I0762586

Iain Matthews

A People's History

Iain Matthews

A People's History

Richard Houghton

First published in Great Britain 2025 by Spenwood Books Ltd

1 Totnes Road, Manchester, M21 8XF, United Kingdom

A CIP record for this book is available from the British Library.

ISBN 978-1-915858-40-5

Design by Bruce Graham, The Night Owl

FOREWORD

In my opinion, Iain Matthews was the first UK Americana artist.

When we talk about musical pioneers, not many people would mention the name Iain Matthews, but that's what he is and has been for the duration of his long career in music. These days, one of the big buzz words in music circles is 'Americana' and the great and the good are all rushing to record American roots music-based albums – but Iain Matthews has been doing exactly that since joining Fairport Convention in 1967.

He was originally recruited to add some strength to the vocals; at the time Fairport Convention were trying to be a British equivalent of Jefferson Airplane, and the male/female shared vocals reflected that. Following Judy Dyble's departure and Sandy Denny's arrival, the band started to turn more towards the British Folk tradition as a source of material, and Iain was 'let go' quite unceremoniously, largely due to Tyger Hutchings' feeling that his voice was unsuited to the new material.

He responded in the best possible way, by releasing his own American influenced album, *Matthews' Southern Comfort.* He would form a working band using the same name and then score a number one hit single with his version of the Joni Mitchell song, 'Woodstock'. He recorded a couple more successful albums and then left his own band (who would record a further three albums without him) to do it all again, releasing two stunning solo albums, *If You Saw Thro' My Eyes* and *Tigers Will Survive*, before forming the formidable Plainsong with Andy Roberts; another band that would continue to hold a legendary position with British roots rock fans.

Looked at in isolation, Iain Matthews' musical career looks like a series of peaks and troughs as he achieves commercial success, only to turn his back on it and move on to something else. But this is an artist whose whole career has been driven by a need to constantly improve – as a musician, as a performer and as a writer. This is an artist who was never interested in being a star, despite various attempts to turn him into one; his focus has always been on becoming the best musician he can be, even if that has meant turning his back on successful projects to better address new, more experimental ones.

When I interviewed Iain for an article for online magazine, *Americana UK*, back in 2022, I suggested that he was ahead of his time in championing Americana music in the UK. With typical modesty, he suggested he was not alone in promoting American roots music in the late 1960s, that all he had done was take the American Troubadour approach that emerged earlier in the decade and tried to write in that style. He described it as 'hearing something that turns you on and developing something of your own from it', but to characterise what he does in such simple terms doesn't explain how successful and innovative he has been at interpreting a style of music that doesn't come naturally outside of the USA, and which he has worked hard to understand and emulate since he first stepped out in front of a public audience.

For me, the album that best sums up Iain Matthews' approach to music is the latterday Plainsong album, *Reinventing Richard* (2015). Iain is on record as saying how fascinated he has been with the songs of Richard Fariña, ever since Joe Boyd brought 'Reno Nevada' to the repertoire of Fairport Convention, way back in 1967.

Iain has said that, in making that particular album, he and the other two members of the band at that time, Andy Roberts and Mark Griffiths, specifically set out to 'conceptualise how his (Richard Fariña) songs might have sounded, if written and first recorded in a twenty-first century electro/acoustic setting'. When you listen to this album (and if you haven't, you really should), the songs sound fresh and relevant, as if they were written just before the band stepped into the recording studio. Yet they were written over 50 years ago, and Richard Fariña himself has been dead and gone since 1966.

This, for me, is what Iain Matthews has always done and it is why he's such an important artist, especially in the context of today's interest in American roots music. He's always taken material and tried to interpret it in a way that makes it fresh and interesting. This is an approach that extends to his own writing, because he's drawing on that American troubadour style while looking to bring it into a modern context. His compositions shouldn't be ignored and he has some excellent songs to his credit, but he is also one of the very best interpreters of a song.

In that same interview, I asked him what drew him to the songs he has covered over the years. His answer was that the common thread was finding a song he could identify with, both as a writer and as an interpreter. Then, having found a song, he had the need to know that he could take it 'someplace else'. That's the key to interpreting a song; you don't just cover it, you find a new way to do it. There's no better example of this than the most recent Matthews Southern Comfort album, *The Woodstock Album* (2023), where Iain and his latest incarnation of the band, involving some excellent Dutch musicians, take on a number of songs closely linked with the original Woodstock festival. It's an outstanding display of taking some very well-known songs in very different directions. As might be expected, some tracks work better than others, but it's the willingness to try something different with well-known material that marks out the true pioneers.

Iain has had a long and varied career. He's made albums with a variety of bands and also has an extensive discography of solo albums. For all his success, you would hardly think of him as a household name and, in many ways, I think he's quite proud of that. He's managed to have a very successful career in music, something that he always hoped for, and he's been able to do it on his own terms, without bowing to fashions and trends, and there are relatively few who get to say that.

His considerable contribution to modern music is long overdue proper recognition and, hopefully, this book will go some way towards changing that.

RICK BAYLES

Above: Iain (left) with Chris Smither in front of HEAR Music in Cambridge, MA (Toby Schwartzman)
Below: Iain appearing with Plainsong at Cropredy, 2000 (Krzysztof Opalski)

INTRODUCTION

Listening to that voice.

I had the privilege of working alongside Iain Matthews when he wrote his memoirs. Over a period of six months, I travelled over to his home in the province of Limburg in the south of The Netherlands. In the mornings we walked the local footpaths with Elvis, Iain's dog, and in the evenings, I sat round the family dining table with daughters Madelief and Luca to eat delicious meals cooked by Marly, Iain's wife. Now and again after dinner, we went out to the beautiful local bar called Cambrinus, a place where Iain had played many a time for the landlord Jan Duijf, who had been a fan since the early 1970s. Other times we stayed in to listen to music or watch football and Marly plied me with strong Dutch bottled beers.

Through the day I listened to Iain telling stories about his life. I followed him from a humble start in a council house in Scunthorpe to landing in Carnaby Street in the middle of the swinging sixties before joining Fairport Convention on their first recording sessions. He told me about his number one record and about appearing on *Top Of The Pops*, his move to America, where he stayed for thirty years, and then back again to Europe, all the while chasing the muse and trying to make a living in the music business.

One morning at his breakfast table, from nowhere, he said, 'I sometimes think my life has been music and I guess music has been my life.' I know that to be true. He won't know this until he reads it, but I looked forward to every morning I woke up in the guest bedroom to hear him doing vocal warm ups, either practising new material or revisiting older songs that he was breathing new life into. It was a great thrill to listen to that lovely voice, giving me my own private concert as the sun was coming up. It was a voice I had first heard all the way back in 1970 when I sang along to 'Woodstock' on morning radio before I set off for school. How strange that going on for fifty years later I would still be listening to that voice, not on radio, but just a few yards away across a landing.

We first met when we exchanged emails in the summer of 2010. Iain had read a book I'd written about how music had been important in my life and got in touch to say how much he had enjoyed it. He told me that he was considering writing his own story about his life as a travelling musician. When I saw the name on the bottom of his message, I wrote back to ask him if he was 'that' Iain Matthews. I was too shy then to say I'd sung along to his famous cover of Joni Mitchell's song 'Woodstock'. I also told him that I was currently enjoying listening to a record he'd made with the Dutch jazz pianist Egbert Derix called *Joy Mining*. He asked me how I knew about that record. It transpired that we both knew David Suff, the owner of the record label that *Joy Mining* had been released on. It was like we were destined to meet.

In September of 2010 Iain was on a short British tour with his guitar buddy BJ Baartmans. He invited me to a gig at Hebden Bridge Trades Club. I couldn't make it that night, but the following week when he had a few days off, Iain came over to my house. We drank some tea at my kitchen table and Iain came out with his idea. 'I want to write my memoir, but I can't seem to get in touch with the same ease and flow that I find when I'm writing a song. Would you consider working with me?' I told him that he ought to write something down and I'd have a look at it with him. I could sense that Iain was a bit crestfallen. I think he'd hoped that I might say that I'd be a scribe for his story. We kept in touch and in 2012 Iain came back to my house with Egbert Derix to play a charity concert that I organised. I asked him if he'd got anywhere with his memoir. He hadn't. The next time I saw him I asked him the same question. He still hadn't.

In the summer of 2015, Iain called me to say he was playing at Cropredy with Egbert and did I want a pair of backstage passes? I went with my old German pal, Volker Bredebusch, who had once managed John Martyn's European tours. On the drive down to Oxfordshire, Volker told me that his lifelong love of English folk and folk-rock music had started when his brother's girlfriend had bought him Iain's *If You Saw Thro' My Eyes* LP as a birthday present.

Volker was delighted to meet Iain in person in the Portakabin dressing rooms. It was a funny meeting as both Iain and Volker were wearing the same blue cotton short-sleeved shirt. They laughed when they told each other that they shopped at C&A. I mentioned Volker's work with John Martyn. Iain told him that he and Egbert were hoping to play in Germany. Volker said 'I can help', Iain said, 'That sounds like an offer' and they shook hands on it there and then. Within a couple of months Volker had organised dates across his homeland. There was even a house concert in Volker's tiny cottage in the village of Sprockhovel. I missed that one, but they told me it was wonderful and intimate.

I have seen many of Iain's concerts over the past fifteen years or so. When he comes to see me, he generally fits in a show near where I live. He played a fabulous set alongside BJ Baartmans in a back street pub in Castleford and another in Pontefract when my lad Edward joined him on piano for a version of the Jesse Colin Young song 'Darkness Darkness'. I think it was on that night in November 2016 that the subject of Iain's memoirs came up again. Iain told me that he'd had an idea. He thought that he might be able to write his story if he had someone alongside him to tell it to. The idea was that I'd travel over to his house and sit with him making notes as he told his story. Then I would write up the notes pass them back to him and he'd go over them. Over time a book would appear. Well, that was the idea.

Another year went by. In the autumn of 2017, I was in Germany celebrating at the retirement party of Volker's older brother, Jurgen Bredebusch, one of my oldest friends. I phoned Iain and told him that if he was up for it, I'd stop off in The Netherlands before I went home to talk about his book idea. Jurgen drove me the one-hour journey from Wuppertal to Iain's home just over the border. Over dinner that night we agreed that we'd give Iain's idea a try. He said, 'Shall we start now then?' And we did.

I asked him to tell me how he first discovered he could sing. He told me that every Sunday when he was a lad, he was packed off to the local Salvation Army where they had a brass band and a choir. Here he befriended a boy called Melvyn who sang his own independent melodies above what everybody else was doing. 'I just copied him, ignored what the others were singing and I could do it too.'

In August of 1967 Iain took that voice to Sound Techniques Studio in Chelsea where Fairport Convention were recording their first single. Joe Boyd called down from the control room, 'Let's do something.' The band recorded an old-time jazz tune, 'If I Had A Ribbon Bow.' Iain told me that he added some 'oohs and aahs'. By the end of the session, nobody told Iain he was in the band but he assumed he must be. In his words, 'And there it was.'

Iain stayed with Fairport less than two years before being asked to leave. He vowed at the time it would be the first and last time he would be put out of a band. Since that chilly February day in 1969, Iain has made his own way and become one of the most prolific singer songwriters in popular music. In a career now approaching its sixtieth year, he shows no signs of slowing down.

I admired Iain's openness and honesty. He wanted to tell a story that celebrated the ups but didn't shy away from the downs of his life. This wasn't a pop star memoir He told his story with tenderness, the same tenderness that we hear in that singing voice of his. Sometimes, when he couldn't remember things, he'd sing a song from the time he was trying to recall and then it came to him. It was as though he was singing his story back to mind.

Just before Christmas in 2017, Iain played Selby Town Hall not far from where I live with the latter-day version of Matthews Southern Comfort. I went along to see the concert with my publisher, Ian Daley of Route Books. We sat backstage and talked about Iain's memoir. Two Ian's and an Iain. Ian Daley suggested that if the book was ready, we might be able to get it out for the following Christmas. Through the spring I followed Matthews Southern Comfort on a short tour of The Netherlands. They played in some beautiful settings, including the old White Church in Terheijden and the Cobblestone Club in Oldenzaal. I travelled in Iain's car. I asked him if after more than fifty years of travelling for a living he ever tired of it. He told me that he was just a pebble in the road and left it to hang. The penny didn't drop straightaway, but he was quoting one of his own songs.

I'm not a complicated man
I simply do the best I can
To be another pebble in the road

When he was a lad Iain's mother had advised him that it was good to stay small. She probably meant do your best and keep out of bother. I think Iain has taken it to mean to be modest and don't show off, do what you need to be doing but keep out of the limelight. Iain's remarkable body of work speaks for itself, but there's more than that. The stories in this book bear witness to a someone who remains approachable and down to earth, a man who values friendship and music by equal measure.

Me I do it for the song
I go in hard, I come out strong
But still, I'm just a pebble in the road

I saw this first hand when I embarked on a tour of the UK with Iain. It was called 'Words and Music'. I read stories; Iain sang and played songs. We found ourselves in a wide variety of venues; a theatre in Barnsley, a socialist club in Wakefield, an oversized shed in someone's garden in Southport, a college in Carlisle and a back street pub in Glasgow. He approached every different setting with the same mantra. 'This is me, here are my songs, is there anybody listening?' And after every show he hung around to talk to people. I admired him for that. Then it was on to the next show for this man whose life has been music and for whom music has been his life.

IAN CLAYTON

A SHOE SHOP
1965, CARNABY STREET, LONDON, UK

JOHN HAYES

I first met Iain while buying a pair of shoes in Carnaby Street in London in 1965. I was working for Radio Caroline, a pirate radio ship, at the time, operating outside the three-mile limit on the south coast of England. At that time, also, I helped build a small recording studio in an upstairs flat in Moscow Road, Bayswater owned by Jonathan Weston – who paid for it! We had the intention of starting a band with two musicians who were friends, Albert Jackson and Steve Hiett. We were looking for a third member to make them a trio, to be called Pyramid. While I was trying on my shoes, Iain and I got to talking music, which was an ambition of Iain's to try his luck in London, having moved from Scunthorpe. I asked him to come in for a meeting with the boys and an audition.

The meeting went well. Iain is a very affable chap, the three of them really got on and their musical tastes were quite similar. Needless to say, Iain passed the audition. There it began, and we have been firm friends ever since.

ALBERT JACKSON

We were in London, the place to be in the mid-1960s. We had high hopes. Anything seemed possible in those days. We had a recording contract with a brand-new label. We had a famous producer and a talented arranger. We had the songs, the sound, the perfect haircuts. We even had matching stage suits. We were going somewhere. Fame and fortune were just around the corner.

Steve Hiett and I had been plucked from a college band by an eager young manager with a plan. We were to become the British Beach Boys. But to do that we needed a third vocalist, preferably one that could hit those high notes. Someone suggested McCartney. But he was busy elsewhere.

Then we were introduced to the 19-year-old Ian MacDonald by a friend who met him selling shoes in Carnaby Street. Ian had

Albert Jackson was in Pyramid with Iain

come to London with ambitions similar to our own. Our voices gelled and the group was formed. We called ourselves Pyramid.

Before long we found ourselves in a commercial recording studio. We were about to make our first single. Only established acts made albums back then. Steve, along with musicians we had never met before, had recorded the backing tracks in the morning. It wasn't until the afternoon that Ian and I were brought in. Together, we made the vocal tracks in just two takes, if my memory serves me well. Hearing 'The Summer Of Last Year' through those studio speakers was a heady moment. Hearing it on the radio in the weeks to come was even better.

To our surprise the record did not go immediately to number one. But that was OK. We were on the way. With our backing band we created a stage act that included several ten to 15-minute continuous medleys of various songs or sometimes just a few bars that made the most of our harmonies. In some venues, these were accompanied by images projected onto a screen behind us by some artistic technicians who were keen to support Pyramid. It was hard work. I am sure we rehearsed longer than we performed on stage, but the shows went down well.

And then along came Procol Harum with their massive hit 'A Whiter Shade Of Pale'. They were newly signed to our management. The single was so successful that it caused rifts between the group and the manager. Contracts were questioned and legal disputes resulted in our manager's bank accounts being frozen. This meant we had no money to pay our band or technicians. We had no transport. Our gigs dried up. There were no more recordings. Pyramid gradually ground to a halt. But youth is resilient. We had no hard feelings. I returned to complete my studies at the Royal College of Art, Steve became a fashion photographer and Ian went on to become Iain Matthews. You know the rest!

SOUND TECHNIQUES STUDIO
WINTER 1967, LONDON, UK

KINGSLEY ABBOTT

I first met Ian, as he was then, outside Sound Techniques Studio on the day that he came down to meet Fairport Convention who were recording there. I was a good friend of Fairport's (I drove them at that point), so I had been aware of the plans to get a new male singer into their ranks. We chatted for a bit with me saying that I knew of his previous group called The Pyramid. I had bought the single, 'Summer Of Last Year', that they had released recently on the Deram label, and Ian seemed to meet someone who had bought it.

Aware that Pyramid had folded, Ian joined the band and took up front line vocal duties alongside Judy Dyble. Their voices blended better on some songs than others.

Interpersonally the relationships between Ian and the rest of the group were cordial, though their various backgrounds were quite different. Eventually though, Ian, Simon and Richard were living together in the flat in Brent. 'Flat' in this instance meant the top floor of a standard North London semi. Simon had the larger front room which doubled as the social space for visitors, Richard had the small bedroom also at the front, while Ian was in the middle room before you got to the kitchen at the back. Here he had his own record player separate from the one in Simon's room. Here was also where he introduced me to playing Scrabble.

By this time Fairport had employed a full-time driver/roadie, so I would drive myself to gigs that were in easy reach, though my close school pal Martin Lamble would often travel with me. On occasion Ian would come with me, most notably on a trip to a gig at Sussex Uni near Brighton. Ian had been unwell during the day, so the band went ahead in their van to ensure timely arrival. Ian had taken special chocolate to relieve the blockage in his nether regions, but had perhaps taken a tad too much. Suffice it to say that we had many enforced stops on the way as things took their course. Just in time for the gig, Ian took to the stage and managed the gig despite having to disappear a couple of times. It says a lot for the man that he persevered that night and completed the gig.

I spent various evenings with him from then on, sometimes over Scrabble, and sometimes listening to the then emerging country rock. Ian was very much enjoying various new artists like Paul Seibel and some established ones like Charley Pride, so it did not come as a great surprise to me when he left Fairport to seek pastures new.

One night we visited Gerry Conway, then Eclection's drummer, and Ian was speaking of how he saw his future. He described a sort of 'staircase' effect where each move he made should take him higher. He was certainly self-motivated. Soon after, as he was putting together his Southern Comfort band, we drove all the way over to the Crystal Palace area to Marc Ellington's flat where he met Marc's friend Carl Barnwell who would join the band.

Ian had left Fairport before their tragic van crash. The day we heard the awful news we went up to the hospital where everyone was, and Ian and I went from bed to bed talking to the surviving band members who were in various states of injury. I can't recall what we spoke about on the way back as we were both quite shaken. I had lost my closest pal Martin, and Ian had seen his injured friends.

After I drove Matthews' Southern Comfort on their very first gig at the famed Mothers Club in Birmingham, like Fairport before them they took on a full-time driver. Ian and I drifted apart at that point, though my girlfriend and I would sometimes socialise with Ian and his girlfriend Chris.

Whilst helping out with Fairport with the driving, there were of course days when there were no gigs to get to. On one such occasion, Iain and I went round to Gerry Conway's flat which was just near North London's Finchley Road. It was the time when headphones were rapidly becoming the must have listening accessory for music. Gerry was getting quite enthusiastic about Bobby Colomby's drumming on the second Blood, Sweat and Tears album, and insisted that we had a listen through the headphones. It certainly was a very positive experience at the time as the drums seemed to dance around your head. I think that this was about the time, or possibly just after, that Iain left Fairport.

The conversation drifted towards what he would do next and Iain explained how he saw his future career path. He described how he saw each move that he made as taking him into new territory, and thus a bit further on and a bit higher. His move to form Matthews Southern Comfort certainly bore this approach out for him when they topped the UK charts with 'Woodstock', so maybe when he decided to leave the band and go solo so soon after the hit it was him taking the next step upwards. Later steps that led to his major US solo hit must have strengthened his resolve.

Over the years he has worked with a very large number of talented musicians with whom he has always taken great trouble to pick the right material for his own voice and the musicians concerned. He also always seemed to include well-chosen steps into his back catalogue.

One of his many collaborations that sticks in my mind was when he linked with Dutch guitarist Ad Vanderveen for the IainAdventure. I saw them at the Norwich Arts Centre where they played two immaculate sets, which included, if memory serves correctly, 'Don't Hang Up Your Dancing Shoes', which has always been a favourite of mine. Ed's playing was absolutely wonderful and Iain's voice was as good as ever. It was another step along the way for Iain, but one that was not to last which I always thought a shame, although soon after Iain did become more enmeshed with Dutch musicians who formed the core for several great albums.

It was also lovely to meet up again at Cropredy, when Iain joined for the 'Early Fairport Convention' set. Backstage we all stood around together. Words weren't needed.

Iain, as he became during the passing time, is a very remarkable artist who has maintained a ridiculously high standard of writing, playing and performance throughout his career. Don't make the mistake of settling on any one era to listen to, because they are all so amazingly good. The musical world is littered with musicians who doggedly stick to their 'name' or 'group name', but Iain has followed his own path and I salute him for it. Well done buddy!

UNKNOWN VENUE
1968, LEEDS, UK

NIGEL BAMFORD

Let's be honest here. When bands in the sixties were putting together their tour schedules, Barrow-in-Furness in the far northwest of England was not first on the list. Or the last. Or, in fact, any date in between. The Kinks and The Who, bless 'em, had taken a wrong turn on their way further north but that was it. No, if you wanted to catch up with current and live music you had to venture beyond the 'longest cul-de-sac in England'. And so it was that as my friends ventured from school to university, leaving me behind, word would filter back of this band and that appearing in the uni refec. Of all these friends, Stu was most musically in touch. He'd seen this band, Fairport Convention, and they were coming back to Leeds; I had to come over and see them.

It was 1968, I stood on the road out of Barrow and stuck out my thumb with very little clue of where the heck I was headed. Nevertheless, a few kindly souls took pity and next thing there I was in Leeds. Fairport were due to appear not at the uni on this occasion but upstairs above a pub which had become a bit of a cool venue. Its name escapes me and it's long gone. Then, there they were on the small stage: I was completely transfixed. The music washed over me in waves: Richard's subtle, beautiful guitar; Martin, Tyger and Simon's tight rhythm; and those harmonies, oh, those harmonies. Ian and Sandy just nailed it. It's a night I shall never forget.

But, as we know, Fairport became somewhat fluid. I tried to keep up: early Steeleye albums; Richard's solo work (who has

Henry The Human Fly in their collection?); *Fotheringay* of course. But it was Iain's direction which truly captured my imagination. I bought the original Matthews Southern Comfort solo album and have been there ever since. *Melody Maker* (RIP) would announce new releases in whatever iteration he chose – solo, MSC, Plainsong – and when that passed, then flicking through record store racks would occasionally surprise me as a new IM album stared back. The internet has changed all that.

I've seen gigs – from sold out to counting the audience on two hands – from London to Fife and they are always rewarding. It's been a long way from the roadside in Barrow and Iain's music has kept me company throughout. Only Barrow AFC and The Kinks have captured my affections for longer. Thank you.

Iain likes reading. He likes football. At a show in Blackburn, I gave him a copy of Nick Hornby's *Fever Pitch*, suggesting he might enjoy it. Fast forward a year or so and we're at his show in Kendal. Mid-intro to a song he stops, points at me in the middle of the audience and says, 'I remember you. That was a great book.'

Maybe a small thing to him, but it meant a heck of a lot to me.

PETER BURKE

Ian Matthews comes from Scunthorpe. His mum and dad lived about half a mile from me. He was in a local band called The Rebels when he lived at 13 Merrion Square in The Borough. When Iain moved out of the flat to live in The Smoke in '67 I moved in.

I later saw him with Pyramid at the Marquee supporting Denny Laine's Electric String Band. Ian was working in a Dolcis shoe shop in Carnaby Street when he was in Pyramid. The grandson of billionaire Nubar Gulbenkian (who rode around in a London taxi fame) also worked there. Legend has it that he would get his weekly wage in a brown envelope (as you did in those days) and never open it.

Ian and I met one night at a party in Dragonby near Scunthorpe. He was with his flatmate Paul Eckersley. Ian told me that Peter Burke was a great name for a rock star. His album *Go For Broke* has a thank you to Peter Burke on the back sleeve (you don't forget these things).

However, after he became famous, I went to see Ian perform at The Venue in Victoria in the early eighties. When I spoke to him, he blanked me and said he didn't know me. A few years later, when I was working for The Pogues, we did a show at the John Anson Ford open air theatre in Hollywood. Ian was there in the audience and we made eye contact and I blanked him!

UNIVERSITY OF EAST ANGLIA

22 JUNE 1968, NORWICH, UK

OLIVER GRAY

It was in 1968 that I saw Iain for the first time, co-fronting Fairport Convention with Sandy Denny at a concert at UEA Norwich at which they opened for Pink Floyd in a double bill arranged by the Bryan Morrison Agency. He seemed cool then and has remained cool in my mind ever since, particularly after reading his enlightening autobiography.

By the time Fairport played their next UEA gig, Iain was no longer in the band as a result of circumstances portrayed all too graphically in his book. That was the famous (in my mind) occasion on which Sandy Denny told me to 'fuck off'.

Fast forward a great number of years to 2024 and I found myself having the pleasure of promoting a show featuring Iain and his Plainsong compadre Andy Roberts in the village where I live. It seemed surreal at the time, but the quality of the music was quite outstanding and I look forward to repeating the experience later in 2025, as well as, remarkably, an eightieth birthday concert for Ashley Hutchings.

UNIVERSITY OF BRADFORD STUDENTS' UNION

6 FEBRUARY 1969, BRADFORD, UK

RON YAXLEY

Life can be full of surprises. But none bigger than a text I received from Iain Matthews one morning in June 2021. That's *the* Iain Matthews, one of my favourite singer/songwriters, whose music I've collected for over five decades, whose concerts I always go to when he tours the UK and who in more recent years I've got to know personally and work with. And what did this text say? 'Hey Ron. My friend John Reed at Cherry Red is putting together a box set of the Rockburgh years and needs help with listening to live recordings. I'm very busy right now and can't assist. Would you be interested in helping him out?'

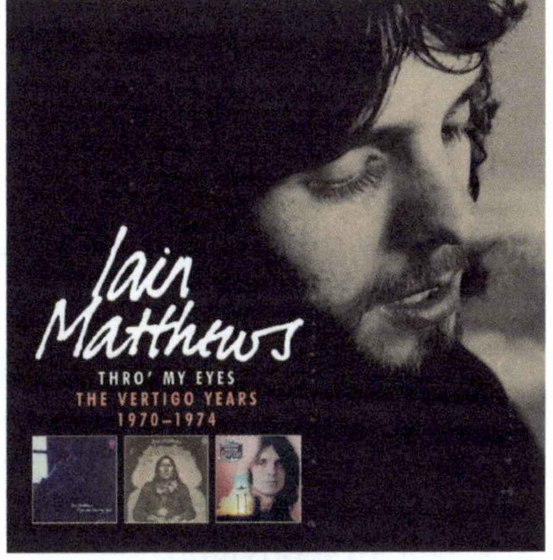

Ron Yaxley has gone from avid fan to authorised compiler of Iain Matthews' albums

It didn't take more than a few seconds to say yes; *carpe diem* as the saying goes.

I've been a fan of Iain's music since I first saw him on stage in February 1969. I was a 20-year-old chemistry student at Bradford University and headed up the Entertainments Committee. The university circuit was huge back then, and as 'Ents Sec' you got to pick and choose the bands that played each weekend. We booked bands like the Moody Blues, Free, Spooky Tooth, Vinegar Joe and Black Sabbath; and we booked *An Evening With John Peel* featuring three acts that he regularly championed on his weekly BBC radio shows.... Bridget St John, Principal Edwards Magic Theatre and Fairport Convention.

Iain of course was one of the two vocalists in Fairport, alongside Sandy Denny. It's hard to envisage now that it was 55 years ago but I remember they sang 'Meet On The Ledge', and did their versions of Leonard Cohen's 'Suzanne' and Bob Dylan's 'Jack O'Diamonds'. And Sandy would no doubt have sung 'Fotheringay' and 'Who Knows Where The Time Goes'. In retrospect, it was probably one of Iain's last few gigs with Fairport as he left them less than a fortnight later.

In the intervening time I've bought pretty much everything he's ever released, from Matthews Southern Comfort and Plainsong to Hi-Fi and More Than A Song, as well as all those solo albums and collaborations along the way. Not to mention collecting hundreds of live recordings, many of them used for the three box sets I've had the privilege of compiling for Cherry Red since that day. Will there be any more? Who knows, but don't be surprised!

FRIARS

23 MARCH 1970, AYLESBURY, UK

JOHN WILSON

The first time I saw Iain live was at Friars in Aylesbury in 1970 with the original Matthews Southern Comfort. I remember enjoying the band's sound and particularly Iain's vocals. I collected records of his various projects along the way, but didn't see him play live again for 30 years when he played the then Phoenix Theatre in Leicester with Ad Vanderveen. A truly mesmeric performance encapsulated in a 'roll the tape' live album recorded in Holland.

Having been blown away by the concert I caught as many of Iain's subsequent gigs as I could, amongst them Plainsong

John Wilson first saw Iain at Aylesbury Friars

when they played Northampton, a random pub in Stoke-on-Tent with Mike Roelofs and Bart Oostindie, and a couple of times at the Hinckley Act, once solo and once with Edgar Derek.

The Hinckley Act was one of the most unusual music venues you could find. It comprised the upper storey of an industrial unit in a business park just off the A5. It was founded by music enthusiast and business owner Keith London and his wife Pam and had a small but loyal local following. The PA system was state-of-the-art and the audience was knowledgeable and appreciative so musicians loved to play there. Sadly, Keith passed away after suffering a heart attack in 2013 and Pam a couple of years ago, and the venue finally closed in 2024.

At the gig with Edgar, Iain was contemplating what he thought would be his final solo recording, *The Art Of Obscurity*. I met up with them in the bar (a side room with a couple of crates of beer on the table) and after congratulating them on a brilliant concert, Iain said he was looking for ideas for the album title. I ventured to suggest *That's All Folks*, but after taking a moment to think about it, Iain politely rejected that idea. Which was just as well because a) I'd probably have been held responsible for the ensuing legal action by Warner Brothers, b) the superb *How Much Is Enough* proved that it certainly wasn't *That's All*... and c) *The Art Of Obscurity* was a much better title... and one that could equally have been applied to the much-missed Hinckley Act.

(Aylesbury Friars pre-show blurb for the Matthews Southern Comfort gig ran as follows:

Next week we have Matthews Southern Comfort who are an incredibly beautiful band. They have some superb four-part harmony vocal arrangements. They also have an LP out which is superb…People will talk about their performance next Monday for months (promise). We will certainly never be able to afford them again so don't be a twit and miss them.)

THE PENTHOUSE

25 JUNE 1970, SCARBOROUGH, UK

ULF DALHEIM

It was the summer of 1970, and my girlfriend and I had decided to travel from Norway to England for a late holiday. One night on our trip we were in Scarborough in Yorkshire, and Matthews Southern Comfort was playing The Penthouse, so we decided to check up this – for us – quite unknown group.

The club was a quite tiny venue at 35 St Nicholas Street, but during the sixties and seventies it also hosted acts like David Bowie, Thin Lizzy, Fleetwood Mac and the Sex Pistols. The house was an elegant nineteenth century Georgian building and for some youngsters coming from Norway, not used to clubs or concert halls, this was a quite impressive venue to visit.

We did not know what to expect music-wise, as Matthews Southern Comfort were new to us. And we had never before seen an act with pedal steel guitar in the line-up. My ears were wide open!

The band started up a bit anonymous, and their sound was not in the style of most of the music we had heard from British bands before. I felt it was original, English folk rock with American roots? After a few songs I was captivated. Gordon Huntley's pedal steel stood out, as did the guitar playing of Mark Griffiths and Carl Barnwell, although it felt a bit like they were challenging each other. Was everything okay within the band?

Ulf Dalheim first saw Iain 55 years ago

The front man, a soft, somewhat shy and quiet young lad, straight away caught our attention with his voice sent from heaven! Among the songs played, Mr Iain Matthews and the group did an amazing rendering of 'Something In The Way She Moves'. And a bit later he introduced a song for the audience with the words, 'This will be our next single.' It was of course their version of Joni Mitchell's 'Woodstock' which, as history showed, later that year went to capture the No. 1 spot in the British charts and gave them an appearance on the famous *Top Of The Pops* programme on TV.

After only half an hour into the performance, Iain suddenly left the stage. The other musicians seemed a bit bewildered, but kept on playing a few more tunes, mostly instrumentals. Then the music sort of faded out, without Iain returning to the stage.

When, after the concert, I approached one of the guys and asked what had happened, he shook his head and replied, 'He did not like the way we were playing tonight.'

Arriving in London the week after, I searched all the record shops in the city to try and get my hands on the 'Woodstock' single but nobody had heard of it. Six weeks later, with huge success in Great Britain, the single was finally released in Norway and I got hold of it. That was my first Iain Matthews record. Today I have them all, more than 60 different albums.

The next time I came upon Iain Matthews was twenty years later, in The Netherlands. I was in Belgium on a work trip and decided to rent a car and drive to the village of Horst, on the other side of the border, to meet up again with the group, now including Andy Roberts, who I knew from some appearances in Norway and who had been invited to join Iain whilst at a party at poet Adrian Henri's house in Liverpool. (They played together in the Liverpool Scene.)

Before the concert in Horst, I sat down with Iain to talk about his music and career. When I told him about the concert in Scarborough twenty years earlier, he said (without thinking for a second): 'That was not a good one!'

That is Iain Matthews in a nutshell. I believe he remembers every single performance he has done, especially the bad ones!

The Matthews Southern Comfort in Horst was a much better experience than the one in Scarborough. The band was tight, the harmonies so beautiful, the songs spectacular. Four guys who loved their music as much as the enjoyed performing together.

Since then, I have travelled to Paris and London to see Iain live again. And I have organised three appearances for him in Trondheim, Norway where I now live. The first one was in 2008, upstairs at Credo Bar, where I also invited Iain to join me for a fantastic meal at a restaurant that now has one Michelin star.

The next time, in 2013, he played at Moskus Bar, getting five on the dice from the reviewer in *Adresseavisen* (Norway's oldest newspaper).

Finally, he came back with Andy Roberts in 2017 to perform

the *Reinventing Richard Fariña* album at Hjorten Club in the cellar of the Radisson Royal Garden Hotel.

Iain has also worked very closely with some Norwegian artists and songwriters. With Henning Kvitnes in 2001 he wrote *July Rain*, which they both have recorded. And in 2019 he made the album *Fake Tan* with the Norwegian group The Salmon Smokers, where the band leader Freddy Holm came up with new arrangements for some of Iain's best recordings, including 'Woodstock'.

SECOND SPRING
RELEASED JULY 1970

RENEE EVERETT

It all began one night in Delaware, in 1972, when I was attending a college party where I met this very musical fellow, Charlie, who introduced me to some of his treasured albums and songs. He and I sat in a room that evening and listened to many of his favourites. The one album that stood out for me was *Second Spring*, by an artist I did not yet know, Iain Matthews and his Southern Comfort band. And the one song I specifically remembered from that night was 'D'arcy Farrow'. Long a favourite in the folk music lexicon, the Steve Gillette and Tom Campbell song caught my attention and made me an instant Iain Mathews fan.

It all began in 1972 for Renee

Charlie (who later became my husband) and I followed Iain's work over the years. The 'M' section of our album (later CD) collection featured many Iain Matthews' contributions. We saw Iain in concert multiple times, but perhaps one of the most

America hears U.S. country music — the Mathews way

MATHEWS' Southern Comfort play American Country music — anl they have been offered a tour of America.

Not particularly startling news until you realise the Mathews' Southern Comfort are an English group who have only been together for a couple of months.

A bit like carrying coals to Newcastle.

"That's just what I thought," said Ian Mathews, founder, leader and vocalist with the group.

"But an American promoter who's heard us play liked the sound we make and said the Americans would really enjoy an English group playing American music."

Mathews' Southern Comfort began life when Ian Mathews grew restless working as one of Fairport Convention. He had appeared on two of their albums.

"I worked with Fairport for a couple of years and I left the group mainly because I wanted to do a different sort of thing.

"I got very interested in the modern electric country music you hear from America today from groups like the Byrds, the Dillards and the Flying Burrito Brothers."

So Mathews quit and made some solo recordings in the Country vein. It was on these sessions he used 44-year-old steel guitarist Gordon Huntley who's since joined the group permanently.

Mathews' Southern Comfort's first album was the collection of these recordings and it was released some two months before the group itself was set up.

Today's band originated on March 16 and it is some sign of their success that they already have a name that's known nationally in such a short space of time.

Ian started off by choosing Gordon Huntley, who agreed to come in with him. Huntley's recognised as one of the best Country steel guitarists in Britain.

Next to join was Carl Banwell on rhythm guitar. Ian's lead guitarist Mark Griffiths was with an underground group called Harsh Reality and drummer Ramon Duffy is from Marmalade.

Finally there's bass player Andy Leigh who played with Spooky Tooth before joining the Country band.

The group are starting to settle down after touring with Ten Years After.

"We're trying to do concerts more than anything," Ian says.

"We're not really what you'd call a raving band so a concert setting is the best for what we do."

Ian thinks the group are over what he calls "the initial stage."

He explained: "For the first couple of months you have the initial stage just getting bet
then come
"We're c
of those spa
nothing s
improving
out everyth
Ian Math
happy man.
"I wasn'
Fairport tov
I wanted t
leader, and
able to cho
myself. I th
I'm enjoyi
much."
He's a be
too.
"I think
to have arr
with our s
There certa
be a marke
"I think
arrival of th
well. This m
drifting slow
America or
people like
people are
ten at last.
"They're a
enjoy the m
Without try
clever or f
I think we m
about 20 g
half of them
play an enc
"It's been
demand for
With a nev
to be release
can tour in t
plenty of den
Mathews' Se
fort are loo
world with h
tion.

Ian Mathews of Mathews' Southern Comf

AIN MATTHEWS ND FAIRPORT CONVENTION

Conventional folk: Fairports (from left) Marti Lamble, Dave Pegg, Judy Dyble, Richard Thompson, Iain Matthews, Ashley Hutching (bottom) the besuited Iain is detached, as Sandy Denny (front) joins; Matthews today (below).

egan as a sofa-surfing enture, but the "you're " severance was a shock.

LLO OCTOBER 1967

guitarist Ashley [Hutchings] and ducer] Joe Boyd were initially ing for a keyboard player who sang. were phoning around record panies where they knew people. Hall at Deram said "Well, this d on the label, Pyramid, are about

Airplane and wanted to explore that kind of male/female lead vocal where each would be singing harmony at the same time. It was really different to most of the bands around London at that time, I was really intrigued by their approach and their repertoire.

They were recording If I Had A Ribbon Bow, and the audition was just to jump in and sing on the track. I never got the nod either way: I was told to come back for the next session, and before you knew it we were pals and I was part of the band. I could only t I was in.

"IT CAME RIGHT OUT OF THE BLUE IT WASN'T MY CHOICE."

E MARCH 1969

t out of the blue. It wasn't ut had obviously been t within the band. We all

MELODY MAKER, October 7, 1972

HAROLD DAVISON on behalf of MAM

PRESENTS

PLAINSONG

MICKEY NEWBURY

HARRY CHAPIN

QUEEN ELIZABETH HALL

SOUTHBANK, S.E.1

FRIDAY, 20th OCTOBER, 7.45 p

Tickets available:
Royal Festival Hall Box Office

Ticket Prices: £1.30, £1.10, 90p, 70p, 5

memorable events was a house concert at the home of Steve Carson who lived just outside of Cincinnati, Ohio. I can't remember the exact date, but it was close to 20 years ago.

Steve's home was open and inviting. We ended up speaking with Iain in Steve's kitchen following the concert. Charlie mentioned we had named our oldest daughter Darcy, due in large part to his 'D'arcy Farrow' song. Surprisingly enough, Iain told us he also had a daughter named Darcy! It was really exceptional to know we shared that bit of history. We later told our daughter all about the encounter and she remembers it to this day. Now almost 42, she remains an Iain Matthews fan, as do we. Music has always been an integral part of our lives and our daughters' lives. We continue to follow Iain and are always looking for another house concert we could attend somewhere near our current home in the Delaware Beach area.

As always, Iain, thank you for your music and inspiration.

JUNE 1971, WASHINGTON DC

MICHAEL OBERMAN

I have known Iain for well over 50 years. As a weekly music columnist with Washington DC's *Evening Star* (DC), I interviewed and devoted a column to Iain in June 1971:

Top Tunes By Mike Oberman

After a successful career with two groups, Fairport Convention and Matthews Southern Comfort, Ian Matthews is going it alone. His first solo album, *If You Saw Thro' My Eyes*, has just been released on the Vertigo label (distributed in this country by Mercury Records). Of 12 cuts on the LP, nine were written by Matthews.

Matthews' vocals are as accomplished as his lyrics. Although electric instruments are used, the basic sound of the album is acoustic and very listenable. Ian, in town last week to promote his album, talked about how his career as a professional singer started. 'I started with a band in London in 1966 called

Top Tunes

By
MIKE
OBERMAN

After a successful career with two groups, Fairport Convention and Matthews' Southern Comfort, Ian Matthews is going it alone.

His first solo album, "If You Saw Thro' My Eyes," has just been released on the Vertigo label (distributed in this country by Mercury Records). Of the 12 cuts on the LP, 9 were written by Matthews.

Matthews' vocals are as accomplished as his lyrics. Although electric instruments are used, the basic sound of the album is acoustic and very listenable.

Ian, in town last week to promote his album, talked about how his career as a professional singer started. "I started with a band in London in 1966 called Pyramid," he said.

"If you can believe it, we did Curtis Mayfield songs with a surfing feel. I stayed with them for a year."

Ian became involved with Fairport Convention through Tony Hall, label manager for Deram Records. "Tony knew some of the people in Fairport," Ian said. "They were looking for a singer.

"I was supposed to do a month's probation period with them. It went on for two years."

Ian left Fairport because of musical differences. "They wanted to do different things," he said. "Sandy (Denny) had joined the band. Our vocals were different. She had a lot to offer. Sandy's direction was the obvious choice."

After leaving Fairport, Ian didn't do much for the next 10 months. He was looking for management and when he found it, he started work on an album. The title of the album probably would have been "Ian Matthews," but he liked an Ian and Sylvia album titled "Southern Comfort," so he changed the title to "Matthews' Southern Comfort."

"The band of the same name came about as a natural extension of the album," Ian said.

Ian's group had a hit with their version of Joni Mitchell's "Woodstock."

"'I picked up 'Woodstock' as a stage number," Ian said. "But it got such a good response after I did it on a radio show, that we released it as a single.

"For three months it didn't do anything. Then a friend of mine got Tony Blackburn (an influential British disc jockey) to play it. With the kind of influence he's got, it took off."

Ian Matthews

On Ian's new solo album he's backed by a number of fine musicians, including Sandy Denny. The title cut, "If You Saw Thro' My Eyes," contains the lines:

I take the blame for where I've been.

On all the ones I've had to lean.

When asked about that song, Ian said, "The whole song is posing a musical question. I find it hard to explain my songs. I take the blame for where I've been.

"I've never been happy with anything I've done. It's no one else's fault. But, I really am satisfied with this album. I find I like listening to it.

"Each time I hear it," he said, "I feel more satisfied with it. Maybe it's because it's just me. I'm not relying on anyone else."

Ian has already started work on his next album. "I like it even better than this one," he said. "It's a little more funky. More electric guitars."

Ian will be touring this country starting Aug. 1 in Columbus, Ohio. The tour will take him to clubs like the Troubadour in L.A. and the Bitter End in N.Y.

If his album is any indication of what his live performance is like, let's hope he'll also be doing a week at the Cellar Door.

Mike Oberman reviewed Iain's *If You Saw Thro' My Eyes* in his column in 1971

Pyramid,' he said. 'If you can believe it, we did Curtis Mayfield songs with a surfing feel. I stayed with them for a year.'

Ian became involved with Fairport Convention through Tony Hall, label manager for Deram Records. 'Tony knew some of the people in Fairport,' Ian said, 'They were looking for a singer. I was supposed to do a month's probation period with them. It went on for two years.'

Ian left Fairport because of musical differences. 'They wanted to do different things,' he said. 'Sandy (Denny) had joined the band. Our vocals were different. She had a lot to offer. Sandy's direction was the obvious choice.'

After leaving Fairport, Ian didn't do much for the next ten months. He was looking for management and when he found it, he started work on an album. The title of the album probably would've been *Ian Matthews* but he liked an Ian and Sylvia album titled *Southern Comfort* so he changed the title to *Matthews Southern Comfort*.

'The band of the same name came about as a natural extension of the album,' Ian said. Ian's group had a hit with a version of Joni Mitchell's 'Woodstock'. 'I picked up 'Woodstock' as a stage number,' Ian said, 'but it got such a good response after I did it on a radio show that we released it as a single. For three months it didn't do anything. Then a friend of mine got Tony Blackburn (an influential British disc jockey) to play it. With the kind of influence he's got, it took off.'

On Ian's new solo album, he's backed by a number of fine musicians, including Sandy Denny. The title cut, 'If You Saw Thro' My Eyes', contains the lines:

I take the blame for where I've been
On all the ones I've had to lean

When asked about that song, Ian said, 'The whole song is posing a musical question. I find it hard to explain my songs. I take the blame for where I've been. I've never been happy with anything I've done. It's no one else's fault. But I really am satisfied with this album. I find I like listening to it.

'Each time I hear it,' he said, 'I feel more satisfied with it. Maybe it's because it's just me. I'm not relying on anyone else.' He has already started work on his next album. 'I like it even better than this one,' he said. 'It's a little more funky. More electric guitars.'

Ian will be touring this country starting August 1 in Columbus, Ohio. The tour will take him to clubs like the Troubadour in LA and the Bitter End in NY. If his album is an indication of what his live performance is like, let's hope he'll also be doing a week at the Cellar Door.

FALLS CHURCH COMMUNITY CENTER

AUGUST 1971, FALLS CHURCH, VIRGINIA

DENNIS HOESCHLER

I have seen Iain and crossed paths with him a few times. Like most, I was turned onto him from listening to Fairport Convention. I had a band in Virginia around 1970 and we performed a number of Matthews Southern Comfort songs including 'Mare, Take Me Home.'

The first time I saw Iain live was at Falls Church Community Center in Virginia. This tour was in support of his *If You Saw Thro' My Eyes*, still to this day my favourite album from Iain's long career.

It's one of the strangest concerts I've been to. The band was Iain, Richard Thompson and Andy Roberts. They were set up on a basketball court with them playing at one end and kids playing basketball at the other end. One of the kids was sporting his father's captured Nazi officer's jacket. Richard was amused by this and made some interesting comments about the choice of apparel. The band was great and it was so great to catch Richard at such an early time in his career. (There is a recording of this band playing at New York's The Bitter End on the *Thro' My Eyes: The Vertigo Years 1970-1974* box set doing pretty much the same set we saw.)

We me Iain's Vertigo A&R man (he's the tall fellow pictured inside the gatefold cover of *Tigers Will Survive* and he's in the middle with a thin cigar in his mouth) and took him to our house and had a party, which I know he enjoyed. We got him back to his hotel as the sun arose over the Virginia countryside.

I next saw Iain when I'd moved back to my family's home in Seattle. Iain had moved there and had a band with David Surkamp called Hi Fi. This was a different sound from what Iain was known for. I approached Iain and asked him about the past but he was not interested in the least about his past at this time. I used to run into him at a record store called Penny Lane (opened in the early seventies by my cousin, it was eventually sold, moved a few doors down, renamed Easy Street and became a world-famous store as Pearl Jam's Eddie Vedder hangs there.) Iain and I had the same musical taste, especially for the great Gene Clark. I have continued to follow Iain's music but noticed he hasn't ever come back to Seattle. It's not on the usual well-worn path.

QUEEN ELIZABETH HALL
20 OCTOBER 1972, SOUTH BANK, LONDON, UK

KARL DALLAS

Undoubtedly, it was Plainsong's night. So much so that a large proportion of the audience didn't bother to arrive at the Queen Elizabeth Hall last Friday until after the interval, a practice that I notice is growing gradually as a reaction to so many promoters who fill up the first half of concert bills with makeweight unknowns. But in this case, the latecomers really missed out for though Plainsong's set was truly superb, Harry Chapin and Mickey Newbury in the first half were really too good to have been missed…

What can one say about Plainsong that hasn't been said before? Have there ever been four voices to blend so perfectly together, coupled with so much instrumental expertise? In Andy Roberts and Ian Matthews, the group has two very individual singers with distinct talents that almost exactly complement each other. Andy's voice wry and slightly acid, Ian's voice soft and sweet.

It was nice, too, to hear Dave Richards taking a brief solo vocal spot.

Most of their songs were from their most recent album, though I spotted a couple of older items. But, for me, the real hit of the evening was the old Jimmie Rodgers number they did as an encore, in which they combined exactly the right proportions of sincerity and affectionate humour, even extending to a sweet ensemble yodel at the end of a lovely but insufficiently promoted and attended concert.

(Originally published in *Melody Maker* magazine.)

UNIVERSITY OF LEEDS

29 JANUARY 1972, LEEDS, UK

DAVID CLARKE

Having listened to Iain's recordings for a number of years, the first time I actually got to see Iain live was with Plainsong at Leeds University as an impressionable teenager. From that day on I was smitten and it remains to this day the most memorable concert I ever attended. The set list comprised many of the tracks from the *Amelia Earhart* LP, which I promptly went out and bought the next day and which remains my favourite record by any band to this day. Of course, my favourite solo recording was the superb *If You Saw Thro' My Eyes*, which is still a masterpiece in all details.

David was an impressionable teenager when he first saw Iain

A couple of years later I wrote off to deejay Johnnie Walker at the BBC, the one and only time I put in a request for a song to be played on the radio, and he graciously played 'Amelia Earhart's Last Flight' for me, one of the only times it has been played on the radio.

Plainsong rapidly disintegrated and for many years I lost track of their output until I suddenly came across a new version of the band which resulted in my working backwards to obtain all of Iain Matthews' recorded material, both solo and in band mode.

It was to be many years before I caught up with Iain again, during a solo tour when I was privileged to see and hear him at a church in Wigan. I was waiting outside for the doors to open when who should come along and wait beside me but the man himself. We had quite a chat together until the doors were opened for him – but I wasn't allowed in!

After the concert, Iain was generous enough with his time to speak to me again and sign copies of CDs and books which I had brought along on the off-chance and to this day they remain treasured possessions.

The last time I saw Iain live was at the intimate setting of a folk club in Pontefract, named the Cat Club, where he reunited with Andy Roberts and resurrected the Plainsong name and I was overjoyed to hear that the magic was still there. I am looking forward with intense anticipation to see the pair of them together again in 2025. Nobody can light up a room like Iain Matthews, either on his own or with his long-time partner. The voice is still as good as it ever was and he is still a brilliant performer. Thanks for all the pleasure he has given over the years.

UNIVERSITY OF KENT

1 FEBRUARY 1972, CANTERBURY, UK

JOHNNY FEWINGS

It's Tuesday 1 February 1972. I'd just turned 19. For one reason or another, (who am I kidding…? it was just the one reason), we weren't really following what was going on. I'd arrived at the University of Kent from Somerset five months earlier, lost my Somerset accent on the train somewhere between Taunton and Canterbury and met some cool people. I thought they were cool then… and I still do!

Johnny was there in '72 (Johnny Fewings)

We're sat in a tiny Darwin College bedroom, probably about six of us smoking and listening to music. There's a knock on the door: 'Iain Matthews is playing live in the dining hall… now!'

This was in the days when a collection of 25 albums was considered to be pretty normal or good-sized for we heads. *If You Saw Thro' My Eyes* was in there in my collection, and pretty high up in the pecking order.

We trooped down to the dining hall. Probably for the same reason I didn't know about it, neither did many other people. It was very quiet. We sat on the floor as we always did in those days. It was fantastic. Andy Roberts of course was there too. What a treat!

It was one of those rare magical nights that you don't quite realise what you've got until you look back on it. 'Ten thousand dollars at the drop of a hat…!', as someone once said.

50 years later, 2022, I'm running the Whitstable Sessions Music Club, just a few miles outside of Canterbury. I've got to know Iain a little and he's played here a few times. He's always good.

'Let's do a gig in Canterbury,' we say. 'Maybe at the University…? 'Yeah, okay.'

At the time the nostalgic significance passed us by. Friday 13th August 2022.

Andy Roberts of course is there too. Then the penny drops… Andy finds that old poster from 1972. It was fantastic, of course, and what a treat.

Turns out our lives can still 'be like that'!

THÉÂTRE BOBINO

MAY 1972, PARIS, FRANCE

JEAN-LUC TEMPOREL

I was handed a concert flyer in the street close to the Bobino Hall in Paris. It was small, piss yellow and badly printed, as everything was back then. It listed Steeleye Span/Incredible String Band/Ian Matthews' New Band/Plainsong/Dick Annegard, etc. As an absolute fan of Ian, I was curious to see this 'new band'.

Steeleye Span refused to play because the audience was too small. Plainsong were announced and then I understood that

Jean-Luc remembers the colour of the concert flyer

Plainsong and 'The New Band of Ian Matthews' were one and the same. I remember Dave Richards testing his mic by counting 'one, two, three… soixante-neuf' as if we were dirty people!

And I remember almost falling off my seat on realising that it was Ian's pure voice I could hear on 'For The Second Time', not to mention the four-part harmonies that would follow.

I also remember a concert in Rennes when Iain pointed at me while I was in the front row shouting out the words to 'Tigers Will Survive' and 'Spot Of Interference'.

When an old childhood friend told me that she lived in the south of France with a guy named Pat Donaldson (*If You Saw Thro' My Eyes* was my Bible for years) and I said, 'It's funny, that's the same name as my favourite bass player,' she told me her man played the bass too. It turned out it was actually Pat!

'I'LL FLY AWAY'

ELIZABETH NORRIS

It was the mid-seventies and I was in my late teens and managing a maternity shop (yes – that's right) in a local mall. I come from a family of folkies who often got together with friends to sing and play music. One of the favourites was the hymn 'I'll Fly Away'. The shop I worked in was never very busy and we were allowed to listen to the radio station of our choice, and often louder than in other (busier) shops. My favourite station was WNEW, which was generally considered a rock station but the folk-rock genre was very popular at the time.

When 'I'll Fly Away' came on the radio that morning, I was alone in the store. Now, I had never called a radio station before, but this rendition was so good… I just had to know who was performing it.

When I got through, I had to make the person who answered tell me the name of the band and the album three times, because I couldn't understand what he was saying. He was aggravated, but I finally understood (no voice for radio!). It was Iain Matthews and Plainsong.

QUEEN ELIZABETH HALL
6 OCTOBER 1972, LONDON, UK

JULIAN CHRISTOU

My first exposure to Iain was way back in 1970 when the 'Woodstock' single was released by Matthews Southern Comfort. I was just 16 and getting into music. I bought the single, which I still have and still play. It wasn't until many years later that I found out it was a Joni Mitchell composition and I heard her version and also the Crosby, Stills, Nash and Young one. For me, neither version can hold a candle to the MSC one.

During the last 54 years I have followed Iain on-and-off. Usually in spurts. I discovered Fairport Convention in the early seventies and, slowly backtracking through their catalogue, I realised that the Iain Matthews in their early line-up was the same as the one in in MSC. What has always attracted me to his music are his covers. He makes others' songs his own, yielding brilliant and original interpretations just as in Joni's 'Woodstock'. Whether it be with Fairport, MSC, Plainsong or solo, those cover versions really stand out. From Richard Fariña's 'Reno, Nevada' to Steve Young's 'Seven Bridges Road' to Peter Gabriel's 'Mercy Street', they are all gems. And, of course, his whole album of Jules Shear's songs. I have admired his work with Andy Roberts in Plainsong and that first album, *In Search Of Amelia Earhart*, opened up Americana for me, a genre of music which had escaped me.

I'm originally from the UK (Wales) and the only time I have seen Iain was with Plainsong when they played at the Fresher's Ball at my first year in university at Queen Elizabeth College in October 1972. It was based on that show that I bought the album and then connected the Matthews name to 'Woodstock'. Hence my enjoyment of the music.

I now live in the States and have done so since 1976 and even though I've never had the opportunity to see Iain again, I have collected the vast majority of his recordings on either LP or CD and also his guest appearances with Fairport at the Cropredy Reunions. Probably the oddest association of his, from my perspective, was with Pavlov's Dog's David Surkamp in *Hi-Fi*, an album I picked up second-hand on a whim because I loved both Iain's and David's music. And I must say I prefer Iain's cover of 'A Hardly Innocent Mind' to the Pavlov's Dog version.

I have turned quite a few friends onto Iain's music over the years and the first album I usually play is either *Pure And Crooked* with its great covers and also the fantastic 'Busby's Babes'. As a youngster, I remember the Munich plane crash and will dig out that song for any Man U fan. The other album I usually play for them is the first Plainsong one. The magic between him and Andy is remarkable and every song on it is a gem.

I eagerly await each new release. Thanks for providing part of the soundtrack to my life Iain.

THE MOUNTAINS

NOVEMBER 1972, PENNSYLVANIA

JAMES M 'JIM' OWSTON

In November 1972, I visited my brother Chuck who had recently moved back to the mountains of Pennsylvania. While there, he gave me 30 albums. One of those was the American release of Fairport Convention's debut LP on Cotillion Records. Of these offerings, it was my favourite and I played it over and over. The following spring, I purchased an import copy of *The History of Fairport Convention*. The cover art was Pete Frame's family tree of the band, and I then learned about Iain's subsequent musical activities as a solo artist, and with Matthew's Southern Comfort and Plainsong.

That summer, I also purchased the second Fairport LP. Two cuts stood out: 'Book Song' and 'Meet On The Ledge'. I also picked up *If You Saw Thro' My Eyes*, *Tigers Will Survive* and the Plainsong LP. Iain's lead and harmony vocals were mesmerising. These LPs were included in the 25 albums I took to college in August 1973, and they remain the favourites of my 5,000-strong album collection.

'Eastern Rain', one of the songs that Iain and Sandy Denny sang on *What We Did On Our Holidays*, became the inspiration for the name of my ASCAP publishing company, Eastern Rain Music, that was founded in 1982.

Jim Owston discovered Fairport - and Iain - via his brother

That same year, I purchased Patrick Humphries' book, *Meet On The Ledge: A History Of Fairport Convention*, which chronicled the history of the band. Over the years, I've had several veterans and members of Fairport sign the book. In the 1990s, my brother Chuck, a musician in his own right, had the opportunity to open for Iain in Pittsburgh. At that concert, Iain autographed my book.

As a 20-year veteran in radio broadcasting, I had the opportunity to play 'Shake it' on WAMX – a 100,000-watt FM station in the Ashland, Kentucky / Huntington, West Virginia market in 1979 and as an oldie at subsequent stations. At WWNR in Beckley, WV in 1987, I hired John Sellards, a high school student, to be a part-time announcer. I had the opportunity to introduce John to Fairport Convention and Iain Matthews. It is quite ironic that both of us were high school students when we discovered the incomparable Iain Matthews.

Coming full circle, John Sellards Design has worked on several projects for Iain and it was my personal copies of three albums that John used for images in two box sets: *In Search Of Amelia Earhart* for *Following Amelia: The 1972 Recordings & More* and *If You Saw Thro' My Eyes* and *Tigers Will Survive* for *Thro' My Eyes: The Vertigo Years 1970-1974*. I was honoured to be named in both collections.

Iain Matthews has been a large part of my life.

SISTER'S HOUSE

AUGUST 1973, JOHNSON CITY, TENNESSEE

CHARLIE HUNTER

I first heard Iain (at that time, of course, 'Ian') Matthews in 1973 at my sister's house outside Johnson City, Tennessee. I was a 14-year-old, coming down from Vermont in August to visit her; she was a reporter at the local newspaper and, after work, she hung with the wordy local freaks (never 'hippies') who enjoyed reading, getting stoned and listening to music.

That year, their albums of choice were Led Zeppelin (the untitled one with those four runic symbols) and Ian Matthews' *If You Saw Thro My Eyes*. She had gotten turned on to Ian Matthews by the staff at The Record Bar, a regional chain that had a store in Johnson City.

My memories of those ten days in August are vivid; reading multiple back issues of *National Lampoon* (a definite step forward in raciness from MAD, my 'outlaw' reading at home), Kurt Vonnegut novels, staring at a black light poster that said 'Dope Will Get You Through Times Of No Money Better Than Money Will Get You Through Times Of No Dope', and listening to Led Zeppelin's 'Stairway to Heaven' and 'The Battle Of Evermore'. And to Ian Matthews.

Charlie Hunter became an Iain Matthews evangelist (Toby Schwartzman)

There was a lot to like about the *If You Saw Thro' My Eyes* package itself – the photos were blurry (mysterious!), the lyrics were printed out, the hand lettering was good (especially the letter 'e') and the record itself – on a Mercury subsidiary called Vertigo – was both very thin (you could bend it!) and had a bit of op-art on the label, so both sides' track listings were printed on the other side!

My sister taught me a rigorous way of listening to music; playing one song over and over and over, dissecting each bit, discussing each turn of phrase, listening for each catch of the voca. Songs subjected to this microscopic treatment had to hold up over time, and the songs we listened to over and over (and over) that summer were 'Desert Inn', 'Reno, Nevada', 'Southern Wind', 'Morgan The Pirate', 'If You Saw Thro' My Eyes'.

And particularly for me, 'Southern Wind'. That vocal! Angelic, but filled with sorrow, with the enigmatic lyric:

So give my love to Augustine and say I won't be long
Say he took a little ride on account of me and wrote us down this song…

That was where I was introduced to the mind-blowing (for a 14-year-old) concept that I didn't have to have any idea of what the songwriter was talking about to know *exactly* what the songwriter was talking about.

I returned home that August and went off to boarding school where I learned that everybody knew about Led Zeppelin and hardly anyone knew Ian Matthews (even though someone named Sandy Denny sang on both their records!). I suppose it's my New England upbringing that instilled in me a strong contrarianism, but, for whatever reason, I became an Ian Matthews evangelist.

I sought out his records (there were cut-outs of *If You Saw Thro' My Eyes* at Discount Records in Cambridge for $1.98!). I made people listen to Ian Matthews in the art building where the secretary let students play music (at a reasonable volume) over the building's sound system. And I was overjoyed when I found another student who knew who he was (I have never forgotten Danny Kahn – a senior! – saying of *Valley Hi*, 'There isn't a bad song on it.'

Becoming passionate about an artist and wanting others to hear their music led, eventually, to my becoming a music manager for a dozen years and even becoming one of Iain's managers briefly in the early nineties. (Our model would have worked, I swear, if the internet had been in place then.)

In the art building one time I remember wondering if, in 30 years' time (50 years being an unfathomable amount of time when one is a teenager), I would even remember who Ian Matthews was? I am pleased to report back to teenaged-me that yes, I do. And that I am still listening to him to this day.

AUBURN UNIVERSITY

25 OCTOBER 1973, AUBURN, ALABAMA

ROY TRIMBLE

Of course, I knew of Iain. I had a Fairport album or two and enjoyed them immensely. But on October 25, 1973, in Auburn, Alabama I decided to go to an America concert. It was my second year of college. I thought of America as a lightweight, acoustic band with pretty singing and playing but not a great deal of depth. But for this concert, supporting the album *Hat Trick*, they obviously were out to dispel that notion. They turned each song into a full-on Neil Young and Crazy Horse rave up. I was surprised and impressed.

Roy Trimble was surprised that Iain was opening for America

But the biggest surprise of the night was that Ian Matthews opened for them. The poster didn't include his name. Opening acts at Auburn were pretty much ignored. Seats were rarely General Admission, so people just showed up for the headliner. So here I was in a vast, partially-filled concrete basketball arena with Ian and his two mates playing down below. It was all beautiful and lovely and I said to myself, 'You need to buy more of his stuff!'

But then he began to play 'Midnight On The Water'. The song is a stunner. It builds in intensity and drops you off a cliff at the end. He was in fine voice and in that echoey, giant space the natural reverb made it soar. I don't think I've ever felt the power of a song so deeply as I did hearing it in that way for the first time. For years after it was always the first or the last song on every mixtape I made.

I finally met Iain at a house concert in Durham, North Carolina a few years ago. He and Andy Roberts were touring the Plainsong album, *Reinventing Richard: The Songs Of Richard Fariña*. I tried to express how impactful that experience was on me (without sounding too goofy) and he assured me I would not experience it that night as they were only playing Plainsong music. As an aside, I believe he said the guys backing him were Richard and Michael Curtis who had written the song 'Blue Letter' on Fleetwood Mac's first album with Buckingham Nicks.

But that was okay. I think the song and space came together in a special moment that could never be recaptured.

JOURNEYS FROM GOSPEL OAK

BOB GALLIE

Journeys From Gospel Oak saved my life and set me on the path of music. It was the early seventies and I was working my way through playing guitar and enjoying everything that came out of Greenwich Village: CSN&Y, James Taylor, Joni and all the usual suspects! And I was infatuated by a Methodist minister's daughter…

We would play vinyl all day and then she said, 'You should listen to this.' It was *Journeys From Gospel Oak*. The voice and the songs just inspired me. Sadly, the relationship with the girl all ended in tears and I was a broken man on the road to ruin, with no true course in life and very close to leaving it all behind.

But one night I put on *Gospel Oak* again and it made me feel like there was more to the life which I had nearly thrown away!

It was only many years later that I discovered that the songs on the album were all covers! It made no difference, as Iain brought so much out of each song. 'Met Her On A Plane' gave me everything I needed to continue writing and performing music.

Bob Gallie was saved by *Journeys From Gospel Oak*

So I thank Iain from the depths of my heart, for being there. I'm just someone who writes and performs my own music, and I've worshipped Iain from afar for many years!

LAGUNA BEACH

SPRING 1976, CALIFORNIA

BRUCE BARROW, FORMER TOUR MANAGER FOR IAIN

The day I met Iain Matthews was, I believe, sometime during the spring of 1976. I was staying in Laguna Beach with my friend Michael Reesberg. Michael had mentioned the previous night at a club, where the Manna band was playing, that this guy Iain Matthews had come into the club with a lead guitar player and bass player in tow, looking to hire Stephen Hooks, who was the saxophone player with Manna at the time. Iain had an album coming out on Columbia Records called *Go For Broke* and needed to go on the road to promote it.

Michael was looking for a second roadie to go out with them and since I was the ripe old age of 25 and had no clue what I was going to do with the rest of my life, I said, 'What the hell – I'll go!'

I'm not sure how many days after that it was that the band met at keyboard player Bobby Wright's house to start rehearsals. It was a bit awkward because it was an eight-piece band with two lead guitar players, two bass players, a keyboard player, sax player and lead singer/rhythm guitar player. Iain showed up with Jay Lacy, his band leader and lead guitar player, and I was introduced to them by Michael.

Iain was very quiet, gave me a bit of a light handshake, quietly said 'hi' and then went about his business. I wasn't very familiar with Iain's music. I was aware of his cover of Joni Mitchell's 'Woodstock' and that was about it. Even though Iain seemed a bit shy around Michael and I, it didn't take long for him to take complete control the band, leaving no doubt as to who was in charge of what he was looking for.

I must say it was actually a hot band, but much better after we ended up losing that extra the guitar and bass player. And little did I realise the day that I met Iain Matthews that that would lead to be one of the most consequential relationships of my life.

THE SAVOY TIVOLI

JUNE 1976, SAN FRANCISCO, CALIFORNIA

CRAIG MATTHEWS

Growing up in the San Francisco Bay Area I was lucky enough to see many of the great bands in the 1970s. I learned to play guitar (poorly) in the seventh grade and played in some garage bands back in the day. So with the popularity of Matthews Southern Comfort back then, some friends would call me 'Whiskey', others 'CC' (for 'Comfort Craig').

I got to see Iain perform at a small club, the Savoy Tivoli in North Beach, San Francisco, the same year I graduated high school. The show was recorded by the Bay Area Music magazine (aka BAM). The cool local underground FM station, KSAN – the Live 95, would play live show BAM recordings on air, so I recorded that show and literally wore that tape out in the Craig Powerplay cassette deck installed in my 1968 Camaro.

Fast forward to 2024. I saw a Facebook post that Iain would be visiting California in March 2025 and was interested in playing some small venues and house concerts. My missus and I have hosted a few house concerts over the years, so I reached out to Iain to offer our help. Iain replied, we spoke on the phone a couple times and we're looking forward to getting together this March for his visit while hosting Iain at a friend's consignment music shop, Mighty Fine Guitars in Lafayette, California.

Craig Matthews first caught Iain at the Savoy Tivoli

ROCKBURGH RECORDS

1978 – 1980, FULHAM, LONDON, UK

BEV PERRIN

I worked for Rockburgh Records from 1978 to 1980, when Iain was signed to the label. I was in my early twenties. There was just me and Sandy Roberton (sadly deceased). We worked out of his house in Fulham opposite the Chelsea football ground, although we later moved to a bigger office around the corner.

Sandy told me a great story about when he was banging on Iain's door and pleading with him (unsuccessfully) to get Iain to appear on *Top Of The Pops* to promote 'Shake It'.

I remember going to studios in Chipping Norton with Iain and his band. It was residential so we stayed the night. I became friends with them, and particularly with Iain's roadie, Gary Perkins, who later saved my husband's life when he had a near-fatal asthma attack in a London hotel room. (Unfortunately, he *did* die of an asthma attack years later.)

I remember Iain's red-haired girlfriend sneaking down to the kitchen in the middle of the night to eat bacon sandwiches in the studio in Oxfordshire. (She was pretending to be a vegetarian.) He probably never knew.

My husband Gary and I later visited Iain and his girlfriend in the US (it might have been Seattle). His friends and colleagues were outraged that he would not allow smoking in his home (which seems laughable now). He was also a vegetarian, and everyone thought that was very odd, although he was simply way ahead of his time. They gave me a lovely retro cashmere jumper for my birthday, and I kept it for decades.

STEALIN' HOME

RELEASED 11 AUGUST 1978

PIERRE-MARIE DUFOUR

Back in 1978, I was 15 years old and I started listening to music.

Back then, there were several evening music programmes on the airwaves, especially on French public radio France Inter and on private station RTL. That year, I remember vividly that my attention was caught be those two British artists' velvet voices and beautiful songs: Gerry Rafferty and Ian Matthews. 'Baker Street' was overplayed and I soon grew tired of it, but after 'Man In The Station' got some airplay, then came 'Gimme An Inch Girl' followed by 'Don't Hang Up Those Dancing Shoes' and 'Shake It'.

Pierre-Marie fell in love with the album cover for *Stealin' Home*

Next thing I did was to eagerly explore the local record store. As I found *Stealin' Home* in the bins, I instantly fell in love with the album cover, a beautiful photo of a young model, with Paris's rooftops emerging from the dark. This vinyl album became one of the very first LP in my collection, which grew to 1,500 albums before it got converted to CDs. And Ian (then Iain) Matthews records have been on my playlists ever since.

LONE STAR CAFÉ

8 MAY 1979, NEW YORK, NEW YORK

RON KURZWEIL

I'm a longtime fan since the early seventies, when *The Bear* album span constantly on my turntable. My brother had season tickets to New York Rangers hockey games, and used to take me on occasion. One of the biggest events in New York hockey history was taking place in May 1979, as the Rangers and Islanders faced each other in the playoffs. My game was supposed to be May 8th... However, Iain was playing with his band The Razorblades at the Lone Star Café that night in Manhattan.

Needless to say, I attended the concert, not the hockey game, and it's one of the highlight shows in the last 45 years of viewing Iain live whenever he played in the Tri-State area. His music has brought me infinite joy, and he's still churning out quality music all these decades later.

Ron Kurzweil is a longtime fan

DINGWALLS
14 DECEMBER 1983, LONDON, UK

DIANE CLARKE

Many, many years of following Iain Matthews and his magical music started with hearing his distinctive harmonies and vocals with Fairport Convention, proceeding to his Matthews Southern Comfort albums from *Second Spring* onwards, and then through the US and the Dutch years! I possess them all on vinyl, CD and downloads. I am a huge fan of his pure voice and the flawless harmonies. I saw him at Dingwalls in December 1983, and it was a fantastic atmosphere and a treat to hear

Diane Clarke loves the purity and wistfulness of Iain's voice

his voice in a comparatively intimate venue.

I was delighted to see him latterly playing at the Hailsham Pavilion on 2 August 2019, another small venue, and to be able to take photos and chat in the interval. He had his Dutch band and played a mixture of old and new. My favourites were the stirring versions of 'Blood Red Roses' and 'Road To Ronderlin'.

My all-time favourite tracks from 54 years of albums? It's so hard to choose, but I love a lot of the songs on *Some Days You Eat The Bear…*, notably 'Keep On Sailing' and Ol' '55'. Also, his version of 'Seven Bridges Road', which I persuaded my choir to cover. I love and frequently replay every track on *Stealin' Home*, particularly the title track and 'King Of The Night'. There is such purity and wistfulness in his voice.

THE MARQUEE

2 MARCH 1984, LONDON, UK

ROB PHIPPS

I may have come to Iain a little late as I didn't really get into his music until I read three articles by John Tobler in three successive *Zigzag* magazines. I then began to collect his albums but by the 1980s I still had never seen him. I was amazed to come across *Mood for Mallards by HiFi* which saw Iain working with David Surkamp whom I'd followed in Pavlov's Dog since their first album (I'm sorry Iain, but I love that period of your work!).

Rob Phipps thinks Iain's work in the eighties is underrated

Fast forward to early 1984 and I saw Iain was playing a gig

at the Marquee in London. I was living in Banbury at the time so was able to drive down. When I got there, I saw that it was being filmed by a German TV company. The gig was absolutely excellent – it was also good to see Mark Griffiths in the line-up. Most of the songs came from *Shook*, another album I really rate. (For me, the Rockburgh period represents neglected classics.)

And to round off this story I am of course a proud owner of the DVD of the gig… and when there is a shot of the audience halfway through, I can just about make myself out in all my six-foot-four glory.

Thanks, Iain, for sorting much amazing music. But don't write off the early eighties!

JEFF SAMUELS

In the late seventies or early eighties, I became friends with Iain and he played basketball with us in Benedict Canyon. As a basketball player he was a good 'football' player. He was aggressive and we all had a great time. At this time, I was an A&R person at United Artists and I seem to recall playing 'Darkness Darkness' for him. I always loved that song and unsuccessfully tried getting one of our artists to record it.

RELAX

1980S, LUDWIGSFELDE, GERMANY

ULLI BEHNKE

I have been fortunate enough to see Iain live several times, including in Berlin at the Quasimodo before German reunification and afterward in a small town called Ludwigsfelde (a place known only for obscure murder cases and its motorway bridge.) It's only a few kilometers from Potsdam to Ludwigsfelde. So I drove there.

The club was called Relax and it wasn't particularly crowded; Iain's great music hadn't yet arrived in eastern Germany. I was standing at a bar table in front of the makeshift stage during

Iain's first set, drinking beer. During the intermission, Iain suddenly came up to me and asked if I had stolen his setlist. I was totally astonished because he meant it. I hadn't, and I never would, but I couldn't shake the feeling that Iain didn't believe me, and the mood was somewhat dampened. Only his version of 'I Don't Wanna Talk About It' reconciled me with the evening.

HALF MOON

6 AUGUST 1986, PUTNEY, LONDON, UK

STEPHEN ROYSTON

I have admired Iain's work, his voice and his songwriting since the first Fairport albums, and I bought his debut solo album, *Matthews Southern Comfort*, when it first came out in 1970. *If You Saw Thro' My Eyes* from 1971 remains one of my all-time favourite albums.

But I didn't get to see Iain perform live until the 1980s. I remember an interesting Fairport line-up, including Richard Thompson, on a hot night at the Half Moon pub in Putney in August 1986.

I also have fond memories of Iain's gig in another pub, the Richmond in Brighton on 3rd March 1990, when he featured songs from his excellent 1988 album, *Walking A Changing Line*.

I loved Plainsong's a cappella arrangement of Richard Thompson's great song 'From Galway To Graceland' from the 1993 charity compilation album of Richard Thompson songs, *The World Is A Wonderful Place.* As far as I know this was the first recording of that song.

I am grateful to Iain for introducing me to the music of Richard Fariña – starting with 'Reno Nevada' from the Fairport days, right up to Plainsong's *Reinventing Richard* in 2015. Thanks, Iain!

CROPREDY FESTIVAL

9 AUGUST 1986, CROPREDY, UK

CLIVE GREGSON

I'm pretty sure that my first sighting of Iain was on the front cover of the 1969 Island Records sampler, *You Can All Join In*. He's standing next to Steve Winwood and he's got a bit of a scowl on. Iain was still just about a member of Fairport Convention at that point, and their contribution to the sampler was the timeless 'Meet On The Ledge'. Iain sings the opening verse. Instantly brilliant voice...

A year or so later, I bought the Matthews Southern Comfort single of 'Woodstock'. Great record… a really classy arrangement of Joni's song and another terrific vocal performance. I also bought the band's albums and their mix of folk, country and pop made a huge impact on me, particularly 'Later That Same Year'. Iain is actually smiling on the cover of that one! Forever musically restless, Iain jumped ship on Southern Comfort and was then also lost to me for a couple of years...

In 1973, I left my native Manchester and went to Alsager College, where my band Any Trouble came together. Turned out that Chris (our guitarist) had impeccable taste in music and he turned me on to loads of great records... he lent me *If You Saw Thro' My Eyes*, a solo album that Iain released in 1971 (still one of my all-time favourite records). Iain's peerless vocals are matched by an awesome cast of supporting musicians. The playout on 'Reno Nevada' has Richard Thompson and Tim Renwick wailing over a stellar rhythm section of Andy Roberts, Gerry Conway and Pat Donaldson... and that's as good as it gets in my book!

Then came Plainsong and *In Search Of Amelia Earhart*, another hugely influential record for me. Iain and Andy's partnership seemed to be firmly rooted and it's hard to believe that this initial incarnation of Plainsong lasted barely a year. Off again, Iain relocated to the States and went back to making solo records, which I frequently bought on the day of release. In addition to being an astute selector of songs (often introducing me to songwriters for the first time), Iain was now a gifted writer and a magnet for brilliant musicians. I still regularly haul out my Matthews vinyl from that period for a blissful nostalgic afternoon...

I think the first time I met Iain was at his Marquee gig in 1983, with Mark Griffiths on bass, Bob Henrit on drums, and Bruce Hazen and Bob Metzger on guitars. Great band, great gig. Our connection was via Sandy Roberton, long-time producer and associate of Iain, who I'd met on a tour where Any Trouble opened up for John Martyn, another Roberton client. Any Trouble were in the process of recording *Wrong End Of The Race*, the final album of our first incarnation, and Iain joined us to sing harmonies on a few tracks. We recorded a re-make of 'Open Fire', a song from our second album and you can imagine how chuffed I was when Iain told me he already knew the song... he'd recorded a cover of it with a band during his time in Seattle! Iain's harmony on 'Like A Man' is still one of my most treasured AT memories. Spare... but perfect.

Iain and I would catch up fairly regularly thereafter... at festivals, Richard Thompson Band gigs... and in 1997, Iain and Andy asked me to replace Julian Dawson in a revived line up of Plainsong. I was thrilled... and we toured the UK and Europe for a couple of years and also recorded *New Place Now*, an album of which I am very proud. We're all smiling in the cover picture, but Iain was not having the best of times personally while we were working on the album. Nevertheless, he trouped mightily...

Sadly, the album, while critically well received, didn't exactly storm the charts and Plainsong disintegrated again. Iain moved to Holland, remained very creative and worked as hard as ever. I don't see him as often these days, much to my regret.

A favourite Iain moment? He joined Fairport at their Cropredy Festival in 1986. Christine and I were there, playing with Richard. Iain asked the three of us if we'd join him onstage for a couple of acapella songs... one of them being 'Woodstock'. There's a YouTube clip of it that somebody pointed me to a while back... it's really special. There's a moment where Iain hits a sublime falsetto note in the last verse... properly spine-tingling. Richard and I smile at each other in admiration...

Ah, happy days.

GOIN' BACK WITH IAN MATTHEWS

Before we actually get down to concluding this epic (for the time being), I feel obliged to tell you about a few items of extra information which various interested parties have sent concerning the various matters so far raised. This explains, he whispered lamely, why this final episode has taken so long to put together.

Anyway, I am indebted to the following (as Cyril Fletcher says - Esther Rantzen can come round here anytime...) for their contributions: Dave Gordon, Nick Jones, Mike Jessop, Nick Ralph (of Dark Star) and Phil Ward.

Let's start with a few things about Fairport Convention, mostly supplied by Nick Jones (currently press officer for BTM - nice to see Climax in the charts, Nick - and who was the first London correspondent for Rolling Stone), and by Nick Ralph.

NJ remembers introducing Richard Thompson to 'Jack Of Diamonds' in 1964, when they played together in a pre-Convention group, and has a notion that Tyger Hutchings was in an Albion Jug Band as long ago as 1964, i.e. considerably pre-Fairport. Nick was one of four 'notables' who attended William Ellis School in Highgate, the others being Richard Thompson, Gerry Conway and Mike Alfandary the promoter. NR provides a list of songs that Fairport played, but which never made it to released record, although some of them were recorded. With Judy Dyble, he recalls 'Violets Of Dawn' (Eric Andersen), and with Sandy Denny, 'Suzanne', 'Bird On The Wire', 'If You Feel Good, You Know It Can't Be Wrong', 'Gone, Gone, Gone', 'Reno Nevada', 'Shattering Live Experience', 'You're Gonna Need My Help', 'I Still Miss Someone', 'Morning Glory', 'High School Confidential' and 'Light Your Fire' (described as a Christmas spoof). Much of this is apparently in Island's vaults, so how about it, chaps?

The more observant among you may have noticed mention here and there of a cassette of early Fairport, which I'm assured by those who've heard it contains a lot of this very same material, and is highly recommended...

Also according to NR, Ian did play with the Fairports for over a year after he left the group, including at a police benefit concert at Little Hadham, which Mr. Ralph claims to be able to authenticate by 'documentary evidence'.

On to the Southern Comfort days. Mike Jessop tells us that Martin Jenkins lives in Coventry, did two LPs on Rubber with Hedgehog Pie, and is at this point reforming Dando Shaft, while the famed Higgy, roadie to MSC, has subsequently worked with Uriah Heep, and is now Andy Fairweather Low's tour manager. Amazing what you can find out...Both Nick Jones and Phil Ward have seen Poli Palmer at the Golden Lion in Fulham recently, while Phil Ward thinks I should have known that Ray Duffy is now drumming with Gallagher and Lyle, before which he was in Cottonwood and a band called Chinook, in which the afore-mentioned Mr. Ward was the bass player. All sorts of famous people write to us - thanks, Phil.

Finally, the prolix Nick Ralph indicates that Plainsong's first recording was of the fabulous 'Along Comes Mary', of Association fame, but that it was never released, although Marc Ellington dubbed his own vocal on the Plainsong backtrack, and put it on his 'Restoration' LP, while a couple of the other tracks that were recorded for the 'Gospel Oak' LP, but didn't make it to the record, were 'Galveston' and 'Turn Your Radio On'. To all you gentlemen, thanks for your efforts, and treat this as your reply.

* * * * * * * * * * * * *

Back to the story - with Plainsong crumbling, Elektra weren't too happy, and the same went for Ian. "I made my displeasure with the band known to the record company, and Ian Ralfini (then head of WEA UK, now head of Anchor) put me in touch with Jac Holzman, who invited me to New York to talk about it. Jac wanted me to leave the band and do a solo thing, and he suggested that I do it with Nesmith. I knew about Nesmith from Bud Scoppa, who was at Mercury, so it sounded great!"

Packing his bags, Ian went to LA where he got involved with the Countryside vibe, staying with Skip Van Leeuwen, the general manager of Countryside, who was also American motorcycling champion, and according to everyone I've spoken to, an ace cat. Nesmith was apparently impressed by Skip's ability to sell things, having bought some motor cycle accessories from him. Just so you know who we're talking about, there should be a picture hereabouts of an almost unrecognisable Nesmith (presumably hung up on hair restorer at the time) with Skip and a mutual interest.

"Michael's an unconscious con man - he doesn't mean to do it, but he's a dreamer, an idealist, with the best intentions in the world. And that's what Skip saw - it was 'Here's a record company, we can sign who we want, and we're going to make a million!' So Skip left".

Having established that he would be making an album with Nesmith for El[...] it came down to details. "When we [...] spoke, he said he wanted to put me [...] on exactly what he was going to do, [...] said that the service he really want[...] perform was to make things availabl[...] me, things that he had access to, an[...] didn't. So I told him the people I w[...] to use, like Jimmy Gordon, and whe[...] back to California (after briefly re[...] to England) he told me he couldn't [...] *any* of them! But he said he had a r[...] good studio band of his own...so I s[...] 'OK'. He never does anything malic[...]

The album which resulted from thi[...] entous alliance was 'Valley Hi', whi[...] simply a magnificent record, and qu[...] essential. It was also the first of la[...] albums where he contributed instrum[...] ally, although with the wealth of mag[...] players in the Countryside band, he'[...] significantly audible. For the unini[...] the band consisted of Nesmith on gu[...] the great Orville J. Rhodes on steel [...] dobro, Danny Lane on drums (now w[...] the one-time Mrs. Phyllis Nesmith i[...] private life), who contributed to the [...] Bert Jansch LP, and also helped ou[...] McTell on the road, Billy Graham (n[...] him) on bass and fiddle, two amazin[...] guitar players in Jay Lacy and Bob [...] ford, the latter acclaimed by Claren[...] White as the best player of Clarence [...] string-bender, and David Barry on [...] boards. A great band, need I say, [...] also to be heard on the Countryside [...] by Garland Frady and Red Rhodes.

The musicians, then, were excell[...] but the songs are maybe even better, [...] an interpretive album, this has few [...] It starts with two Plainsong remnant[...] 'Keep On Sailing' and 'The Old Man [...] The Mill', the latter of which I consi[...] be the only blot on an otherwise nea[...] perfect escutcheon, because it's dr[...] boring, with little to commend it to [...] 'Keep On Sailing', on the other han[...] great, with a beautifully layered ba[...] complementing a finely recorded and [...] appealing vocal. 'Shady Lies' is a [...] from the pen of Richard Thompson, [...] not very old. He wrote it when he w[...] with the Albion Country Band. Rich[...] used to call Sandy's album 'The Nor[...] Gasman and the Raver'! But I hear[...] do that song on a gig, and said I'd l[...] record it, and he wrote it down for [...]

Next comes what I consider to be [...] son Browne's best song, obviously [...] diamond among a positive hoard of p[...] stones, 'These Days'. Ian claims t[...] been one of the earlier of the dozens [...] people who've recorded it, only bein[...] preceded by the Nitty Gritty Dirt Ba[...] Tom Rush and Gator Creek, and in a [...] sequent discussion of Tom Rush, Ian [...] that 'No Regrets' is constantly on hi[...] list to record, and he reckons he'll [...] ually do it, which is something to lo[...] forward to indeed. 'These Days' is [...] followed by another Matthews song, [...] time not a previously recorded effo[...] called 'Leaving Alone', which apart [...] its inherent excellence, also has so[...] good use of the string-bender from [...] Warford.

Side two starts with the brilliant '[...] Bridges Road', written by Steve Yo[...] and apparently recorded on both of [...] first two LPs. (The first of these w[...] called 'Rock Salt and Nails', and I [...] that the fine Mr. Rod Buckle at Sone[...] acquired a Steve Young album, from [...] Blue Canyon label, which should be [...] shops by now, and is heavily recomm[...] Frame reckons that Steve Young was in a group called Stone Country with Don Beck, who visited Europe as a member of the Burrito Revue, the main part of which was Country Gazette.) Then there's 'Save Your Sorrows', another ex-Plainsong, a Randy Newman thing called 'What Are You Waiting For', which could only have been written by the man who did write it, 'Propinquity' by Nesmith, which is nearly as good here as in the original, and finally 'Blue Blue Day' by the great and underrated Don Gibson. "It was one of my favourites, and everybody had done it too fast. I wanted to show it the way it was, like Neil Young did with 'Oh Lonesome Me'".

Don Gibson remains a remarkable song-

Ian Matthews
Stealin' Home

Ian Matthews has had a long and varied musical career beginning with a Deram band called Pyramid who had just one single released, "Summer Of Last Year". In late 1967, he joined Fairport Convention and stayed with them for three albums but left when the material was tending towards English traditional and away from what he wanted to do. His first solo album, "Matthews Southern Comfort", was released in 1970 and he went about forming a band of the same name. With Southern Comfort, they released two further albums that year, "Second Spring" and "Later That Same Year". The band had a huge hit with a single, Joni Mitchell's "Woodstock", which took Ian by surprise. Unprepared for success on such a scale, he left the band and once more embarked on a solo career.

After two more solo albums, Ian teamed up with Andy Roberts and formed Plainsong who recorded two albums under Sandy Roberton's production. The first was the excellent "In Search Of Amelia Earhart", but the second was never released. Presumably disillusioned, Ian left Plainsong and moved to the States, recording his next album with Michael Nesmith producing. Four more solo albums followed, which brings us up-to-date with the release of "Stealin' Home" on Rockburgh Records with Sandy Roberton again producing. I.M. spoke to Ian two days before the start of his recent British tour.

102

GOIN' BACK WITH IAN MATTHEWS

it was your real name, and your mother remarried or something, and there's another which said that Judy Dyble (original Fairport lady singer) went off with Ian McDonald of King Crimson.

IM: That's the real reason - I didn't want people to think it was me! ...

apparently taking with them the B-side of the single, 'If (Stomp)', a pleasantly lightweight jugband-like affair, which appears on their first album, devastatingly titled 'Fairport Convention'. There are, of course, no original members left in the new Fairport group.

Ian Matthews
May 15, 1988
The Bayou, Georgetown, DC

On a very nice summer night Paul Hartman and I had the pleasure of seeing Ian Matthews at the Bayou in Washington, DC. The proverbial "small but enthusiastic crowd" enjoyed a very heartwarming show. Ian showcased music from virtually every facet of his career.

Opening the show was The New St. George, who did a nice job-- and for the first time in their career they were louder than the headline act.

Knowing that I had not seen Ian since 1978, I was not sure what to expect-- to be honest I was a little bit more than surprised. Ian's voice was in superb shape and his choice of material and musicians were top notch. We were fortunate to see the talents of Mark Hallman on guitar and vocals, who vastly helped Ian on his new album. Also along on all keyboards was Craig Negolson, who did a great job.

For the first time in a long while Ian was doing an acoustic set and some older material came off very well, as well as some new songs from his Windham Hill album, *Walking a Changing Line*.

From the way Ian talked with the audience obviously the man is a grizzled veteran of the music business who was having fun but also had a tremendous tongue in cheek when it came to talking about hit singles and life past. I think everyone enjoyed his talking to the crowd immensely.

If you are an Ian Matthews fan the set included music from Fairport, Matthews Southern Comfort, Ian Matthews' early & later solo material, Plainsong, as well as a new song now released.

Highlights were-- "Seven Bridges Road", "Alive Alone", "Woodstock" a cappella, "Shadows Break", "If You Saw Thro' My Eyes", "Meet on the Ledge", and "Sights of Manhattan" (new song). The other songs were: "Old Man/Squirrel Hill", "Keep On Sailing", "Man in the Station", "Except for a Tear", "Reno, Nevada", "For the Second Time", "Following Every Finger", and "Standing Still".

-- *Bill Martin*

IATTHEWS IS NOT STANDING STILL! Ian's latest album
A Changing Line" has been released on Windham Hill Records and
imported into Australia by Festival Records. The album feat-
songs written by Jules Shear, who is maybe a new name to some of
JN PENHALLOW asked Ian some questions about the album...

Ian, what's Jules Shear's background?
es is a singer/songwriter who I've known since 1975. At that
, he had a band called Jules & The Polar Bears. They had two
ms on CBS, then three solo albums on various labels. I was an
initiate to his songwriting and collected his demos avidly.
tly, Jules has been known for the hits he wrote for the Bangles
She Knew What She Wants") and Cyndi Lauper ("All Through The
").

you give us some comments about the songs on the album?
her than go through each song, I can tell you that they were
en for their (a) lyrical content (b) adaptability and (c) be-
e in my opinion they are the best things he's ever written.
irrel Hill" was written at my request - I wanted something
-sounding.

's the girl with the great voice that you duet with on the
m?
girl singing on
ve Alone" is a
nd of mine. Her name
liza Gilkyson and
has an album of her
on Goldcastle, dist-
ted by Polygram. We
t tour together,
gh we have shared
same bill before.

sleeve notes men-
Roger Swallow. Is
our old drummer?
, Roger was in both
hern Comfort and
nsong and was also
he Albions. He now
s here in Los Ang-
and he's one of my
friends who also
a collection of
s' demos.

what's the plan for

e started thinking
t the next album. I
a half dozen orig-
songs finished. I'd
it to be 70% orig-
and some single-
covers. I'm touring
y month here in the
es. In fact, this
h (Oct.'88), Richard
Thompson and I are playing some shows together. In December I hope to
be recording demo songs.

JP - Has your back catalogue been issued on CD yet? I'd like to get
some of them again.
IM - "Stealing Home" and "Shook" are available in Germany on Line Records. I got mine from Virgin Imports in London - they also have "Siamese Friends", one of my favourites.

JP - Well Ian, thanks for your answers and we'd love to see you down
here in Australia.
IM - Thanks, I've never been to Australia and always wanted to. I tour
as an acoustic duo with my co-producer Mark Hallman. It's quite magic
al, even if I do say so myself!

Since doing this interview, I learnt that there is a proposed "Evening
With Windham Hill" tour due in May '89 and we're crossing our fingers
that Ian and Mark will be included in it, along with Michael Hedges, the
brilliant guitar player. If it happens, we've just got to get as many
friends there to the concerts as possible - buying a ticket and going
on your own isn't good enough! (JP)

COMPETITION TIME!

Name the Jules Shear song Ian recorded on an earlier album and the album's title. First correct answer wins a copy of Ian's single "Following Every Finger", and a full colour poster. Entries to John Penhallow,
21 Perrett St, Rozelle, NSW 2039.

COMPETITION TIME PART TWO!

We also have an autographed cassette of the Roaring Jack "Cat Among The Pigeons" album, as described in detail in the last issue of Fiddlestix (NB: I erroneously forgot to credit Alistair Hulett as the co-author of that particular piece - sorry!).

Anyway, to be in the running to win this cassette, just name the band's first mini album which was released last year.

Entries for this competition go to P.O.Box 110, Stepney, SA 5069.

These competitions are for subscribers only. See what you miss out on by not subscribing?

The first correct entry recieved will be the winner, so be quick!

If you don't win, go out and buy the album, it's great Gaelic thrash!

THE BOTTOM LINE

MAY 1988, NEW YORK, NEW YORK

RONALD STEWART

Iain was playing his Jules Shere songs in NYC. I had no way to get there, and no money at the time. A guy I disliked who I worked with was bragging about how great a bowler he was. I offered to bowl him a two-game total at his lanes for 50 bucks. (I didn't have 50 bucks, but I figured I'd win anyway.) I destroyed him in both games, took the dollars and took the bus in, paid for my ticket and had an amazing concert experience. I love Iain.

Ronald bowled for money to win the cost of an Iain concert

EDMONTON FOLK FESTIVAL GALLAGHER PARK

5-7 AUGUST 1988, EDMONTON, CANADA

MARK HALLMAN

I first discovered Iain's music in 1970 via two different yet converging paths. FM radio was in its infancy, and I was captivated by Fotheringay's version of Gordon Lightfoot's 'The Way I Feel', which in turn led me to explore Sandy Denny and Fairport Convention. At the same time, Matthews' Southern Comfort had a radio hit with 'Woodstock', which I adored. Thus began a long run of buying records by these bands, as well as Iain's solo records.

By the mid-eighties, I had become a record producer and moved to Austin, Texas. I got a call at my studio one day and

Mark Hallman was surprised to receive a call from Iain

the voice on the other end of the line said, 'This is Iain Matthews.' I instantly replied, 'THE Iain Matthews?!' After a humble response, he told me that he had heard my work, and was interested in working with me on a new project. He came to Texas, we met, we played together and decided to go forward. Iain had a collection of Jules Shear songs – demos that Jules had given him. He wanted to do a record of entirely Jules Shear songs. I had never heard of Shear, but quickly recognised what an amazing talent he was, and together with Iain's voice and musical sensibilities, I knew something great was about to happen. The result was our first record together, *Walking A Changing Line*, and a musical partnership, as well as a lifelong friendship, was born.

We subsequently recorded a number of records together and began touring as a duo, with Iain performing his material accompanied by my harmonies and guitar work. He could have done solo shows, but he chose not to at this time.

My story pertains to a performance at the Edmonton Folk Festival in Canada. Back in those days, North American citizens could use IDs such as drivers' licenses, rather than passports, to cross each other's borders. I had not realised that my own license had expired, and so I was detained upon our arrival in Canada. We decided that Iain should go ahead and that I would join him later for our scheduled performance that afternoon. Unfortunately, clearing me into the country was an hours-long process. After an agonising delay, I was finally allowed in and somehow managed to get a ride to the Folk Festival. As I arrived, Iain was already on stage, about to sing his first note, when I walked on. It was quite a testament to his dedication to his music that he was going to do his first ever solo show right then and there, even though I ultimately managed to plug in at the last second, and we did the set as a duo after all.

There are countless other stories of our exploits on the road, some fun, some not so fun, but our friendship endures, and we still sing together whenever we can. Playing and singing with Iain is always a musical treat for me.

IRON HORSE CAFÉ

12 SEPTEMBER 1988, NORTHAMPTON, MASSACHUSETTS

BOB YOUNG

It's the seventies and I am a young teenager with a love of music and not much money to spend. Collecting records meant trawling through the cut-out bins at Woolworth, where you could get ten singles for a dollar, including 'Woodstock' by Matthews Southern Comfort. As I got a little older, I started collecting LPs. At Grand Way, a long-gone department

Store, I started picking up a few albums for nine cents apiece. It didn't matter if I had never heard of the artist; it was music. One day I came home with two albums by this guy, Ian Matthews. One was *If You Saw Thro' My Eyes*. The other was *Tigers Will Survive*. I loved them and played them incessantly.

By 1979, I was working for Bradlees, another now defunct department store. I walked past an album display and did a double take. There was Mr Matthews on display with *Stealin' Home*. I immediately bought it and added it to the collection.

Later that year, I joined my college radio station and started exploring the production room, where old records went to die. I found the Elektra records, then the Columbia albums and began dropping them into my sets on the air. Another jockey pulled me aside and asked me if I had ever heard of Fairport Convention?

Nope.

Well, it has the same guy. And Matthews Southern Comfort and Plainsong? That's him, too.

By the early eighties, I was placing the occasional classified ad in *Goldmine* magazine looking for IM-related material. One day, an album showed up in the mail, unsolicited. It was *Go For Broke*, signed by Iain. He had seen my ad and asked a record store friend to send it to me. Holy crap! I was thrilled.

In 1988, Iain was touring the northeast United States and I got tickets for the show at the Iron Horse Café in Northampton, Massachusetts. I saw him walking up the hill carrying his guitar case and burst out the door to meet him. I managed to blurt out something about the album he sent me. He said, 'Oh, I remember. You're the *Goldmine* guy.' That became my moniker for a few years whenever we communicated.

I told Iain I had been collecting his stuff. A few months later, I got a huge package in the mail. It was all of Iain's personal scrapbooks. He had entrusted them to me to photocopy whatever I wanted. Of course, I copied everything. But seriously, who does that? How did he know I wouldn't damage anything? Why did he trust me to send them back?

Over the years, I continued to collect IM. I have what may be the most complete collection of his physical media: 45s, LPs, CDs, cassettes, eight tracks, posters, promo packs and even obscure Polish flexi-discs. I have his safety reels of a few of the Rockburgh/RSO albums. Through Goldmine and the internet, I've met some great fellow collectors and fans, especially Barry Eaton and Ron Yaxley. We share recordings of old radio shows and interviews. And Iain has shared his time, his recollections and his good humour with all of us.

Being an Iain Matthews fan is like being a member of a select club. We pretty much all know each other, even if we have never met. Very few outsiders know who Iain is or can fathom why we like him so much.

But we know.

BARRYMORE'S MUSIC HALL
18 JANUARY 1989, OTTAWA, CANADA

BRYAN BANCE

I recall it being a chilly winter's evening and the beginnings of a snowstorm that would emerge over the next couple of days. As such, I was part of a small but appreciative mid-week crowd who got to witness one of the music world's premier entertainers in an intimate setting. If he was fussed by the smallish crowd, he certainly didn't let on and, with support from Mark Hallman, proceeded to give one of the best shows I have ever had the pleasure of seeing. Iain was in fine form, performing a cross selection of tunes from his entire career to that point, including the recently released 'comeback' album, *Walking A Changing Line*.

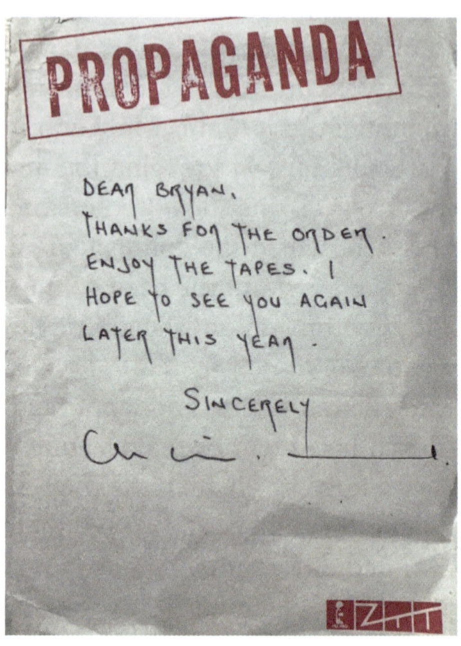

PROPAGANDA

DEAR BRYAN,
THANKS FOR THE ORDER.
ENJOY THE TAPES. I
HOPE TO SEE YOU AGAIN
LATER THIS YEAR.

SINCERELY

Bryan Bance was out of cash on the merch stall

Barrymore's was a hub of musical activity in the 1980s, and being a converted theatre from the turn of the century meant that the sound quality and sight lines were exceptional, especially for acoustic-based artists. This was exemplified during an a capella rendition of 'Woodstock' where everyone sat mesmerised by the sheer clarity of the notes being sung.

Well, nearly everyone. Barrymore's had a policy whereby at a certain time in the evening, they would open the side doors and allow people to come in from the bar next door and watch the rest of the show for free. As it turned out, two boisterous patrons from the pub next door wandered in and, recognising the song they were hearing, began hooting and hollering and attempting to sing along in the loudest, most unmusical manner they could muster. Iain, being the consummate professional he was, without missing a beat or even opening his eyes, simply raised his hand in the air as a polite means of asking the two new attendees to refrain from talking until he could finish the song. To everyone's surprise, they did and proceeded to listen politely for the remainder of the song and even joined in the applause afterwards. I don't recall whether they stuck around after that, but there were no more interruptions and Iain had successfully defused the situation with a simple gesture and some powerful singing.

After the show, I got the chance to meet Iain and chat briefly with him. They say that meeting your heroes can be somewhat disappointing, but not in this case. Iain was very charming and friendly and although I'm sure he would have preferred to be heading back somewhere a bit warmer, he stayed and spoke with all who stopped by to say hello.

He was selling homemade cassettes of what eventually became the *Nights in Manhattan* CD a couple of years later. As I didn't have any cash on me and the nearest ATM was out of order, Iain suggested I could just mail him the cash and he would send me a copy, it being the pre-internet days! He wrote out his mailing address on the back of the venue flyer and a couple of weeks later, I received a copy of the cassette along with a personal note thanking me for supporting his music.

I don't think Iain travels to Canada very often and I haven't had the opportunity to see him in concert again. I do, however, still have the note, the cassette and even the flyer, and 36 years and many, many CDs later, I still am amazed at how consistently pleasing and vital his music continues to be. He is a legend!

EARLY 1990s, SAN FRANCISCO, CALIFORNIA

PAT THOMAS

I first met Iain Matthews in the early 1990s in San Francisco. By this point, I was a major fan and Iain was in a particularly prolific phase. There were new albums, rarities compilations, videos, and even a snail-mailed newsletter. I sort of 'demanded' an interview and the next day, I was invited up to Marin County where we spent a pleasant afternoon reflecting on Iain's career, gossiping about the Cropredy Festival, and comparing notes on John and Beverley Martyn's two albums.

In the early 2000s, our paths crossed again – this time, mostly by email. I organised the release of his two Elektra solo albums onto one CD. And then we did an expansive Plainsong two CD set (for Water Records), putting every known recording from the original line-up in one place. Iain was always helpful and eager to answer my questions about the history of these recordings – he helped make my liner note essays that much better.

Around 2012, Iain and I found each other again – he had a new album that needed a home and I connected him to Omnivore Recordings. We did several releases (new and reissues) together and, again, our conversations led to some detailed liner notes inside of those packages. I got involved in the Wild Honey organisation and I encouraged Iain to start coming to LA and participating.

One time he brought Andy Roberts with him – who regaled me with Roy Harper stories. Iain and I went on a California tour together (which he discusses in his memoir) and besides playing percussion for him, we had hours long chats about all sorts of groovy topics and laughed a lot as well.

That road trip included a delightful backstage hang (and gig) with me, Iain and Richard Thompson. It was heartwarming to watch those lifelong comrades compare notes on music as well as play together. And on the way home, Iain and I hatched the plan for the Richard Fariña tribute album!

Personally, I think he's a very underrated songwriter (most people think of him as a vocalist), but he's got a fine stack of songs that stretch back to the very beginning. In recent years, he's written more than ever and become a very solid guitarist as well. And if that's not enough, besides the fact he looks and sounds at least 20 years younger than he is, he's quite charming.

I love the guy.

CARLETON CLUB

5 MARCH 1990, MORECAMBE, UK

DAVID SUMMERS

Like many British people of my generation, I first became aware of Iain Matthews in 1970. I was a music-mad 13-year-old in those days, and spent most of my pocket money on records. Mostly singles, as I recall; albums were still largely unaffordable. During the course of that year, I got to know three versions of a Joni Mitchell song called 'Woodstock', which referred in some way to a music festival in the United States, although I couldn't make out from the lyrics precisely what the connection was. Joni Mitchell's version of her song sounded like a meditation, and I was initially put off by her acrobatic melodic leaps, although I eventually grew to love them. Crosby, Stills, Nash and Young's version sounded like a wild celebration, and I loved the soulful lead vocal, which I later discovered was Stephen Stills. Matthews Southern Comfort's version, which came out a few months after the others, was totally different and completely won me over from the start.

Beautifully sung, in a clear, pure, and slightly mournful voice, it sounded like an elegy to the 1960s, although I wouldn't have known what an elegy was at the time. I just loved the song, the arrangement and the voice. I don't think the group survived long after the single, but the singer, Iain Matthews, appeared a few times on BBC2's *Old Grey Whistle Test*, so I was able to follow his progress, and I became a fan, although I never saw him in concert in those days. By the time I was old enough to attend gigs on a regular basis, he had moved to America.

I have been lucky enough to see Iain Matthews several times since then, mostly in the last couple of decades, since he started returning to the UK more frequently. One gig stands out. It took place in Morecambe on a Monday night in March 1990. It was the first of a handful of gigs by established singer-songwriters offered at the Carleton Club in an unsuccessful attempt to diversify the clientele and pull in the punters on quiet weekday evenings. I don't recall any publicity apart from a single A4 poster at Lancaster University, where I worked at the time. It read: 'Ian Matthews, tonight, 8:30pm, Carleton Club, Morecambe' (he had just one 'i' in his name in those days).

There was no photo and no further explanation. Could it be him? Well, I was obviously intrigued enough to want to find out, but when I arrived there was no audience. Maybe just a dozen of us. Eventually, Iain emerged, along with accompanist Mark Hallman, and asked us to all draw our seats close together in a circle around him. He said, 'I'll sing you a few songs I've prepared and then, if there's anything you particularly wish to hear, I'll see if I can do that too.' What could have been a disaster turned into a magical intimate gig. Nowadays it might be called a VIP experience. We all felt we had been invited to hear Iain play to us in his sitting room.

He sang a lot of favourites from throughout his career that evening, including 'Close the Door Lightly When You Go', 'The True Story Of Amelia Earhart', 'Busby's Babes' and, of course, 'Woodstock'. There were not many of us there, but the privileged few went home in the knowledge that Iain was not just a classy singer, but a classy individual too.

VARIOUS VENUES

1990, VARIOUS CITIES

BILL MARTIN

For a few years I was involved with booking Iain for some tour dates. I also worked with him on the *Orphans And Outcasts* CDs, volumes 1 and 2. I set up national distribution throughout the US for both releases, as well as selling them through *Dirty Linen* magazine while I was working for it.

When I was booking and working a tour with Iain for the *Pure And Crooked* album, I had set up several dates on the East Coast, with just a few dates open for extra booking. I was in my office one day when the phone rang. It was the promo director from the Denver Zoo. He explained that the zoo did two concerts a year and that, as a big fan, he would like to book Iain. I explained that Iain was on an East Coast tour and had very few dates open and logistics were not good for this. But the director really wanted to do this show. He offered to pay for and fly Iain in, pick him up in a limo, wine him, dine him and pay him a sick amount of money for the show (basically, five times what I was getting for Iain to play).

I asked him to hold on for a moment. I had to put the man on hold because I was doing all I could do to not crack up from laughing so hard. This was just too good to be true. I composed myself and accepted the gig. Henceforth, we had a gig in Pittsburgh one night, I dropped Iain off at the airport the next morning and picked him up three days later for a gig in Baltimore for *Dirty Linen* and life was good!

On the same tour, I had booked a gig on the campus of Johns Hopkins University in Baltimore through a student there. Iain did the gig and when it was time to get paid, Mr Promoter was nowhere to be found and we were left high and dry. Paul Hartman from *Dirty Linen* magazine was with me and with the help of a few students we tracked this guy down to his apartment. After threatening to beat the hell out of him, we got paid and all was well with the world.

Once again on the *Pure And Crooked* tour, we were doing a gig in State College, Pennsylvania. Iain told me he was going to try a new song out that night. It was the first rendering of his classic folk/rap song, 'Back Of The Bus', and it was a fine moment.

One of the two times Iain was booked at the Bridgeton Folk Festival in New Jersey, he was sharing the bill with Jesse Colin Young. I asked Iain if he would be up for doing 'Darkness, Darkness' with Jesse (who wrote the song) as a nice surprise moment. Iain was. But I asked Jesse and he said 'no'. He told me his set was 'pre-made' and that he couldn't do it. I didn't quite understand that until Jesse took the stage. His back-up band was pre-programmed computers. The funny thing is, they broke down and started repeating themselves like a broken record. Very

TONIGHT, SATURDAY, MARCH 17, 1990 11

THE Critics

VENTS
TON BAPTIST
URCH
ton Road.
18, 10.30 a.m. and
Rev. Tony Sargent.
Illustrated talk on
ilisation in China.
45 p.m. - Operation
in the Indian
ontinent.
45 p.m. - Operation
afloat. Illustrated
Doulos and Logos
2.

S & ARTISTS
equired for Heavy
el. (0454) 773611.
quired for rock
gs waiting. — Tel.

VENTS

ere's
Ball?

The Fleece and Firkin, Bristol: Ian Matthews

Two decades on from topping the charts with the Joni Mitchell anthem *Woodstock*, there is nothing of the gone-to-seed rock star about Ian Matthews.

Neat and well-preserved, he entertained a sparse but appreciative Fleece crowd with a likeable, nostalgic blend of acoustic material from the four main phases of his career to date.

There was the majestic *Meet On The Ledge* from his days with the seminal, folk-based Fairport Convention; several clean-cut offerings from his commercially successful Matthews Southern Comfort period; a nod towards his Plainsong collaboration with Andy Roberts; and, most interestingly, a selection of his more recent solo work.

Deftly-supported by Texas guitarist Mark Hallman, Matthews swiftly proved that though he has been out of the limelight for most of the 80's — last night's show was part of his first British tour for 12 years — his characteristically clear, mellow vocal style and ability to write a pretty song both remain intact.

He set the tone with a gentle opener, *On Squirrel Hill*, and moved smoothly on to John Martyn's brisker *Man In The Station*, before unveiling several of his own new compositions.

This Town's No Lady, from his forthcoming LP, and *The Bridge At Cherokee*, a tribute to revered American jazzman Charlie Parker, were both fine. But the highlight for me was the beautiful, haunting *Busby's Babes*, written with obvious love in memory of the eight Manchester United players who died in the Munich air disaster of 1958.

It turns out that Ian has always been a United fan. In both music and football, he's clearly a man of impeccable taste.

Ivan Ponting

Colston Hall, Bristol: Nailsea Music Centre Concert

This was a rarity: a concert where the audience grew ... the evening progressed. As each of the five ... and the chorale vacated the stage they ... own enthusiasm to the

Lyttelton, Royal National Theatre, London: *Sunday In The Park With George* by Stephen Sondheim and James Lapine.

Sondheim lovers have ...

most of the all-conquering

...rt bass player
(who has also
...vely with The
...ent times) and
...ngwriter/multi-
...ilian Dawson (of
...re will be heard
...ong '92 will be
album, again for
. Meanwhile, not
Taxim has just
...e previously
...rial by the 1972
...oup (demos for
...ld have been the
...cond album, plus
Titled *And That's*
...les interesting
might have been,
calling card for

...all this, another
...s CD has been
...unction with an
...ock magazine,
Orphans &
...69-1979, it's a
...in of demo
...dio sessions,
...idence of
talent as a
...elf-conscious
Southern
...lly-realised
played on
...entally, the
...hich he has

...s well as the
..., Nights In
...on Keys - a
...rphans &
for release
...ll bad for
...en largely
...r the past
...and Taxim

Matthews returned to Britain for a triumphant appearance at the 1990 Cambridge Folk Festival

Manchester United football team of the time). The album was another

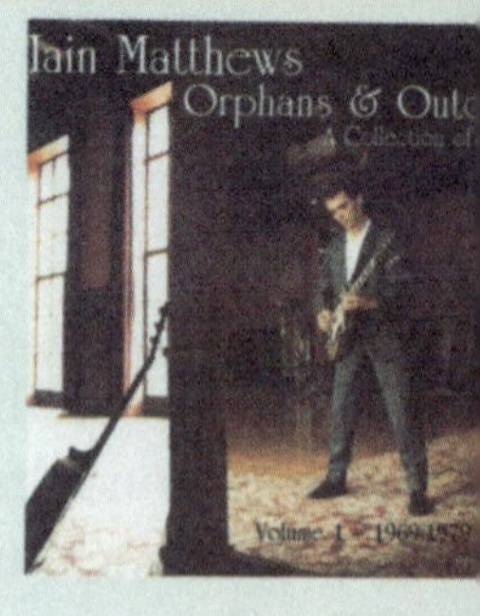

LOOK for...

The following titles are currently available on CD

Fairport Convention *(Polydor 835 230-2)*
What We Did On Our Holidays *(Island IMCD 97)*
Unhalfbricking *(Island IMCD 61)*
Best Of Matthews Southern Comfort *(MCA 251 839-2)*
And That's That *(Taxim TX 2002-2)*
Journeys From Gospel Oak *(Mooncrest CREST CD004)*
Discreet Repeat *(Line LICD 9.00560)*
A Spot Of Interference *(Line LICD 9.00060)*

GENERAL

Iain Matthe...
Orphans & Outcasts Vo...
1969 - 1979. Dirty Linen ...
(also on cassette)

With interest in times past never greater than at present, this 70-minute-plus collection, of previously unheard goodies by one of the finest vocalists this country has ever produced, is a timely release.

Featuring the work of such songwriters as Neil Young, Jesse Winchester, Gram Parsons, Chris Hillman, Gene Clark, Richard Thompson (who also plays on several tracks), Bob Dylan, George Harrison, as well as seven Matthews originals, this album arrives as Matthews, and his longtime cohort Andy Roberts, are about to reform the shortlived but amazing Plainsong, a group they launched in 1972 before Matthews left to live in America.

There's a superb radio session by Plainsong here, from 1972, featuring the heartbreaking Commander Cody classic, **Seeds & Stems**, the excellent Matthews original, **Tigers Will Survive**, and a couple more, but the best thing on the album, which has been released by Dirty Linen, an American magazine devoted to folk/rock, is a version of Richard Thompson's **Poor Ditching Boy** with beautiful violin by the great Richard Greene.

The opening tracks, out-takes from when Matthews fronted the Woodstock chart-toppers, Matthews Southern Comfort, are the least vital, but thereafter (55 minutes worth), this is extremely worthwhile. Available from London megastores, or tell your favourite record shop that it's distributed by Projection.

John Tobler

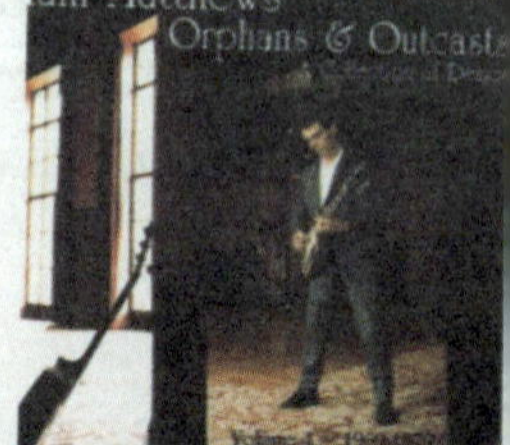

…HE SURVIVOR

…n Tobler's complete history of Iain Matthews

…onally speaking, a major highlight …his year's Cambridge Festival was …re-emergence of a Great British …out who has been languishing in …colonies on the other side of the …antic for far too long – in fact …ut seventeen years, although he …ventured back for, mainly under…d, visits from time to time. Quite …e only real change in this artist …at time has been that he now …first name with an extra 'i' – wel…, Iain Matthews.

…od deal of his early career has …documented elsewhere so, in an …to save space, this is a brief …of what should be quite well …Matthews fans. Born in Scunthor…ne 1946, Ian (as he was then …as apprenticed to Bradford F.C., …l for a musical career, joining a …known as Pyramid, who recorded …sfully for Deram before folding. …name is Ian Matthews-Macdonald, …arents had dropped the Matthews. …wishing to be confused with Ian …d of King Crimson, dropped the …ld and reinstated the Matthews. I …ve got that…

It was, in fact, fairly crucial as the next band he joined, Fairport Convention, was eventually signed to Island, whose roster also included King Crimson – but we're going too fast. The first recording line-up of Fairport included Messrs. Thompson, Nicol, Hutchings, Matthews and Martin Lamble, plus Judy Dyble. They did a single for Track, produced by Joe Boyd, of *If I Had A Ribbon Bow*, an old song discovered in Boyd's record collection and *If (Stomp)*, written by Matthews (credited as Macdonald) and Thompson. The single stiffed, but Polydor signed the band for its debut album *Fairport Convention* (how do they think of these titles?). Good album, but this was the Summer Of Love and there were literally dozens of great albums around, so it didn't even do well enough for Polydor to commit to a follow-up. In fact, the album is now available on CD and sounds rather good (despite the absence of *If I Had A Ribbon Bow*; as others have noted, it wouldn't have been that hard to add it).

After that album, Judy Dyble left the band and was replaced by Sandy Denny, of course. Ian stayed on for *What We Did On Our Holidays* but left during the recording of *Unhalfbricking* – on it, he's only on the wonderful Dylan cover, *Percy's Song*. Both these fine albums are now on CD from Island, by the way. Ian was then approached by the dynamic starmaking duo of Howard and Blaikley, who had already struck oil with Dave Dee & Co. and The Herd (with a young Peter Frampton and Andy Bown, now of Status Quo). They signed him for a solo album titled *Matthews Southern Comfort* (which also featured Thompson, Hutchings and Nicol), and it was then decided that he should form and front a band named after the album. 'Ere long, the result was a chart-topping cover of Joni Mitchell's *Woodstock* (probably not inspired by the place in Oxfordshire) and two more albums in quick succession which, to be honest, were only OK (and he agrees: "The only member of the band I speak to these days is Mark Griffiths. Gordon Huntley has died, I understand, and I didn't like the others much.") What *is* OK is a *Best Of...* CD recently released by MCA.

After that, Matthews properly went solo, signing to the very trendy Vertigo label for whom he recorded three albums although only two were released on Vertigo. *If You Saw Through My Eyes* (1971) and *Tigers Will Survive* (1972) have both stood the test of time better than, for example, the Southern Comfort albums, but they're about as rare today as a *Folk Roots* cover. These albums have probably been deleted fifteen years and, since Iain's summer visit, efforts are being made to get them on CD (maybe both on one disc) – their availability again would be no hardship to anyone. Before he had completed his three album deal, Ian had formed Plainsong with Andy Roberts, Dave Richards and Bob Ronga and Vertigo found themselves in the difficult position of having an artist who was signed as a solo artist forming a group they decided they didn't want. *Journeys From Gospel Oak*, which is considerably better than many so-called contractual obligation albums, was sold by Vertigo to Mooncrest two years after it was made. Vertigo simply never released it, although they did put a track which was going to be included, *Christine's Song (Devil In Disguise)*, on a sampler titled *Suck It And See*, but then excluded the track when they sold the album.

Plainsong signed with Elektra and were brilliant (from one lucky enough to see two staggeringly excellent gigs just after they released their album *In Search Of Amelia Earhart*). At one, they topped a QEH bill opened by Harry Chapin followed by Mickey Newbury (who had a cold). They had completed a second album, *Plainsong III* (referring to the fact that the band was a trio after Dave Richards departed due to personality clashes, rather than it being a third album), when Matthews decided to knock it on the head. He was invited to discuss his future plans with Jac Holzman, who told him that maybe Michael Nesmith would help him make a solo album. The result was *Valley Hi*, another splendid album rarely seen in ten years. The same is true of the follow-up, which bears the great title *Somedays You Eat The Bear* (and somedays the bear eats you and somedays you both go hungry).

Something which may not be known outside *Hokey Pokey* circles is that Thompson's *Poor Ditching Boy* was originally scheduled to appear on the album. It was removed by order of David Geffen, who had taken over from Holzman, and who made Ian replace it with Tom Waits's *Ol' 55*, a great song indeed but one, Ian notes, which the Eagles, whom Geffen had helped to stardom, would record within a month of his version. "Asylum was much more of a priority for David Geffen than Elektra after they merged and he took them both over. It wasn't a huge surprise that they didn't pick up their option for a third album, although I rate *The Bear* as one of the best albums I've done". He's right – but finding one these days is like getting a civil word out of Ken Hunt. The two Elektra albums really should be on CD but, if they are, it can only be imagined that it is as a result of a clerical error.

However, there is interesting news of a fresh Plainsong album, though it's not, as yet, confirmed. Andy Roberts, with whom Matthews toured this summer, has found some master tapes of both studio demos and an early gig. A London independent label with generally impeccable taste may release an album, which Iain is pleased about, although he has not been involved in negotiations. Especially after hearing him working with Andy Roberts at Cambridge, some additional Plainsong recordings would be most welcome.

To return to the story, Matthews waited out the Elektra deal and then signed with CBS after submitting demos to famed Nashville producer Norbert Putnam. Curiously, as Putnam is a big cheese in country, *Go For Broke* was, according to its star, "pretty much a pop album as by that time I had veered away from folk and country). Hard to deny, but it still retains the two main qualities which make Iain Matthews a continuing contender – his superb voice and excellent taste in songs. Not only does the album include covers of Van's *Brown Eyed Girl*, *Groovin'* by The Rascals and other familiar classics, but also Matthews originals of the calibre of *Lonely Hunter*, which he still performs. *Hit And Run*, the final CBS album (1977) includes John Martyn's *One Day Without You*, but a personal view with which Matthews does not immediately disagree, was that the CBS era was when he lost the plot. Nevertheless, the albums have been overlooked in the search for mid-price CD repertoire and, like the vast majority of his oeuvre, are by no means disastrous.

After the second album, Matthews took the band who made *Hit And Run* on tour: "It was a rock'n'roll band, and I was thinking of moving in that direction anyway. Then Sandy Roberton, who managed Plainsong, got in touch with me and offered to make a new album with me, which he described as a pivotal LP which would resurrect my career". It was apparently also the only game in town, so Matthews worked with musicians with whom he had never previously played on *Stealin' Home*, released on Roberton's Rockburgh label in 1978. Not that they were bad musicians as Matthews admits – Bryn Haworth, Pete Wingfield, Rick Kemp and Phil Palmer among others. "The LP worked, but it's not a favourite of mine," he says today. What was the most significant about it was that Roberton licensed the album for North America to a Canadian label, Mushroom, which was hot having launched Heart (the same band which today is a big selling stadium act). Mushroom took a single of *Stealin' Home*, a funky item called *Shake It*, which went Top Ten in the U.S. A memorable gig at Dingwall's was at least a sight of Matthews, but it was a one-off. "We were on tour in Europe when we heard that the man who ran Mushroom had died and that Mushroom was virtually a one-man company. They couldn't follow up a Top Ten single so it was all over, which is a shame because I think our next album, *Siamese Friends*, was one of the best ones I ever did".

This was also sad in view of other great songs on *Stealin' Home* like John Martyn's *Man In The Station* (Iain's favourite) and Jeffrey Comanor's *King Of The Night* (my favourite). *Siamese Friends* was already complete when the bad news about Mushroom became known and Matthews feels that it was perhaps a victim of life's circumstances (whose album title was that?): "I think it's one of the three or four best albums I ever made, but it didn't do anything anywhere". An unlikely inclusion was a cover of Jona Lewie's *The Baby She's On The Street* (a title which is unforgettable because of its clumsiness), another John Martyn song, *Arena*, which Matthews particularly rates, as he does an original title *Heatwave*, which he co-wrote with Mark Griffiths, who plays bass on the album. The rest of the band included Jim Russell on drums from *Stealin' Home*, guitarist Bob Metzger (a longtime Matthews associate), Craig Buhler on saxophones and Mick Weaver (also credited under his Wynder K. Frogg alias) on keyboards. For Matthews, one of the albums most significant features was that it featured the first occasion on which he covered a song by Jules Shear (of Jules and The Polar Bears, the Funky Kings etc.), *Home Somewhere*. If you ever see the album, the inner sleeve may induce a smirk...

In 1980 came another album for Ro…burgh, *Spot Of Indifference*. Never a pers…al favourite, and rarely (if ever) playe… Matthews says he enjoyed doing it at t… time, but thinks its style is rather dated: "…really punk". This one was apparently re…sued by Line in 1983, perhaps a questi…able decision. Also in 1980 came a 'Be… Of...' compilation, *Discreet Repeat* on Ro…burgh. This 27-track double album effecti…ly started after Matthews Southern Comf… and includes four tracks from *Thro'* … *Eyes*, two from *Tigers*, four from *Gosp… Oak*, two from *Amelia Erhardt*, one fr… *Valley Hi*, five from *The Bear*, three from … *For Broke*, two from *Hit And Run* and fi… from *Stealin' Home*. If you can find it, … pretty good, although a more wide-rangi… 'History of...' album would actually ma… more sense, rather than this non-chronolo…cal approach.

By that time, Matthews was living … Seattle (the American city most l… Britain?) and had become one of the t… vocalists in a band called Hi-Fi. Alarmin… (until you hear the records) the other voc… ist was David Surkamp, who became kno… for his vocals when fronting a band kno… as Pavlov's Dog, who are probably unkno… to the vast majority of those who've got t… far (and are unlikely to appeal to those o… nervous disposition) – it seemed like an o… partnership. "David also lived in Seattle a… couldn't sing harmonies, but I could s… harmonies for him, and we could sing … unison. We both wanted to play in cl… and bars, rather than a dues-paying proje… tion, you might say, and we had no int… tion initially of recording. Then PBS di… 30-minute special on a Seattle band, and … were chosen". (Public Broadcasting Servi… the vaguely U.S. equivalent of the BBC – … obliged to make a profit). "It was recor…

…with little… …ore the words "a musical test of …ographic performance" and this …e inaccurate. The five tracks on …? include *Savage* (The Shadows!) …nother version of John Martyn's …*Station* (now with an indefinite …was previously on *Stealin' Home* …lefinite article), plus a song writ…nips' (Steve Parsons, once of …ith Chris Spedding). This was …as promising enough for Hi-Fi to …omplete studio album, *Moods For* … "I don't do any of those songs … …*When You Were Mine*. The style …nd grew out of *Spot Of Indiffer*…hich seems to suggest that it also …ted. The track *S.O.S.* is not, by the …hing to do with the Abba song of … name – do not forget that Clive …n Any Trouble did an Abba cover! …s wrote four of the other songs, …the remaining five.

…t came an album which even this …atthews follower had never heard …, let alone seen, until he told me …bout it. *Shook* was apparently an …bum released in 1983 by Polydor …n continental Europe: "Sandy …obertson called up again one day, …y which point Hi-Fi had changed. …rkamp had left and been replaced …hesiser player, which was the fash…thing to do at the time – in fact, …ee played synth on *Shook*, which …e good material on it. I was signed …or International in Germany via a …on deal with Robertson, and when …ldn't release it in either Britain or … I thought 'What's the point?' – I …lisappointed that I decided to give …work in the administration side of …c business. I'd moved to Los Ange…983 and started working for Island … October 1984, initially for the pub…company, Island Music, but eventu…

…little-publicised visit, the reasons for which seem obscure, and while he was here was filmed gigging at the Marquee. Once again, the results were hardly over-publicised, but are in fact readily available on video under the title *London Revisited* (released by Hendring, available via Castle). The one-hour tape included eleven songs – from the Hi-Fi catalogue come *I Can't Fade Away*, *Blue Shirt* and the Snips song, *9 O'Clock* and (of course) *Man In A Station*. *Lonely Hunter* first appeared on *Go For Broke* (see above) and no doubt most of the others were on *Shook*, although it's hard to know if that applies to *Over Under Sideways Down* (as in The Yardbirds) or Duncan Brown's *Wild Places*, which are on the video. On it, Matthews is backed by Bob Metzger (misspelt on the sleeve) and Bruce Hazen (from Hi-Fi) on guitar, long-time compadre Mark Griffiths on bass and ex-Argent drummer Bob Henrit. It's interesting, if not vital – it was done at a time when Matthews was evidently uncertain of his direction.

In 1985, he was laid off by Island and spent nine months thumb-twiddling and in 1986 appeared at Cropredy. "That was when I realised that I still enjoyed singing and being on stage, but shortly before that, I'd got a job with Windham Hill". Aargh! But that's New Age music! "I'd been listening to ambient music for years before that, people like Eno, Jean-Michel Jarre, Vangelis. I pursued that job – I wanted to do it, not expecting that it would necessarily be a big thing. I actually joined Windham Hill to work on Open Air, which was intended to be their vocal label, but Will Ackerman soon lost interest in having a vocal label. I signed Fred Simon to Windham Hill, but he was the only act I found that they were interested in. I left after about a year to pursue the concept of an album which had been offered to Windham Hill but which they'd turned down. It was by an artist named Barbara Higbie, who was in a band called Montreux.

Photo: Dave…

Photo: Dave Peabody

Matthews re-united with old Pla…

I liked the idea of a con… vocal album and I decide… The idea was to use a di… siser player on each trac… which interpreted the son… er. The eventual result … *Changing Line*, which … written by Jules Shear… Matthews, with synth backin… ber of notables in that field… aforementioned Fred Sim… Parks and Patrick O'Hearn… man. "I considered other so… as Van Morrison and Rich… but eventually decided … unspoken reason seems to … less well-known than the… became involved, sending… chord sheets and he wrote … which I sing acapella on … what has Jules Shear been d… made an album for IRS, *The*… I think *Walking A Changing*… thing I've ever done from… worked even better than I'… it. I made some acoustic d… ham Hill liked them enough… album".

It was originally goi… either *The Soul Of Many F*… *In The Rain* but was finally… as *Walking A Changing L*… fact a line from *On Squi*… adopted at Windham Hill… was a critical success, b… enough of a commercial su… sold 30,000 copies and it… New Adult Contempora… New Age radio, if you like… were confused because W… known as a vocal label… another album for them,… keen". However, in 198… duced a cut-down versio… *Repeat* compilation, fitti… single CD, cutting off th… *Home* tracks and three o… worth getting as a Matthe… as mentioned above, it p… – but we don't live in a…

embarrassing, and eventually Jesse had to abandon them and just played acoustic, but there was no duet.

Iain wrote a song as promo for one of the guitar companies many moons ago, entitled 'Wings'. It's a kid's song. It appeared on the reissue of *Pure And Crooked* many years later as a bonus track. He sang the song in my living room on my couch with my son Iain when he was three years old. That was a very special moment. (My son's name is Ian Matthew Martin.)

BRIDGETON FOLK FESTIVAL

JUNE 1990, BRIDGETON, NEW JERSEY

JIM FOGARTY

I first met Iain Matthews very briefly at the 1990 Bridgeton Folk Festival in New Jersey. I had been a longtime Fairport and Richard Thompson fan, and while I knew some of Iain's work, his set that day with Mark Hallman simply blew me away. Perfect harmonies, intertwining guitar parts, and a set of classic and new songs that were stellar and inspiring. My wife Lindsay Gilmour and I had performed earlier that day and felt that Iain's folk/pop was akin to what we were striving to achieve. Very inspiring.

After his set, he came to the CD/record tent to sign merchandise and we said hello, and met Bill Martin (from *Dirty Linen* magazine) who was driving Iain, selling his CDs and had begun to book him. We mentioned to Bill that we'd love to do a show with Iain in the future, meaning sharing a bill as the opening act. Bill replied with, 'How big's your house?'

That began our relationship, hosting a few house concerts in our little musician's commune in Philadelphia's Roxborough section. Iain's first house concert for us turned out to be his first solo acoustic house concert ever, and he wasn't quite sure of the format. So, he proceeded to play almost three hours, including all the songs he knew....and some he didn't!

At one point, he asked if I would come up and accompany him for a few numbers. It worked out well, we ended up becoming friends and eventually touring and recording together on and off for the last 35 years.

As an accompanist, if you can't work with Iain Matthews, you can't work. Aside from his legendary voice, his guitar playing is always rock-solid and exactly what the song needs. While we rehearse and work out some of the recorded parts for live shows, he also encourages you to find your own place in his music and be creative. In all those years, Iain has never once told me to play less or to pull back on what I'm doing. Like any artist, he has his preferences, but is willing to consider new ideas, even on classic songs that have been set in stone for years.

We may argue about it occasionally, but always for the betterment of the music. Additionally, he's generous with credit and billing, which is extremely rare. After a while many of our duo shows were booked as 'Iain Matthews and Jim Fogarty', despite the fact that we all know who the audience was really there for. On his shows he's encouraged me to use ambience and electronics in creative ways, bringing in left-of-centre sounds. Once we even did an entire tour with me playing Dobro, an instrument I'd never played before. I learned on the road, and now I'm a Dobro player.

All in all, I'm a better musician, who is taken more seriously, for having worked with Iain Matthews. More importantly, we're friends and I've been glad to know him these past 35 or so years, even through some ups and downs.

QUASIMODO

11 SEPTEMBER 1990, BERLIN, GERMANY

CHRISTOPH DESCHNER

In 1990 booking agent Wolfgang Sedlatschek gave me a call, asking if one of his acts could be booked in Berlin. I picked Iain Matthews and Andy Roberts, because I am a huge fan of Plainsong's *In Search Of Amelia Earhart*. So I went to the Quasimodo, which at the time was West Berlin's premier jazz club, and convinced its manager Giorgio Carioti to book the acoustic folk-rock duo on 11 September after assuring him they would receive good airplay in advance.

Music critic and radio host Wolfgang Doebeling, himself a Plainsong fan, scheduled two exclusive shows on SFB Radio 4U: one two days before the concert and a second a week later.

STAGE DOOR

1991, SCARBOROUGH, UK

RICHARD PEARSON

I moved from Muswell Hill to Scarborough, North Yorkshire, in 1991. Sometime after settling in, it came to my attention that my old pal Andy Roberts was playing a local with his former Plainsong colleague, Iain Matthews. I'd admired Andy since his days in The Liverpool Scene, whose 'Batpoem', had been covered by my band, The Strawberry Jams, at Heckmondwike Grammar School Christmas Party in 1971. I'd managed to catch him live in Bradford, where I think he was supporting Fairport Convention or Free – but it could have been somebody else!

Richard Pearson met Iain through Andy Roberts

I first met him in the flesh when he was buying guitar strings for a rather splendid green Gretsch Country Gent on the corner of Denmark Street, London's Tin Pan Alley, in 1974. We were introduced by my friend Julian Hardwick, who was a guitar demonstrator at Francis, Day & Hunter, a well-known music store in the area. Julian knew a lot of the musicians who frequented Tin Pan Alley and introduced me to several, including Rod Argent, who had a keyboard shop on the corner of Denmark Street and Charing Cross Road, and with whom I subsequently worked, on a couple of TV shows.

It was several years before Andy and I met again. By that time, I was working for BBC network TV, booking music for a couple of shows and I went to see The Hank Wangford Band at The Pegasus in Stoke Newington, with a view to booking them for a BBC 2 evening show. I booked them for that show and another BBC 1 show, so got to know Andy and the other members of the band fairly well.

Whilst I'd never met Iain, I'd been a fan for many years. I'd bought the first four Fairport Convention albums out of sequence, so my earliest exposure to Iain was when 'Woodstock', by Matthews Southern Comfort, went hurtling up the hit parade! Whilst country music was uncharted territory to me, I fell in love with the sound of Gordon Huntley's pedal steel and that was most definitely a sign of things to come. *In Search Of Amelia Earhart* by Plainsong was one of the most frequently heard records in the flat I shared with Peter Townsend in Fallowfield, Manchester in 1973 and I must confess I became a bit obsessed with both the album and Amelia, even going as far as reading the book mentioned in the lyrics, *The Search For Amelia Earhart*, by Fred Goerner. Via the track 'Raider', I was also introduced to the wonderful (if somewhat weird) world of Judy Henske and Jerry Yester and, most notably, their album *Farewell Aldebarran*, which has gone on to become one of my favourite albums of all time. Judy Henske is a name I don't think I've ever heard mentioned in compilation lists of favourite female singers but, for me, she was one of the greatest.

Fast forward to 1991. I headed down to Scarborough's Stage Door, where Iain and Andy played a great set to a small but enthusiastic audience. I went up to Andy to say hello at its conclusion and he introduced me to Iain. We sat down for a chinwag and a bit of liquid refreshment, but were soon interrupted by a man with long white hair, a white beard and a noticeably red face called Brian. Brian was a devoted fan of Iain's. He had personally sponsored the gig and was putting Andy and Iain up at his house in the Old Town. Or, it turns out, that had been the intention. There had been a bit of a bruhaha between Brian and his lovely wife, who it seems had lodged serious objection to Brian's open house policy, meaning our two troubadours were rendered homeless for the night. My wife and kids were away for a few days, so I did the honourable thing and offered them the use of my humble abode. After finishing our drinks, we all departed for number 10, Londesborough Road.

Once installed, we chatted for quite some time, over more liquid refreshment and played a few records. I recall going up in Iain's estimation when he discovered I had records by Robert Earl Keen Jr and Mark Germino in my collection; two of his favourites at the time. He also recounted the woeful tale of his record company, Rockburgh, going bust, the very day his single 'Shake It' went top twenty in both the *Billboard Hot 100* and the *Cashbox Top 100* charts, meaning he earned zilch from what was probably his biggest commercial success. Iain took down my address and phone number and vowed to stay in touch, but I didn't hear another peep from him, until we met backstage at the Cropredy festival a few years ago. Andy and I remained in intermittent contact and now I've moved to Hastings (he lives in Brighton) a reunion lemonade is on the cards!

I coffee'd and breakfasted the pair the following morning and Andy offered to give me a lift to work, en route to their next gig. I was more than fascinated by Andy's new-fangled, after market CD player, which was a floor-mounted tower, powered by way of the lighter socket; state of the art, in all its glory!

When the kids got back home, they were duly impressed to discover their beds had not only played host to a former number one chart topper, who'd been on *Top Of The Pops*, but also to a man who did music for plays and films and stuff and had also been a member of the legendary Hank Wangford Band, who got a lot of play at Londesborough Road.

ROYAL FESTIVAL HALL

24 APRIL 1991, LONDON, UK

NICK SHEARS

I spent my teenage years in South Africa, with Iain's magnificent if *You Saw Thro' My Eyes* and *Tigers Must Survive* as close to my heart as Dylan's and Cohen's records. My first opportunity to see him live was when he supported Al Stewart in London. I had no interest in Mr Stewart's work, but I hung on every word and note of the man whose folk rock had so inspired the younger me. Several years later, those early albums were on the iPlayer that kept me company for a year in hospital.

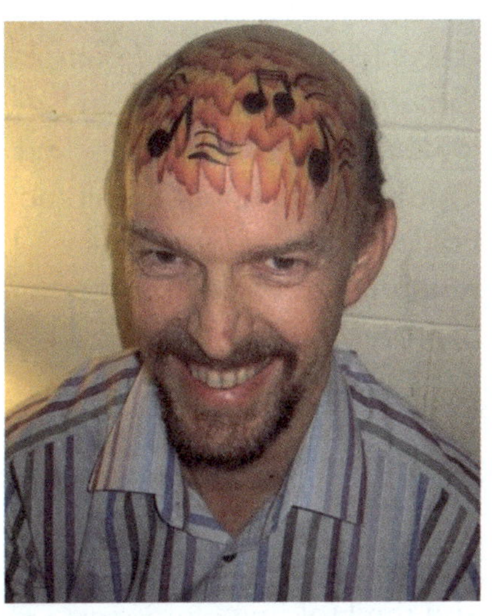
Nick listened to Iain's music in hospital

I remain forever grateful.

1992

PHIL MCMULLEN

My memories of Iain date back to early 1992, although I was familiar with his music long before that. From 1989 on, I was the editor of a fanzine named the *Ptolemaic Terrascope*, and Iain was high on our list of people we wanted to talk to and feature. I'd heard (either through my good friend Pete Frame at *ZigZag* magazine or one of the guys at *Dark Star* magazine) that Iain was a lovely bloke, but could be a little bit tetchy sometimes if you inadvertently asked the wrong question – understandably! – so we approached it not really knowing what to expect.

The result was absolutely brilliant. I had no idea Iain had worked on A&R for the Rain Parade, for example; one of my very favourite bands. I think we probably got off to a good start when Nick Saloman (of the band Bevis Frond, and my co-conspirator on the *Ptolemaic Terrascope*), who is no mean football player himself, opened by asking Iain about his all too brief career in football. The resulting interview appeared in *Ptolemaic Terrascope* issue 11 in 1992, alongside interviews with Arthur Lee from Love, guitarist Robin Trower and members of the Yardbirds, Kaleidoscope, and Big Brother and the Holding Company. Iain also very kindly gave us a lovely unreleased song to use on our compilation EP, given away free with that issue as well ('Rains of 62').

Iain Matthews

Iain in Austria, 1990

LATER THAT SAME CENTURY...
THE IAIN MATTHEWS INTERVIEW

Phil remembers an interview Iain did for his magazine

What a lovely guy.

UNKNOWN VENUE

1992, MONTCLAIR, NEW JERSEY

ROBERT DOYLE

Most kids leave college with expanded musical tastes, though quite often it seemed to me like it was based on following the pack. When I graduated in 1990, for most kids that was U2, REM and that sort of vibe. Then there were the pop music kids listening to whatever the flavour of the day was, or the retro-alternative kids who were immersed in Television, Talking Heads and The Cure. There were also the metal kids who, though they were holding on to the eighties hair bands, held Metallica to the highest level in that genre. I was certainly the only kid in Worcester, Massachusetts who left college listening to Fairport Convention.

I had seen them live in 1987, and in those pre-internet days scoured articles about them in the library, scanned every bin of every record store nearby looking for anything I could find by the band. I also had a VHS copy of the documentary produced about them for their twentieth anniversary, and got a better sense of the many ex-members, and added all those names to the list to search for as well. One of those names was Iain Matthews, whose voice I immediately latched onto. I wore out my first copy of that tape, because it was a collective music that sent me off in so many directions. The traditional side from the band and Ashley and Swarb sent me searching deeper into my Irish roots and exploring English folk. Richard's music sent me off into a different sort of rock music, with those wonderful lyrics and blistering guitar.

Which leads me to Iain. Other than the Fairport recordings, I believe that it wasn't until 1992 that I finally heard a proper solo Iain Matthews album. It was *Skeleton Keys*, which I am listening to as I type this. It was purchased at what was also my very first Iain Matthews' gig, in Montclair, New Jersey, which if memory serves correct was in a church 'coffee house'-type setting. I was alone (as I usually was in those dreadfully shy introverted days). The show was just Iain and guitar, and I was held spellbound. I remember my jaw dropping at the same clarity of voice coming through in 1992, scarcely different from that 1967 clip of Iain singing 'Time Will Show The Wiser'.

Speaking of being shy, during the break between sets, I could only gather the courage to watch Iain speak to members of the audience from a distance. Happily, I have overcome that fear since, but this was literally the first gig where I witnessed a musician willingly speaking with the audience! I remember purchasing both *Skeleton Keys* and *Pure And Crooked* that night, and I remember popping them both into the CD player on the ride home. *Skeleton Keys* remains my go to Iain album to this day. Though there are so many more, well... as the saying goes, you never forget your first! I vaguely remember Iain saying with pride that it was his first completely self-penned album, and 'Jumping Off The Roof', 'God's Empty Chair' and 'True Location Of The Heart' are deeply important songs to me.

Time went on, and I subsequently picked up every new album, as well as going back to the archives. I wore down my cassette tape of *The Soul Of Many Places*, because that largely country vibe was something that I had been loving for quite some time. There was *Journey's From Gospel Oak*, *The Dark Ride*, *Excerpts From Swine Lake* and so many more. Not to mention the excursions into Matthews Southern Comfort, Plainsong (both old and new), Hamilton Pool and the album with Elliott Murphy. I remember the day at a record store when I found *Hit And Run*. All together I think I have what amounts to more than a full day listening to Iain's music.

I continued trying to see him perform any chance I could get in and around the New York area. The Bottom Line, Turning Point and various smaller venues. It did not matter! Another memory I have is when Iain guested on a music forum, and I asked him about the story to the 'Ballad Of Gruene Hall', which ranks up there as one of my most favourite Iain songs. Based on his answer I could surmise that I think he thinks it is too, after such a tragic yet true story.

But then again, every song of Iain's is a favourite. His cover of 'Brown Eyed Girl', 'I'm Alive', 'Bridge Of Cherokee', 'Something Mighty', 'God Looked Down', 'Keep On Sailing', 'Sing Me Back Home', 'Evening Sun', 'The Rat And The Snake'...

Iain Matthews. The voice, the interpretations, the songs, the unflashy yet always tasteful guitar playing (which no one mentions), the direction changes, the location changes... His music is a big part of my life. In my loner days, his songs were my accompaniment on long drives, whether there was an actual destination or not. Iain, next time you come around, I'll summon the courage to speak to you in person and thank you.

STABLES BAR, UNIVERSITY OF LIMERICK

JULY 1992, LIMERICK, IRELAND

JOHN O'REGAN

The first thing that got me was that voice, a distinctive mix of silk and honey with just enough high lonesome of the bluegrass tenor kind to make for a sound that weaved its way from the radio into my consciousness. The year was 1970 and the song was Joni Mitchell's 'Woodstock', a forlorn lament written for a festival she did not attend but had written from the distance of her Californian seclusion.

The version of 'Woodstock' that chimed from the radio was different to Joni's solo eclectic piano lead reverie from her *Ladies Of The Canyon* album. This version was by a band – a country rock band at that. The pedal steel guitar chimed and the bass and drums were almost molten, there and not there as the song demanded it. It was the epitome of cool, from a distance and close up.

That voice and that sound made an impression on me. I heard 'Woodstock' on our TV pop show *Like Now* on RTE television, produced by the genius Bill Keating and presented by the flamboyantly effervescent Danny Hughes, an Austin Powers cast off hip to the trip and with enough pep talk to trip on.

It was an almost unreal experience but it was part of the light in the upgrowth of someone in the youthful undergrowth in modern Ireland. The occasional sliver of light in an otherwise uber dark black and white existence overseen by Church and State, intertwined in bedfellow-like movements to prevent the light of progress and enlightenment of the permissive society from corrupting the sweet innocence of a younger generation whose peers wanted to keep them dancing at Lughnasa permanently.

Still slivers of light broke through and 'Woodstock' was one of them. And a bright shining beacon it was. One of contained cool it was. I learned that the band was called Matthews Southern

IAIN MATTHEWS by post:

IAIN MATTHEWS ~ LIVE ALONE. Recorded direct to DAT, Mr. Matthews solo. Fifteen songs from his solo repertoire late '91. First release in a series of 'notebooks' on Iain's own label: for sale mail order and at gigs. On CD @ £13·00. Imported from Perfect Pitch in the USA.

NEW IAIN MATTHEWS ~ SKELETON KEYS. An all new album from Mr. Matthews, his first ever collection of all-original material. Recorded in Austin with Mark Hallman, Scott Neubert, Gene Elders, Paul Glasse and Julian Dawson. Arguably the strongest album yet from Iain Matthews.

NEW Imported from Line Records, Germany, on CD @ £13·00.

IAIN MATTHEWS ~ NIGHTS IN MANHATTAN. Recorded completely live at the Bottom Line New York City in May 1988. Iain Matthews with Mark Hallman and Craig Negoescu. Twelve songs, over 54 minutes. Imported from Taxim Records, Germany on CD @ £13

IAIN MATTHEWS ~ ORPHANS & OUTCASTS volume 1. A fine collection of demos and out takes spanning the years 1969 ~ 1979, a great selection all previously unreleased. Compiled by Iain and the chaps at Dirty Linen, includes material from Matthews Southern Comfort, Plainsong and the first songs recorded in America. Musicians include Richard Thompson and Andy Roberts. Imported from the USA on CD @ £13·00 and on cassette @ £8·50.

IAIN MATTHEWS ~ ORPHANS & OUTCASTS volume 2. A further delve into the Matthews tape chest, this time covering the period 1980 ~ 90. A collection of demos and outtakes from Hi-Fi, 'Shook' and 'Walking A Changing Line' ~ including some more Jules Shear songs not recorded for the album; together with song-writing memos. Volume 2 is a further insight into the recording career of Mr. Matthews.

NEW CDs imported from Dirty Linen are expected in late February @ £13 Place your order now.

PLAINSONG ~ AND THAT'S THAT (The Demos). Recorded in 1972 and finally released in 1992. Eleven songs intended for the second album by Plainsong, plus four live tracks. Sleevenotes by Andy Roberts, full song lyrics and many previously unpublished photographs. Imported from Taxim Records, Germany, on CD @ £13·00.

Plainsong

DARK SIDE OF THE ROOM

PLAINSONG ~ DARK SIDE OF THE ROOM. First album from the new Plainsong: Iain Matthews, Andy Roberts, Mark Griffiths and Julian Dawson. Fifteen songs including some great new Matthews' songs: 'Toscanini's Darkhorse', 'Bluebird Morning' and 'Evening Sun'. The album includes a cover of Julian Dawson's 'Welcome To London Town' and a further song about Amelia Earhardt.

NEW Imported from Line Records, Germany, on CD @ £13·00.

HOKEY POKEY* A subscription to the new slim-line HOKEY POKEY newsletter costs £4.00 (UK), £5 (Elsewhere). Please write to Colin Davies, 43 Stroud Road, Wimbledon Park, LONDON SW19 8DQ. Please enclose an s.a.e.

Out the Blue Jim Boyes

We have copies of the first two releases from our friends at No Masters Voice. Both are highly recommended. JIM BOYES 'OUT THE BLUE' Debut solo collection from Swan Arcade singer. A great collection of songs, produced by John Tams. Contributors include Rick Kemp, Barry Coope and Sam Smith. Now on CD with 3 bonus tracks. On CD @ £11·00 and cassette @ £7.00.

Token Women

THE RHYTHM METHOD

NEW TOKEN WOMEN ~ 'THE RHYTHM METHOD'. First album from this marvellous new seven piece, all female band: Jo Freya, Fi Fraser, Becky Palmer, Carly Rose, Heather Vigar, Jacky Rawlinson & Kathryn Locke. A wonderful collection of tunes, together with songs by Pete Coe, Steve Ashley and John Tams. All-in-all an impressive debut album. On CD @ £11·00 and cassette @ £7.00.

HOKEY POKEY Records Ltd P.O Box 547 LONDON SE26 4BD

HOKEY POKEY

Yardbirds • Arthur Lee • Iain Matthews
Robin Trower • U.S. Kaleidoscope
Big Brother & the Holding Co. • Pat Orchard
Magic Mushroom Band • Hampton Grease
Skooshny • Magic Carpet • Sneetches • Petals
+ free E.P. (McCarty Band, I. Matthews, Magic Mush., Cul De Sac)

After a decade of undeserved neglect, singer/songwriter Iain Matthews is about to come back with a new solo album. John Tobler anticipates his re-emergence

Iain Matthews

The name Iain Matthews may look familiar, but may also appear to be mis-spelt. In fact, this is the very same Ian Matthews who topped the UK chart in 1970 as leader of Matthews Southern Comfort, but as yet, has been unable to rediscover similar commercial success. However, he is about to re-emerge with a new solo album, *Skeleton Keys*, on the pioneering German label, Line Records, whose products have recently become readily available in the UK.

An advance hearing of the album suggests that Matthews' past glories could easily be renewed, as this is his most accessible release in some time. More to the point, he appears to be fashionable again in this country - it's a sad reflection on record buyers of the last two decades that his often excellent work has too frequently been ignored. Now much of his extensive back-catalogue has been re-issued on CD, in preparation for a substantial revival of interest in his often uniquely clear and accurate vocal performances, and his excellent taste in songs.

Matthews first emerged as a member of Fairport Convention, appearing on their impressive self-titled debut album released on Polydor, and on their subsequent two albums for Island, *What We Did On Our Holidays* and *Unhalfbricking*. He left Fairport before the latter album was completed, accurately sensing that the group was about to embark on a major change of musical direction (to traditional folk) which would have left him isolated.

He made a solo album, *Matthews Southern Comfort*, with

He left Fairport, accurately sensing that the group was about to embark on a major change of musical direction

erstwhile Fairport colleagues like Richard Thompson, Simon Nicol and Ashley Hutchings, and then formed a Matthews Southern Comfort band to promote the album. This MSC line-up made two more albums plus the chart-topping *Woodstock* single. While the original albums may never be released on CD, an excellent compilation, *Best Of Matthews Southern Comfort*, features most of the vital tracks (including

Woodstock). Matthews then the band, which briefly contin without him as simply South Comfort, while he signed w Vertigo, making two good alb which have yet to be digitali plus a 'contractual obligation' *Journeys From Gospel Oak*, wh has been released on CD. obligation occurred beca Matthews, while still ow Vertigo an album, had forme group which he jointly led w fellow singer/songwriter, and guitarist, Andy Roberts.

Plainsong, as the group w known, signed with Elektra (he Vertigo's ire) and made a brilli album, *In Search Of Amelia Earl* However, they split up during recording of their second alb and Matthews then moved to USA, where he has been resid ever since. He next made t superb solo albums for Elekt *Valley Hi*, and *Some Days You The Bear*, and while these personal favourites, curiou enough neither the Plains album nor the other two have b re-issued on CD - except in Jap

RHYTHM of the WES

GLOBAL EDITION — THE IAIN MATTHEWS NEWSLETTER — SUN

REFLECTIONS ON GOSPEL OAK

It's funny the way things turn out sometimes. "Gospel Oak" was recorded as a contractual obligation. I wanted to do Plainsong. Vertigo wanted one more solo album. I waived my advance, gave them a low studio budget and went in totally unprepared. Something I hadn't done before or have since. The record was cut in 5 days. Mixes and all. I wanted to save my new originals for Plainsong, so I put together a list of stuff I liked at the time, added a couple of my own and ended up with a recording that 20 years later, is one of my favorites. Even the title was a throw-away, Gospel Oak being the area of London I lived in. For you vinyl junkies out there, a single of "Met Her on a Plane" with strings was released, and a sampler came out from Vertigo with the Burrito's "Devil in Disguise" on it (not on the album). Vertigo ultimately sold it to Mooncrest, who released it in 1974. Two songs I'd planned on cutting and didn't were "Witchita Lineman" and "Dark End of the Street". I probably never will either. The record never did come out in the USA. I still get a real kick out of hearing my "5 Day Wonder."

— Iain

"Return to Zero" Review

-Dirty Linen, June/July 1995

As writers and lead singers, the trio are a study in stylistic contrasts. Fracasso's twangy "Apple Pie" starts things off in a rollicking fashion. Matthews' songs like "The Taker" and the gentle "Evening Sun" work wonderfully in the sparkling, three-part harmony arrangements offered here. Hallman contributes some muscular pop rock with "Secondhand Love" and "Jewel." The album's sound is enriched by the instrumental contributions of guitarists Robert McEntee (whose Dobro perfectly frames Fracasso's plaintive reading of Jagger/Richards' "Back Street Girl"), accordionist Michael Ramos, and Hallman, who plays everything in sight as well as serving as the project's producer. Hamilton Pool is a folk-rock supergroup that makes artistic sense, enhances the talents of each of the participants, and makes gorgeous music in the process.

— Michael Parrish

NEW T-SHIRT ARTWORK!

TOUR DATES

6/30 Pittsburgh, PA - Rosebud w/ Leslie Smith
7/01 Gallipolis, OH - River Recreation Festival
7/03 Dayton, OH - Canal Street Tavern
7/07 Columus, OH - Barley's Underground
7/08 Newport, KY (Cincinnati) - Southgate House

Look for West Coast dates in late July, Plainsong dates in Europe in Sept., and Texas Songwriters Tour in Europe in Oct./Nov.

HELLO AGAIN, FRIENDS!

As promised, we're back with our 2nd newsletter of the year. I can't tell you how much Kim and I have enjoyed getting to know all of you who have called, written, or faxed. The response to the last newsletter was great. We feel like we've made friends all over the world.

As you can see from Iain's letter, it's been a busy year so far and shows no signs of letting up. Hamilton Pool is recieving great reviews (see article) everywhere. We hope you were able to catch them on their brief tour in May. Keep calling your local radio stations to request they play the album "Return to Zero". You can make a difference!

Once out of the studio with Eric Taylor, Iain will hit the road again (see dates). Many of us who are fans from the Fairport days are hopeful we'll see Iain and old band mate, Richard Thompson, do a few songs together at the Bridgeton Festival. Come out and show your support when Iain's in your area. We'll keep you European fans posted as tour plans are finalized.

There are a number of items of interest on the sales end of things. We have acquired Iain's 1972 CD, "Journeys From Gospel Oak". This has, at least in the states, been very tough to find. It happens to be one of my personal favorites and we are pleased tomake it available to you (see Iain's comments). We also have promotional t-shirts from Iain's last solo record, "The Dark Ride". The front of the shirt is the pencil drawing of Iain by his daughter Darcy for the CD booklet and it has the Watermelon Record logo on the back. It is a great shirt and is available in sizes large and extra-large.

For all of you European fans, you'll be pleased that we have finally been able to convert the "Compass and Chart, Vol. I" video to the PAL format. For those of you who don't know, this video chronicles Iain's career from Pyramid through 1977's "Hit and Run" album. It is filled with interview footage shot exclusively for this video and contains full performance clips from Fairport Convention, Matthews Southern Comfort, and the 70's era Plainsong. A must for any Matthews fan. And, by the way, our good friend, Michael Soloman, is busy at work on Vol. II as we speak. We'll keep you posted.

We are also carrying the new releases of 3 of Iain's personal favorite artists. You all know Michael Fracasso from Hamilton Pool. His new record is "When I Lived in the Wild". Betty Elders and Leslie Smith are also familiar names to our readers. Betty's new release is entitled "Crayons" and features Iain singing backgroung vocals on "New River" and playing shakers (aka. the Golden Egg) on "The Futon Song". As for Leslie Smith, her new CD is "These Things Wrapped". I had the pleasure of seeing Leslie perform at the SXSW Music Festival and can unequivocally say it was the finest set of the fest. She writes some of the most poignant lyrics you'll hear and sings in an achingly beautiful voice. I strongly recommend this wonderful record.

Lastly, many of you have asked exactly what the Notebook Series CDs (ie. "Live Alone" and "Intimate Wash") are. These CDs were produced by Perfect Pitch and are exclusively available from us or on tour from Iain. The idea was to reproduce, for fans, what they are hearing on stage at Iain's solo shows without the hassle of trying to record shows on the road. So Iain took his guitar into the studio and, in one day, recorded, live to DAT, the songs for theCD. The "set list" was chosen to mimic what one might hear on any given solo night. Thus, it includes newer songs (some of which later appeared on "Skeleton Keys" and "The Dark Ride") as well as vintage Matthews' material such as "Call the Tune" and

A LETTER FROM

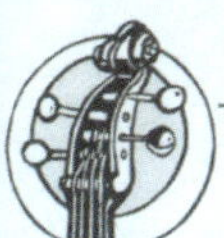

Dirty Linen

The magazine of folk, electric folk, traditional and world music.

P.O. Box 66600
Baltimore, MD 21239-6600
USA

Tel: (410) 583-7973
FAX: (410) 337-6735
CompuServe: 74020,47

FOR IMMEDIATE RELEASE

Dirty Linen, the magazine of folk, electric folk, traditional and world music, announces the fifth release on the *Dirty Linen* label:

Iain Matthews
Orphans & Outcasts
(A Collection of Demos, Volume II - 1981-1989)

Iain Matthews has long been an important influence on the British and American folk scenes. He was a member of the British folk-rock band Fairport Convention in the '60s, then went on to form Matthews Southern Comfort, who had a U.K. hit, "Woodstock." An extensive solo career followed. Iain's most recent release, *Skeleton Keys* on Mesa/Bluemoon, is enjoying much critical acclaim. Elektra has issued another compilation of material from the '70s, *Soul of Many Places*.

Orphans & Outcasts, Vol. II is the second installment of never-before released demos, radio shows, and "songwriting memos" that span Iain's career. The music ranges from the techno-rock of his Hi-Fi band, to demos of Jules Shear songs for the *Walking a Changing Line* album on Windham Hill after his three-year hiatus from performing and recording, to demos and alternate takes of songs from the *Pure and Crooked* [Gold Castle] album that have a decidedly Texas singer/songwriter feel.

Iain Matthews
Orphans & Outcasts, Vol. II - 1981-1989
Dirty Linen CD (CDL104 - $15.00 + $1.50 p&h)

← Available from Hokey Pokey & Projection Records (CD only)

For more information or review copies of *Orphans & Outcasts, Vol. I*, contact:
Paul Hartman
Dirty Linen
(410) 583-7973
FAX: (410) 337-6735
CompuServe: 74020,47

For interviews, contact:
Toby Goldberg
Young/Hunter Management
(617) 643-2773

ATTHEWS • INTIMATE WASH • The next collection in Iain's Notebook Series. 15 songs, just Iain uitar. Includes new versions of 'Call The Tune' and 'Desert Inn', along with five new songs includ ove' and 'Evening Sun'. Intimate Wash is an anagram of Iain Matthews, in case you were wondering
Imported from Perfect Pitch in the USA, on cd at £13·00

HEWS SOUTHERN COMFORT. Iain Matthews first post-Fairport album from 1969. Guests inc. Thompson, Ashley Hutchings, Simon Nicol, Marc Ellington and Dolly Collins. Songs include 'Colorado ternal', 'A Commercial Proposition' and 'Please Be My Friend. Cd has one song less than original
Imported from Line Records, Germany, on cd at £13·00

HEWS SOUTHERN COMFORT • SECOND SPRING • 1970 debut of the Southern Comfort band with well, Ray Duffy, Mark Griffiths, Gordon Huntley, Andy Leigh and IM. Includes a version of James Taylor's 'Something In The Way She Moves' alongside the traditional 'Blood Red Roses' and 'Jinkson Johnson'.
Imported from Line Records, Germany, on cd at £13·00

ROSPECT • BEFORE • US •
LBION DANCE BAND

)) MATTHEWS SOUTHERN COMFORT LATER THAT SAME YEAR
Second album from 1970 and Iain Matthews last with the band. Includes bonus single version of 'Woodstock'.
Imported from Line Records, Germany, on cd at £13·00

MATTHEWS' SOUTHERN COMFORT
Scion
(Strange Fruit BOJCD 007)

Ian Matthews' voice always sounded a little too pure, the aural equivalent of the sickliest chocolate (it's as high as Colin Blunstone's, but without any of the angst and passion). When he left Fairport Convention it was a relief, as it brought the group's more idiosyncratic voices to the fore. Even so, many consider him one of Britain's finest folkies, and will doubtless be overjoyed at this compilation of previously unreleased material.

Though MSC recorded no less than nine sessions for John Peel, only nine songs remain, collected here alongside four out-takes from 1970's *Later That Same Year* album. The Country material is all pleasantly melodic (if too reliant on pedal-steel guitar), but is also, mostly, instantly forgettable. ● **3**

Peter Hogan

MC5
Black To Comm
(Receiver RBCD 185)

IAIN MATTHEWS NEWS

from the horse's mouth

in has been as busy as ever lately, as this recent letter explains:

've been playing a lot of solo in the past year. My book is called t's About Time'. 437 pages from my scrap book, all kinds of stuff. 's $35 (US dollars) and postage $23 by air or $8.65 by surface.
dy (Roberts) and I are getting ready to do a new Plainsong album. rk griffith is the third member. We have a CD of the demos from e unreleased second album out in Germany on Taxim.

've just finished a new solo album for release in Germany initlly, with licensing around the world on Polygram. it's called "Sketon Keys". All my own songs, first time ever. Dirty Linen are prering "Orphans Vol.2" for a July release."

a PS, he adds "There's got to be someone over there to tour me!". ll, isn't there?

Comfort and the singer was Iain (then Ian) Matthews. My journey had begun.

Fast forward to 1973 and the young ears that beheld 'Woodstock' in 1970 had moved on and grown into a curious pairing that soaked up music like a sponge. Those ears had developed a taste for mixing traditional folk music and rock and roll. Somewhere along the way they encountered the name Fairport Convention and by 1974 had been exposed to songs like 'Meet On The Ledge', 'Book Song' and 'Mr Lacy' from *What We Did On Our Holidays*. The voice of silk and honey still sounded out from the vinyl and the male tones again registered. It was *that* voice and it sounded good.

1974 saw the issue of the compilation album, *The Best of Matthews Southern Comfort*, and once again an acquaintance was made… the voice beckoned again. 'Woodstock' sang again but also 'Something In The Way She Moves', 'Blood Red Roses', 'Tell Me Why', 'Once Upon A Lifetime' and 'I've Lost You', all special moments lit up with that voice out front. My Iain Matthews discovery journey had begun in earnest.

In early 1975 I encountered the wonderfully titled *Some Days You Eat The Bear, Some Days The Bear Eats You*. From the first notes of 'Ol' 55' I was hooked on that voice weaving tales of lost love, disappointment, desire and homesickness, evocatively recalling scenes in 'Biloxi' and 'Home'. There was also the definitive version of Danny Whitten's 'I Don't Want To Talk About It' with that lonesome harmonica leading the way and capturing the wistful hopelessness of the original much better than any other version. 'Keep On Sailing' hit my ears for the first time, as did Steely Dan's 'Dirty Work' and Pete Dello's 'Do I Still Figure In Your Life?' It was an emotional smorgasbord, all delivered in that distinctive voice still sounding as good as before. I loved this voice and I wanted more.

Valley Hi soon came my way with Mike Nesmith's production and Red Rhodes' steel guitar and dobro leading the way on 'Seven Bridges Road', 'Keep On Sailing' and Don Gibson's 'Blue Blue Day' and Mike Nesmith's 'Propinquity'. The album became a firm favourite; the version of Jackson Browne's 'These Days' equalled the original while the traditional 'Old Man At The Mill' caressed my ears.

Later that year, a borrowed copy of *If You Saw Thro' My Eyes* came my way, exposing me to 'Desert Inn', 'Hearts' and 'Southern Wind', as did the Plainsong album *In Search Of Amelia Earheart*, with the gems of songs that were recollections of love lost and the aftermath of romantic fall out: 'For The Second Time', 'Call The Tune', 'Even The Guiding Light' and 'Side Roads'.

Next up were *Go For Broke* with Van Morrison's 'Brown Eyed Girl' and Jesse Colin Young's 'Darkness Darkness' and the jazz/funk/sounds of *Hit And Run* with John Martyn's 'One Day Without You', 'The Frame' and revisits to 'Tigers Will Survive' and finally another overdue hit single in 'Shake It' from *Stealin' Home* in 1978. There were more albums like the rockier *Siamese Twins* and *Spot Of Interference*, but I jumped off the train for a while.

So did Iain, to the world of A&R for some years before returning in 1987 with *Walking A Changing Line*, dedicated to the songs of Jules Shear. This escaped me as did much of his late eighties' output, and save for a cover feature in *Folk Roots* magazine in 1989, coverage of his career wasn't exactly every day.

Next up was a real-life meeting in 1992 when I heard Iain Matthews was touring Ireland and performing in Limerick at The Stables bar in the University of Limerick. Here I not only heard one of my heroes in person but also met him in the first of a series of meetings we have had down through the last couple of decades. Touring with Julian Dawson, I heard again that voice which had lit up my teenage life. It was quite an experience as a fan, bringing some albums for signing and a cassette recorder to interview him. It was too good a chance to miss.

That voice hit me again, sounding as good as ever, and while the songs were new and for the most part unfamiliar, that voice made them sound like classic tracks I had known for years. We met after the show and recorded our piece as planned and soon I picked up some pieces missing from his back catalogue; *The Soul*

Of Many Places compilation, some CDs from *The Notebook Series*, a reissue of *If You Saw Thro' My Eyes*, and *Tigers Will Survive* and *Pure And Crooked*. I noticed that the voice was still as strong, melodic and powerful as ever.

Since then, there have been more meetings at Fairport's Cropredy Convention in Oxfordshire, further recordings and more examples of that wonderful silk and honey voice with that high lonesome tenor. Iain Matthews' voice can touch a stone and melt the heart in a way few singers can. He has still got it and I am proud to know him as a friend and hero.

THE CANTEEN

9 JANUARY 1993, MANAHOY CITY, PENNSYLVANIA

DAVID WEISBERG

Whilst I've now known Iain for over three decades, I first met him in the early 1990s when I booked him to play a concert in an old bank that had been converted into a recreation facility in the tiny town of Mahanoy City, Pennsylvania. I made myself the opening act that evening for what was an amazing show (by Iain, not by me), and Iain stayed at my house that night.

I had boxes and boxes of vinyl records in my basement that had been recovered from a home that an old colleague of mine had bought at a tax sale. He had given me the records in hopes that I could sell some of them, but I was also free to take whatever I wanted.

Iain and I spent a lot of time down in that basement going through those records, with Iain taking some. I recall him saying about one record, 'I'm going to ask first if I can have this before telling you about it, or else you'll want to keep it.' It was an original pressing of the *Eclection* album featuring former Fairport Convention member, Trevor Lucas.

But most important to Iain was a stack of children's (perhaps Disney) 45s. He and I struck a deal that, if he could have those records, he'd trade me a collection of every Iain Matthews 45 in existence to have for a jukebox I owned at the time. So now I remain the proud owner of Iain Matthews singles that include not only promos but also test pressings of songs that would never be released as a 45 (including, I believe, 'Rains of '62').

I have many good memories of Iain over the years – celebrating his fiftieth birthday backstage at the Columbia Folk Festival, attending a Phillies game together, and tons of kindnesses over the years – but those first couple of days together are a time I will never forget... and I have the vinyl to prove it!

IAIN MATTHEWS IN CONCERT
With Special Guest — David Weisberg
Saturday, January 9, 1993
8:00 P. M.
THE CANTEEN
20 East Center Street
Mahanoy City, PA
Proceeds to Benefit United Cerebral Palsy
$5.00 Per Person
No 110

When David Weisberg booked Iain he booked himself as the opening act!

LOBBY BAR
29 JANUARY 1993, CORK, IRELAND

DAVE BURKE

Iain Matthews and Julian Dawson came to the much-respected Lobby Bar in Cork in January 1993. The Lobby was a haven for folk and traditional music and for singer-songwriters. The bar was run by Pat Conway and hosted the cream of local and international artists, both upcoming an established, from 1988 until it closed in 2005.

The night Iain came was special. I am an admirer of his music and feel he is an influence on my own writing. *Skeleton Keys* was his current album at the time and has remained a personal favourite. I recall getting Iain's two-LP compilation, *Discreet Repeat*, in Uneeda, the local music and book shop, about a week later.

I was unaware of Julian Dawson's music but I vividly remember sitting on the window sill during the break and chatting with him.

CONGRESS HOUSE STUDIO
1993, AUSTIN, TEXAS

KIM SIMPSON

One way to get to the Congress House Studio in Austin is to take a little street called Foremost Drive from the I-35 feeder road. Stop where it crests and you've got a strangely elegant view of an auto junkyard. Not long after I moved to Austin from Salt Lake City in 1993, I thumbed through the Yellow Pages and booked a session for a quick demo at Congress House, which sounded reputable. I took Foremost to my session and had to pull over for a sec when I saw that junkyard.

At the session I did a song of mine called 'Simon St Claire', which I wanted to come off like a medieval English ballad. In the middle of doing the vocal, the engineer Bradley Kopp (a fine musician himself) said through the studio mic, 'Hey Kim, have you met Iain Matthews?' I said, 'No, but I'd like to someday.'

'Well, he's right here,' said Bradley, and I looked up through the glass and there was Iain sitting next to him.

I was a British folk obsessive at the time and had known Iain's work with Fairport Convention and also through his Vertigo albums. I knew him first, however, via 'Shake It' on AM radio, so I knew he wouldn't likely be carrying himself as a folk pioneer. Even so, I wasn't able to muster more than *er, um, wow*, and *hi*, before gathering myself to do the rest of the vocal with him there taking it in.

This is not an I-met-Iain 'and the rest is history' story, because I walk too circuitous a road for that. But, actually, it kind of is, because the man I met in the control booth after the session was one who not only took my own creative efforts seriously, but also creative effort itself. He lifted my spirits, yes, but most importantly I met a model of persistence, artistry and human warmth in Iain that I've admired as a fan and observer to this day.

Well, hello, that reminds me of the auto parts term 'like-kind-quality', where the initials come from in the name of that junkyard (LKQ Pick-Your-Part) near the Congress House studio where Iain made so much good music. (My favourite from his Austin years is *Pure And Crooked*, which Iain handed to me at the studio and which is a lovingly-produced work of mature songcraft, with hooks to

Kim Simpson looks out at the auto junkyard

spare and his ever-soaring vocals at top flight.)

Iain doesn't know that the times he would see fit to greet me at his own gigs, including one at the Cactus Cafe (where he welcomed a surprise guest named Richard Thompson), made me feel some much-needed camaraderie during some low times. One day he called me to see if I'd participate in a songwriter in the round gig, and he'd reached me when a number of things were going haywire in my world, and I was having a meltdown. I'm not sure what prompted me to pick up the phone in such a state, but I did, and I'm glad, because he took some time to talk and worked some magic that was at once momentary and lasting.

Iain Matthews's voice saying 'everything's OK' on the phone that day still rings in my ears, and the fact that he continues to carry himself as though everything's OK is the farthest thing from a liability.

I continue to stop at the top of Foremost Drive to take in the junkyard view when I'm in the neighbourhood. I brought up two boys in Austin, and that became a favourite thing for all of us to do, gazing out and identifying broken cars. Whenever I'm there, I have thoughts of Iain, not only because of that first studio association, but because he's come to represent for me a guy whose car, in fact, never stops running.

SOUTH BY SOUTHWEST

MARCH 1994, AUSTIN, TEXAS

PETER HOLSAPPLE

When my friends and I were sixteen, *Tigers Will Survive* by Iain Matthews was released, and we all played his a capella cover of 'Da Doo Ron Ron' by The Crystals ad nauseum. It was letter-perfect, and Iain's clear tenor bore that kind of repeating as he sang every glorious harmony. Admittedly, that year's most-lift-the-needle-from-next-track award went to 'Hope You Know', which fifty years later really is a great song, of course. Blame it on callow youth.

My intro to Fairport, from whence Iain sprung, was the post-Sandy Denny *Full House* album. Once that was fully digested, I started looking back and listening, finding gems like 'Tale In Hard Time' and 'Book Song' alongside covers he piloted the band through, like the Merry-Go-Round's 'Time Will Show The Wiser'. Then 'Woodstock' and then 'Shake It' and so on, and now it's a discography with dozens of sterling albums, both solo and as an ensemble player, at which he is very gifted.

Continental Drifter Peter Holsapple has worked with Iain over the years

I finally met Iain in Austin during South By SouthWest in the 1990s when he was a labelmate of Continental Drifters on Blue Rose Records out of Germany. We were deep in our Fairport Convention-appreciation-society phase that was born from a tribute to Sandy Denny we did at St Ann's in Brooklyn with a raft of vocalists; Iain was not among them, but Edgar Heckmann from our label saw the possibility/need of getting his two artists together. Band and Iain clicked immediately, and we backed him up on a show in New Orleans at the Howlin' Wolf as part of our guest-star series. He had us singing his all-vocal rendition of Richard Thompson's 'From Galway to Graceland' and we were in harmony heaven.

Over the years, Iain and I would find ourselves in the same

place at the same time, including concerts in Los Angeles, Durham and Winston-Salem. And Iain has become a beloved fellow moving part of the Wild Honey Foundation family, lighting up tributes to the music of his favourites, The Lovin' Spoonful, The Band and Buffalo Springfield.

My admiration for the guy just grows, and I'm grateful for our friendship. Imagine my delight to receive a note from Iain recently, which read, 'I always felt that of all the bands I've worked briefly with, I would have loved to have become a Drifter too.'

The feeling is mutual; maybe we could work up 'Hope You Know'!

SCHUBA'S

12 MAY 1995, CHICAGO, ILLINOIS

PHILLIP ZISOOK

Sometime in the mid-nineties I rediscovered Iain Matthews' music. I loved Iain's early work, but somehow had lost track of him over the years. I became aware of Iain's then-current work primarily as a result of getting turned onto Watermelon Records, an independent Austin label, which was signing several artists I followed, most notably the Silos and its founder/leader, Walter Salas-Humara.

Phil Zisook rediscovered Iain's music in the nineties

In 1992, Watermelon released the album by indie-supergroup the Setters (Walter Salas-Humara, Alejandro Escovedo and Michael Hall, with Gurf Morlix, Scott Garber and Lisa Mednick), produced by Gurf. In 1994, Watermelon released two Silos albums separated by several months, the wonderful *Susan Across The Ocean* followed by their previous album, first released in Germany on Normal Records, *Hasta La Victoria*. I had to find out what other music this company was releasing!

Around the same time, I learned that Watermelon released a new album by Iain, *The Dark Ride*. Iain at the time was living in Austin, Texas. I ordered the album, was blown away, and the rest is history. From there, I got his previous album, *Skeleton Keys*. Then I signed up for Iain's newsletter and discovered his wonderful *Notebook Series* albums, released through Perfect Pitch – *Orphans And Outcasts*, *Live Alone*, *Intimate Wash* and *Camouflage*, each of which I consider to be cherished components of my music collection. Not only did Iain still have 'that voice', his compositions and performances were deep, artful and musically interesting. He also continued to do great interpretations, including Richard Thompson's 'From Galway To Graceland'.

In 1995 I learned that Iain was forming a trio comprised of himself, Michael Fracaso and producer/guitarist Mark Hallman, called Hamilton Pool, and that the band was releasing an album, also on Watermelon, *Return To Zero*. That was probably the sixth Iain album I bought that year! And, the band was coming to Chicago's great music room, Schuba's. I bought tickets the minute they were available. There was just one little glitch; the date of the show, May 12, 1995, was not the best night to be playing at a club in Chicago. The Bulls were playing the Orlando Magic in the NBA semi-finals that night. Chicago is a big sports town, particularly when the Bulls at the time consisted of Michael Jordan, Scottie Pippen, Horace Grant, Steve Kerr, B.J. Armstrong, Ron Harper, etc. To make matters worse, Schuba's space consists of two rooms. The first is a large bar, with TVs over the bar. Needless to say, when there was a Bulls playoff game, the room was packed, with Bulls fans. May 12th was one of those nights.

The music room, adjacent to the bar, however, was not packed. Suffice it to say, it was an intimate performance. So intimate, that when Iain, Michael, and Mark looked out in the audience, you had the impression that they were looking right at you. And yet, what a performance! In addition to Hamilton Pool songs, we were treated to Iain solo material from throughout his career. It was riveting and inspiring, hearing his diverse repertoire, the depth of those songs, and that powerful, clear voice, in-person. In addition to putting on a generously long show, the band met fans in front of the stage and talked for an extended period. It was absolutely wonderful, notwithstanding that many more should have been there.

From that point through the present, I've continued to see Iain play whenever he's come to Chicago and that has included a show with Andy Roberts, where they concentrated on Richard Fariña songs and selected Plainsong material, as well as a recent solo show at Space, in Evanston. Each has been an inspiring music experience.

Looking forward to the next time!

THEATER HEERENLOGEMENT

1990S, BEUSICHEM, THE NETHERLANDS

DIANE VAN GALEN

In the 1990s, Iain Matthews toured The Netherlands with his music for the first time. An enthusiastic booker alerted theatre programmers to Iain's musical tour. Not only that, but organisers were explicitly invited to book Iain for a performance at their theatre. A performance was offered at the theatre where I was volunteering at the time, Theater Heerenlogement in Beusichem.

The programme manager at the time announced that a certain Iain Matthews would be performing at his theatre. I wondered if

Diane Van Galen has seen Iain perform many times

we were talking about *the* Iain Matthews. We were! Iain Matthews from Matthews Southern Comfort, was coming to Theater Heerenlogement. His first performance at our theater, and the first of many, by the way. We've since seen him perform with Plainsong, with Fairport Convention, with Matthews Southern Comfort and solo...

The unforgettable performances had an unexpected sequel. Eric Taylor joined Iain for one performance. They were staying in a holiday cottage in the Utrecht town of Scherpenzeel during their tour of The Netherlands. The question was, 'How do we get from Beusichem to our accommodation in the middle of the night, in a region we've never been to before?' (Over 30 years ago, wayfinding electronics hadn't yet been invented…)

After some deliberation, we quickly found the solution. I live in Veenendaal, near Scherpenzeel, and because explaining the route was too complicated, we simply led the way and Iain and Eric followed us. Throughout the drive, we were aware that our musical heroes were in the car behind us, following us to their holiday cottage.

Another special memory: during the annual Friends' Evening at the theatre, we sold raffle tickets to win a house concert. I won the grand prize and of course I chose a performance in my living room by none other than Iain Matthews. The musician whose LP I had at home as a teenager was now performing in Veenendaal, in *my* living room.

BRIDGETON FOLK FESTIVAL
17 JUNE 1995, BRIDGETON, NEW JERSEY

BOB ROSE

I was born in the USA in 1954 and grew up during the fifties and sixties. I was very fortunate to enjoy great music from artists from both sides of the Atlantic. This inspired me to work in music, but that's another story. Part of that great music while growing up were the sounds coming from the UK which included many folk-rock bands, among them the Fairport Convention. After his stint with the band, Iain Matthews released Matthews Southern Comfort and I became a fan for life and still cherish these early records. Years later, when I was fortunate to organise a folk festival in my hometown of Bridgeton, New Jersey, I booked Iain in 1990 as one of our featured performers.

Not only did Iain delight the audience with his well-crafted songs but he was joined on staged by Philadelphia-based artist Lindsay Gilmour who was on the same bill that year. Five years later, Iain returned to the festival which happened to be headlined by his former bandmate Richard Thompson. We had hoped for a reunion of sorts but it wasn't to happen that time, but I was glad it did happen later when they shared the same stage at another festival. Over the years I have remained friends with Iain and have worked with him a few times. He is not only one gifted and talented artist but such a fine individual who I am proud to call a friend.

THE SANDTRAP

15 JUNE 1996, LIMERICK, PENNSYLVANIA

GRAHAM CROUSE

I was booking music at a new venue called The Sandtrap at a golf course in Limerick, Pennsylvania. I was looking at the back of Iain's *The Dark Ride* CD and saw 'for bookings contact so and so…'. I debated whether to call it, thinking, 'What's the chance of getting one of my favourite singer-songwriters at The Sandtrap?', but I did and, lo and behold, I got a call from his agent who said Iain was interested in performing at our venue.

I was putting on entertainment during Friday 'Happy Hours' at the time, when people consumed a lot of alcohol. It was not the best scenario for a solo folk artist. Nonetheless, Iain put on a great performance and I couldn't have been more pleased. I proceeded to book Iain for future dates and he soon picked up local guitarist, Jim Fogarty, to accompany him. Jim continues to perform with him on his US East Coast tours.

Graham booked shows at The Sandtrap

One show I will always remember was when Iain played up in our Banquet Room. This area was much more conducive (and quieter) to one of his shows. He performed with Ad Vanderveen and it was just incredible.

Another time, Iain was scheduled to be at The Sandtrap on his sixtieth birthday and my wife Debbie and I got him a cake and helped celebrate it with him. I also had the pleasure of meeting a lot of great people there who also shared my love for Iain's music.

After moving on from The Sandtrap, I made it a point to attend as many shows as possible at other venues when Iain was in the area. Most recently, I was able to get the Raven's Claw Golf Club to help me host a couple of his shows in 2022 and 2024. As always, these were fantastic and appreciated by everyone who attended. My son Jon, who has known Iain since he was a boy and has always considered him an inspiration, thought it a privilege to open up for him at these two showings.

I have to say all of my experiences with Iain have been good ones. He's not only one of my favourite musicians but also one of my favourite people. He's a great soul creating meaningful music. My whole family and I are happy to have known Iain for all these years and I'm proud to call him a friend.

HOUSE CONCERT

23 JUNE 1996, DOWNINGTON, PENNSYLVANIA

JIM MARKS

I have just finished Iain's compelling book, *Thro' My Eyes*, last night. In some respects, it was like the first view of a music video from the eighties. You know, where the band's visual

RHYTHM of the WEST

GLOBAL EDITION | THE IAIN MATTHEWS NEWSLETTER | May, 1996

A LETTER FROM TEXAS

And I thought last year slipped away! Here we are, one third gone already and I'm just getting my bearings. I'd better get out there before you forget me!

I decided at the beginning of the year that trying to book myself was too time consuming, and I went out fishing for an agent. I'm pleased to report that I found someone. Ironically, the man who sent me on my second Japanese tour 3 years ago, Geoffrey Blumenauer, at GBA. Just in case you have any grand performing ideas for me (house concerts, etc), his phone # is 818-893-1896. Fax is 818-893-2796. That's a load off me. Thanks Geoffrey!

I've just returned from recording a new Plainsong CD, This one was done in Suffolk, Andy's neck of the woods. During the recording, I was reading Peter Guralnick's "Sweet Soul Music", which may have coloured a couple or so tracks. I'll be going back there at the end of July for a few festivals, plus some in Germany.

Right now the task at hand is to finish my new solo CD. It's a little different–more electric. All originals. I don't like to give too much away. Some songs you've seen me perform in the past twelve months, some not. It's called "God Looked Down".

This should see me through May. Then we hit the road again! Kerrville on the 7th of June, then the east the 13th through the 24th. I'll be doing a cool little festival in Columbia, PA on June 16th. Isn't that someone's birthday?? Put on by my pal, David Weisberg. Maybe see you there!

Lastly, thanks to everyone who said "Hi" from Kim and Greg to me in Europe (and I suppose to all those that didn't). Just keep coming, okay!!

Iain

Swine Lake

May 1996

P.S. Before I forget. There is also a compilation due out on September 10th, on the Varese-Sarabande label, of my Rockburgh recordings. This set was compiled by me, with the guiding hands of Cary Mansfield at V.S.. It's called "Carefully Taught": The Seattle Years. It contains tracks from "Stealing Home", "Siamese Friends", "Spot Of Interference", and "Shook". Hmm, all esses. I should have called it "The Sounds Of Sibilance" (joke). None of this material has been available on CD in the US until now. Once again, I've dug into my archives for more unpublished artwork.

See and Believe!

U.S. TOUR DATES

June 1996

7 - Kerrville Folk Festival - Kerrville, Tx

14 - Turning Point - Piermont, Ny

15 - Sandtrap - Limerick, PA (ph: 610-495-6945)

16 - Columbia Folk Festival - Columbia, PA

18 - World Cafe Taping (sorry, no audience)

19 - Rosie's Cabaret - Washington, NJ

20 - Ellicott Theater - Ellicott City, MD

21 - Tin Angel - Philadelphia, PA

22 - Godfrey Daniels - Bethlehem, PA

23 - Private Party

Please call venues for confirmation, ticket info, times, etc.

NEW RELEASES DUE THIS SUMMER

Sorry it's been so long since the last newsletter. We're still here!! We wanted to wait until Iain was back from Europe to send this out. We hope all you fans in England got to see him play. We will continue to let you know dates as they occur.

There's a lot to tell you about and a lot to look forward to this summer.

First, Iain's trip to England was primarily to get together with Andy, Mark, and Julian to record the new Plainsong album, "Sister Flute". The sessions went great and I think you'll all like the results. The tracks include 4 new songs by Iain, 4 Dawsongs, 2 by Andy and three covers including a way cool acapella version of the Who's "I Can't Explain". European release will be in August. Right now there is no firm date for a US release, but we will, as always, have copies of the European version as soon as they come out.

If that's not enough, final mixes are being completed on "God Looked Down", Iain's new solo record on the Watermelon label. As of this writing, the ever evasive Mr. Matthews has not sent me a tape, but he promises this will be as good as "Dark Ride"–perhaps a bit more electric. A couple of staples from his recent solo dates like "Southern Wind" and the title track will get a full band "fleshing out". Should be fun to hear!! Players on the new record include David Grissom (Joe Ely Band) on electric guitars, Michael Ramos (Bodeans) on keyboards–including lots of Hammond B3. Production, as always, is by Mark "Punchmaster" Hallman. Tentative release date is July 23rd in the USA.

Lastly, we still have copies of "Camouflage" available. We think this is a wonderful record we've put together (see review, this issue) and hope you all order a copy soon, It's the support you show by purchasing these CD's that allow us to continue producing the newsletter, which now goes out to about 3800 fans at a cost of about $2000 per mailing. So help us continue to keep you informed and hear some great music at the same time.

Peace-

Greg and Kim

LATE NEWS FLASH:

We have some late-breaking Hamilton Pool news for you. We are pleased to announce that the very talented David Halley has been added to the line-up. David has two records to his credit, "Stray Dog Talk" and Broken Spell", the latter of which was produced by Ham Pool's own Mark Hallman (and made my personal top ten list). In addition, after some soul searching, Michael Fracasso has decided to rejoin the fold as well. We welcome he and David back to the band. Look for them to be recording and performing before the years end.

CAMOUFLAGE - A REVIEW

This man has one of the purest and most beautiful voices in music today, as anyone who has sat in a small room and got chills from hearing him perform can attest. So, this latest in his self-released "notebook series" is quite a treat - a chance to hear some highlights from the past five years of live shows.

But first, there's a great unearthed BBC tract from 1971, "There's A Woody Guthrie Song", with Richard Thompson and Plainsong's Andy Roberts (and featuring Iain's now nearly extinct British accent). Then it's on to revisit '70's songs "Keep On Sailing", "For The Lonely Hunter", and "And Me", all of which benefit from the stripped down acoustic arrangements.

Even the more recent material, like the autobiographical "Compass and Chart" and "True Location Of The Heart", seem more effective in these Spartan surroundings. And while there's no question that Iain's records have never really done his voice justice, this is about the best Iain Matthew's record ever, in that sense.

Though it's true that Iain's songwriting skills have grown over the last decade, it's a cover that steals the show–Mark Germino's "The Rat And The Snake". Go ahead, listen to the original versions first, and see how this man can make a song his own, with seemingly little effort.

A delicate beautiful souvenir of the last five years.

-review by Dewey Gurall

-Reprinted by permission of PORTHOLE, a Fairport Convention Quarterly. Subscriptions: $20 US and Canada/$28 overseas. Write to: PORTHOLE, 212 Farmington Road, Pittsburgh, PA 15215, USA

READERS POLL

Iain and I have been discussing new merchandise ideas and thought we should go right to the source and ask you for your input. So get out your paper and pens and drop us a line.

Here are the ideas we had. Let us know your preferences And, if you have other ideas, send them along for consideration too.

1) A reprint of Iain's book "It's about Time"- This is a thick soft-cover book filled with clipping and photos spanning Iain's career. It was available a few years ago in a very limited number and could be reprinted if there's ample interest.

2) A series of "vintage" T-shirts based on artwork form old LP's, etc (e.g.: we've kicked around the idea of a shirt from "Some Days You Eat The Bear" or "Hit and Run")

3) A series of historic posters– Iain has old Southern Comfort and Fairport posters that could possibly be reprinted.

4) Postcards (sets of 6) made from archive photos- the postcards would also be a series and issued chronologically.

5) A Songbook - transcribing songs from throughout Iain's career for guitar. Of course, photos and comments would be included.

Well, what do you think? Do any of these set your mouth watering? Or is there something you've been hoping for that I haven't mentioned? We look forward to hearing your responses. Stay tuned for our final decision.

IAIN MATTHEWS

As Bob Dylan once noted, "He who is not busy being born is busy dying" Iain Matthews is living proof of that adage. For after thirty years of ma music - during which he's released some thirty four albums, both solo otherwise - Iain Matthews is creating the best music of his career right now. latest album "The Dark Ride" is ample evidence of that fact.

•

Born in Scunthorpe, Iain Matthews was a founder member Of **Fair Convention** alongside **Richard Thompson**. He left them in 1969 to forn own band, **Matthews Southern Comfort**, and had an unforgettable No with a version of **Joni Mitchell's "Woodstock"**. Iain has long had a reput for having a keen ear for the work of some of the finest songwriter's of our c Jesse Winchester, Tim Hardin, Gene Clarke, John Martyn and Tom Wai name just a few. More recently though Iain has become a songwriter t reckoned with. His album "**Skeleton Keys**" was his first entirely self-pe album and it brought him as much praise for his incisive writing as fo trademark breathtaking vocal work.

•

Iain went through a period of disillusionment in the early 80's and lef performing and recording to become a talent scout for Island Music Wyndham Hill. Fortunately for his loyal fans, an incendiary performanc Cropredy in the late 80's, sparked a return to making music and also to a w lot of new fans. Iain has spent many years now living in The States and the 5 years in Austin Texas which is renowned for the high quality of m produced there. It is not surprising that Iain has soaked up some T influences.

•

Few other artists with such a proud legacy can still hit such creative high n but as Iain explains, "I've always felt that the best part of my life is yet to co What gets you first with Iain Matthews is the voice. An instrument of h desire, disillusionment and dreams; a voice at once ancient and time gorgeous and emotive. What Richard Thompson is to folk-rock guitar, Matthews is to folk-rock voice.

•

An original. Unique, unforgettable.

Iain's latest solo album has just been, released. It is called GOD LOOKED DOWN. Also available is PLAINSONG'S latest album SISTER FLUTE. Iain has also contributed a track, a live version of Rains of '62, to the Westbury Park School Compilation CD THE PARK CONNECTION.

You are invited to an evening with...

Iain Matthews

2nd Biennial Backyard Concert Series

Date: Sunday, June 23, 1996

Place: Marks' backyard
29 Lafayette Circle
Downingtown

Time: 7:00 - ?

Special Notes

Please bring a blanket and lawn chairs. BYOB. We'll supply the munchies. (I'm sure a keg will show up for the beer lovers)

ADULTS ONLY

English folksinger Iain Matthews is considered one of the great vocalists in folk/rock history. Beginning with Richard Thompson and Fairport Convention in the 60's, Iain branched out with the formation of Matthew's Southern Comfort (where he made a hit of Joni Mitchell's "Woodstock" and three excellent records). Iain's solo career includes more than 20 outstanding recordings, including the excellent Electra series (most notably "Valley Hi") and his classic Windham Hill recording of Jules Shear songs (Walking a Changing Line) which is highly recommended. Iain records often and tours Europe every year to large crowds. His recent collaboration with Michael Fraccasso and Mark Hallman called 'Hamilton Pool' combined three unique talents into an eclectic folk/country sound.

RSVP By June 1 458-5741

EUROPEAN TOUR INFORMATION

BRITAIN

July 19 Carlisle Folk Festival (Plainsong)
21 Half Moon : Putney (Plainsong)

*for additional dates in Britain, call Janet or Keith at S 161-370-7248

GERMANY

August 2 Gottingen Festival (Plainsong)
3 Bardentreffen Festival (Plainsong)
4 Salzburg, Austria (solo)

*for additional dates/info call Christian Thiel at 49-40-

SEPTEMBER - MUNICH RECORDS SONGWRITERS TOUR

Featuring Iain Matthews, Bob Neuwirth, Eric Taylor and Dates in Scandinavia, U.K., Germany, Austria, Switzerlanc Belgium.

*for exact dates call Arnold Wegner at Tornado Concert 31-20-627-5875

PLAINSONG - "SISTER FLUTE" TOUR

October 2-12 Holland

*for further information Frank van der Meijden at 31-18-363-6880

October 13-27 Germany and Austria
13 Kito : Bremen
17 Cafe Hahn : Koblenz
18 Die Halle : Reichenbach
19 Ducsaal : Freudenburg
20 Festhalle : Schwabisch
21 Cafe Balzak : Heidenheim
22 Neu Welt : Ingolstadt

Matthews - Orphans & Outcasts Volume 3
More Undiscovered Gems

een a while since our last O & O, six years actually, and I apologise for the slight delay. I didn't
n it would appear, only that it undoubtedly would. The truth of it is that I've been so caught up in
with Plainsong, and solo and recording both, there hasn't really been a lot of time to consider an
elieve it or not, it's quite a time consuming commitment, scrambling through boxes of boring old
ch of 'just' the right thing. Sometimes I cannot believe how many of these things I have. If my memory
ht, the last time around, I flirted with the idea of a live 'Hit and Run' band disc. Well, I listened to
his time through, and they still sound quite tasty. But it has to be heard as a complete set, rather
or two stings here and there. But, one day it will appear.
s.
Texas. 1999.

ted edition release Iain has collected together unreleased recordings including his 1965 debut as the
duced by Denny Cordell + a different mix of the classic Matthews Southern Comfort hit Woodstock. The
eatures radio recordings made in 1970 with Richard Thompson, Andy Roberts, Viv Stanshall and more
ings with Plainsong as well as a selection of unreleased solo recordings.

bout You, Woodstock, Hearts, Home, Never Ending, I'll Fly Away, Sing Senorita, On The Beach, This
Except For A Tear, Next Time Around, God's Empty Chair, Jaques And Tambo, Spirits, Sing Sister Sing.

his CD is a mail order only release and is available from Unique Gravity at £12.99 UK £13.99 ROW.

SONG AT THE PICTURE PLAYHOUSE, BEVERLEY
AY, 11th MARCH 1999 (REVIEW BY ADRIAN BOOTH)

ws was back in his home territory when Plainsong played their gig at The Picture Playhouse
in the lovely East Yorkshire market town of Beverley. Although he was born in
his childhood was spent at Barton-upon-Humber, not fifteen miles from Beverley. It was a
newing old acquaintances for Iain, who spent pre, mid, and post-gig breaks chatting to
his old mates. From the stage he also asked if anyone in the audience knew the
s of an old childhood friend whom he was trying to trace, but sadly nobody could help.
nsong, whose original line-up included Iain Matthews and Andy Roberts, came to
in the early 1970's, after Iain's spells in Fairport Convention and Matthews Southern
n 1972 Plainsong released the critically acclaimed 'In Search of Amelia Earhart' album, but
on split up to further solo careers. The band lay dormant until 1993, when Matthews and
eased the album 'Dark Side of the Room' under the Plainsong monicker, while the current
has Iain Matthews and Andy Roberts joined by Mark Griffiths (ex Matthews Southern
and Clive Gregson (best known for his erstwhile duo with Christine Collister, and
of the Richard Thompson Band).
Beverley gig kicked-off with Iain Matthews taking lead vocal on his own composition 'And
may be found on his solo 'Live Alone' album. It was a good start, but the performance
awry with a version of a Hollies hit from the 1960's, the relevance of which to Plainsong is
nceive. Andy Roberts then took lead vocal on a disjointed song with a strange melodic
re was also early troubles with the sound mix (the guitars coming through very thin), and it
ntil after a three song medley about Amelia Earhart that a fully rounded guitar sound
cked-in. Thereafter it was highlights all the way...
ey returned to their heritage for 'YoYo Man' (off the first album) and performed acapella
l Thompson's sad 'Galway to Graceland'. Iain Matthews mentioned his admiration for the
he late Richard Farina, and the band played two Farina compositions, including a fine
the strangely titled 'House un-American Blues Activity Dream'. There was plenty of stuff
ng's brand new CD release, and each of the band's three lead vocalists was able to perform
om their respective solo back catalogues. Clive Gregson told an amusing anecdote when
his song 'Tatoo' (off his excellent 'I Love This Town' solo album). He related how the song
d by him seeing a sign in the USA offering 'Tatooing while-U-wait', although he declined to
rm behind while he went shopping!
sically, Plainsong were a hot quartet. During the concert Andy Roberts (guitar, mandolin,
dulcimer, and bodhran), and Clive Gregson (guitar, slide guitar, mandolin, banjo, and
stage prescence) constantly changed instruments to keep the sound fresh; while Iain
played rhythm guitar and Mark Griffiths bass guitar. On a few numbers the band's tour
illed-out the sound on percussion. They finished with an eight minute version of Iain
'Back of the Bus' (also on 'Live Alone') and then, after prolongued warm applause, returned
e song encore. They did an acapella version of the traditional 'Souling Song' followed by
ur Radio On' and an unidentified song which they performed acoustically - without
on - sitting on the edge of the stage. In total they played 1 hour 55 minutes and, after the
t, it had been a superb concert.
terwards I spoke to the very friendly Iain Matthews. We reminisced about our mutual
of Barton-upon-Humber, about the old brick works and, when we were young(er), both
he ancient paddle steamboat which used to plie across the River Humber between nearby
and and Hull. A Fairport Convention fan asked Iain to autograph a vinyl copy of the very
ort album, and then pose for a photograph holding the said album: the hero obliged. Andy
as chatting to fans, and I was pleased to be able to speak to him for a couple of minutes
early solo albums and his subsequent theatre music career. He told me that he is very proud
rent Plainsong. So he should be; they are a talented lot - catch 'em if you can.

PLAINSONG - "SISTER FLUTE" TOUR continued

October

23 E Werk : Erlangen
24 Barenswinger : Dresden
25 Folk Clupp : Luxembourg
26 Zehntscheuer : Ravensburg
27 Star Club : Oberhausen

*for additional information call Christian Thiel at 49-40-47-6993

ENGLAND

November 15-30 Solo tour

*for dates call Janet or Keith at 161-370-7248 (tell them HI! from Iain!)

Jim Marks organised a backyard show featuring Iain

interpretation of a beloved song doesn't quite match the one in your own head? As I read about his journey, I found myself reflecting on where I was in my own life when his music crossed my path. It was so much fun to look back, remember, put some pieces of his timeline together, and separate fact from starry-eyed fandom.

My bond with Iain Matthews began on New Year's Eve in 1975. I was looking forward to a great night of music, friends, beer and girls, at a private gig my older brother was playing in Jersey, when I came down with the flu. Feverish, lonely and sad, I stayed home. I played a new record, *Valley Hi*, over and over to escape. It worked! That record became a favourite and a 'go to' pick-me-up.

But even before then, in high school, I was drawn to *Later That Same Year*. I had a love affair with the pedal steel guitar. That started it all, and I later collected all of Iain's records. I made dozens of mix tapes in my day, many of which included the fantasy Webb crush ballad, 'Met Her On A Plane'.

It wasn't until the eighties that I first saw Iain play live. Our 'history' was likely the impetus for my first visit to the Philadelphia club called the Tin Angel. It was there that I first introduced myself. I later saw him again a few times at the same club where I heard *Pure And Crooked* and *Skeleton Keys* selections for the first time. After that, I never missed a show anywhere near South East Pennsylvania. And he always remembered me.

Married with kids and scampering in the rat race, I was looking again to music to keep centred. So my friend Larry and I held our second neighbourhood concert in my back yard, this time featuring Iain and the talented Jim Fogerty. I wanted everybody to meet Iain and share my joy for the music. The show was intimate and a big success. Iain opened cold with the a cappella tune 'Squirrel Hill' and all jaws dropped. It was a goose bump moment.

Amongst Iain's stops here in PA were golf course ballrooms. I heard about the shows through Graham, another fan of Iain's, who contacted me and who also attended my backyard show. I have been to several of them, including one in autumn. Graham told me Iain was considering retirement. So this time I brought with me yet another favourite record (perhaps my favourite of all), *Walking A Changing Line*.

I was fully prepared to say farewell, choke back my emotion and get lost in the music one last time. Before I asked him to sign the record (yes, he remembered me again) I said, 'Iain, I feel like I have known you my whole life.' Iain heard this, hugged me and inscribed my album with the following: 'To Jim, I feel like I have known you my whole life.' What a guy.

Thank you, Iain, for understanding how fans feel. And thanks for accepting the love! You have returned it in more ways than you will ever know.

SWINE LAKE

MARCH 1998, AUSTIN, TEXAS

RONALD HOOIJENGA

'Yes, this is Swine Lake!'

Horses, cats, and dogs, and a donkey to kick the coyotes away. 'Yes, this is Swine Lake!' was a handwritten sign on the gate. When I first entered that gate of Iain's ranch near Austin, Texas, it was March 1998. After listening to his records since I was fourteen in 1971, starting with his then just released masterpiece *If You Saw Thro' My Eyes*, I used my first trip to the States to interview him for the Dutch newspapers I wrote for. We had a lovely conversation on the porch, overlooking Swine Lake, in the lukewarm Texas spring.

Ronald Hooijenga first met Iain when he interviewed him for the Dutch press

Later that same week, during the closing day of music festival South-by-Southwest, Iain and his then wife Veronique threw a Sunday party. Where else could you see your lifelong idol throwing horseshoes in the yard, together with Mark Hallman and other musical friends?

It was a wonderful week, and I have been back to Austin at least a dozen times more. To write about SXSW, record some of my own songs, and to interview one great Texas artist each year. After Iain came Eric Taylor, Slaid Cleaves, Sam Baker, Brandi Zdan and others. The late great Jimmy LaFave stood high on my wish list, but I met him literally every year I was in Austin, mostly by chance, and at his own showcases.

Both Iain and Jimmy starred in my own song about South-by-Southwest: 'Charlotte Street', which I wrote immediately after my first trip to Austin:

Man, I met Iain Matthews, and Jimmy LaFave
And that guy from Binky Records nearly every day
I danced cheek to cheek with Veronique
But I dearly missed the girl from Charlotte Street

They both posed later quite proudly with the single, mainly because it was the first song ever with their names in it, I guessed. To hand the record to Jimmy, I had to wait for another SXSW in Texas. Iain made it a lot easier: he moved to The Netherlands!

I have seen him perform here frequently since 1998, interviewed him a couple of times more, and now play one of his old guitars. On the porch of Swine Lake, he gave himself another five years, tops, as a creative and performing artist. But here he is, in my own country: still writing, still playing, still singing with that beautiful voice. Thanks for more than 50 years of music! And counting…

CAFÉ DE AMER

7 MAY 2000, AMEN, THE NETHERLANDS

ARTHUR TICKNOR

Living in Oregon in the USA, I first became aware of Iain when 'Woodstock' was a big hit in 1970. The beauty of his singing got my full attention. As the years passed, I gradually lost awareness of him until I got a computer and in 1998 joined his mailing list. He was living in Austin, Texas at the time. He let us hear songs from his latest releases such as 'A Tiniest Wham'.

Iain Matthews (left) with Arthur Ticknor, May 2000 (Koen Hottentot)

Our first meeting was a non-event due to my shyness in the presence of greatness. In August 1999 I went on Festival Tour's England and Scotland trip, and saw Iain at a lunch event. I said 'hi' but quickly moved away again because he was one of the important people there and, surely, he had other people to talk to?

I made a Dutch friend on that trip from the Fairport Convention

Iain (left) with Judy Dyble at Cropredy, August 2002 (Arthur Ticknor)

mailing list. Having wanted to see Europe all my life, the following May I put together a holiday starting in Holland. Fortuitously, Iain moved there at the same time. My new Dutch friends were fans too so we all went to Amen in the least populated corner of the country to see him live.

It was a wonderful venue for an intimate performance. I met Iain again, talked a bit, and a picture was taken of us. It was a memorable show made all the better when he released a recording of that very concert, *The Iain Ad Venture* CD. What a perfect souvenir of my Dutch holiday!

Returning to Britain for the Cropredy Festival, I saw Iain perform with Fairport Convention on 6, 9 and 10 August 2002. I returned to the Netherlands where I saw the Iain Ad Venture perform *If You Saw Thro' My Eyes* in its entirety live for the first time on 28 October 2003. I got there early and had a front row seat where I turned out to be sitting next to his manager and his soon-to-be wife. Another fantastic show, and once again he released a CD of it. I can't get over my luck. I saw him two more times that decade, in New York City and Philadelphia, and he was always a joy to experience, and I had no more shyness about talking to him. Since then, I haven't gotten to travel much. I don't mean to sound patronising, but those travelling days when I crossed paths with Iain really were some of the best times of my life.

COLWALL VILLAGE HALL
15 OCTOBER 2000, MALVERN, UK

ROY BURTON

I first became aware of Iain back in the Fairport days and then with Matthews Southern Comfort and his great interpretation of 'Woodstock'. I have always liked Iain's professional approach to any song he sings. He has such a unique sound, both in his voice and in his guitar playing. When a song of his comes on the radio you cannot confuse him with anyone else. I got to see him locally for the first time at Colwall Village Hall, near Malvern, with Ad Vanderveen. It was such a great night.

Roy Burton considers Iain 'a true legend'

He then played in 2001 with Andy Roberts and Plainsong, which was another unique show. During his show, Iain gives a bit of insight into how the songs come about and the way he puts everything together. 2002 saw Iain return with Ad Vanderveen to play Huntingdon Hall in Worcester, my local venue.

There are so many great songs. 'Funk And Fire' is a particular favourite and I have heard a few variations from the original CD.

It was 2017 before I got to see Iain live again, at the Kitchen Garden in Birmingham, a lovely place that was absolutely perfect for Iain's acoustic music. After the show, I had a short talk with Iain who is always willing to speak to his audience. He really is a top-class act.

I last saw Iain at Huntingdon Hall again, in 2023, where he appeared solo and played 'The Ballad of Gruene Hall', another great song. He's coming my way again with Andy Roberts on the Plainsong tour in October 2025. I'll be there and I'll bring as many others as I can muster so that they can all see a true legend of music.

THIRSTY EAR TAVERN
4 JANUARY 2001, COLUMBUS, OHIO

DEBRA WATKINS

I can't imagine my life without Iain Matthews. His music is so honest and real and it touches me down in my soul. Since 1976, when I first heard the album *Go For Broke* on my future husband's record player, his voice and music have captured my imagination. Through the eighties, married, children, no budget for records, we lost track of Iain (Ian). When my husband purchased his first computer (for work) at the end of the nineties, the first thing I said was, 'Look up Ian Matthews! It would be great if he's still alive and still making music!'

Debra Watkins almost fell out of her chair when a Plainsong concert was announced

Much to our delight there was a huge discography that we had been completely unaware of. On January 4, 2001 we travelled to Columbus, Ohio to see Iain at the Thirsty Ear Tavern for our first in person concert. It was surreal after all those years of not knowing what had happened to him. We met him and I think we told him we thought he was dead! (Oh dear!)

He was so sweet and the performance was so beautiful. Now,

after having read *Thro' My Eyes*, if I had known what he was going through, I wouldn't have been such a dork!

Our next concert to see Iain was September 2002 in Nashville at the Douglas Corner Cafe with Ad Vanderven. It was awesome! Then there was an October visit to the outskirts of Atlanta where he appeared alongside David Olney and Jeff Black. (I still have the poster.)

A special treat closer to home was a private house concert in Durham, North Carolina where he appeared with Andy Roberts. They started with 'Raider' and I almost fell out of my chair when Iain said it was a Plainsong concert. (For years we only had *Go For Broke* and Plainsong's *In Search of Amelia Earhart*. We had that Plainsong album on a cassette tape and it got played on every road trip we ever took. It's still our favourite album ever.)

That evening Iain and Andy featured the songs of Richard Fariña. Then we saw Iain again in 2019 in the NODA district of Charlotte, Virginia. Iain let me give him a hug and we told him how much we loved him. Again, so sweet! We saw him again two days later, once more in Durham, this time for an awesome solo performance.

Our last journey to see Iain was 10 October 2021 in Ardmore, Pennsylvania at The Living Room where he was joined by Jim Fogerty. It was such a special night.

'The Letter' is the greatest anti-war song ever written. The only thing really on my bucket list is to see Iain in person again. How much is enough? I'm counting on Iain continuing to make music as long as I live!

CAFE CAMBRINUS

11 SEPTEMBER 2001, HORST, THE NETHERLANDS

HENNY SMITS

My partner, Jan Duijf, is super-nervous. One of his musical heroes, Iain Matthews, is playing on his stage that night. Our regular helper has called in sick so we have asked someone else to

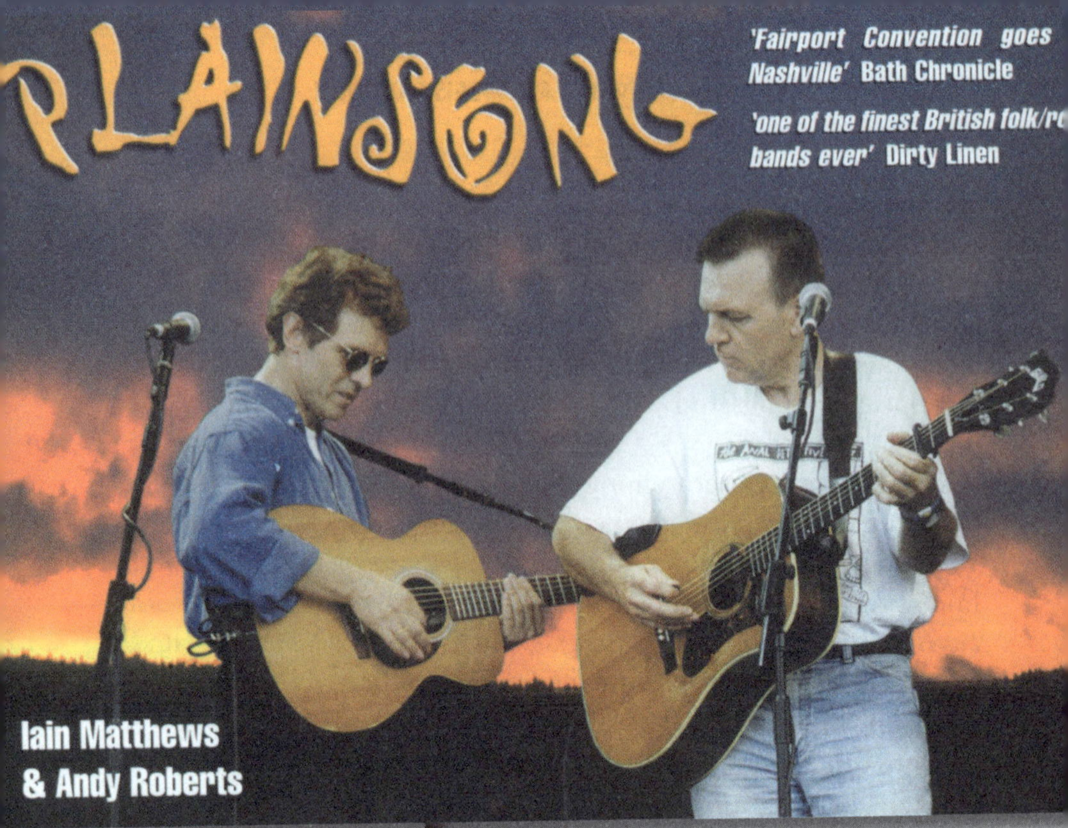

'Fairport Convention goes Nashville' Bath Chronicle

'one of the finest British folk/r[...]
bands ever' Dirty Linen

Iain Matthews
& Andy Roberts

Press Release

Release Date: March 27th 2000 **UK Distribution: Proper/Direct**

Iain Matthews
releases a new solo album
A Tiniest Wham
(Perfect Pitch PP006)
initial release comes with live bonus CD

As a founding member of Fairport Convention back in 1967, along with Richard Thompson, Ashley Hutchings and Simon Nicol, Matthews appeared on the bands' first three recordings (Fairport Convention, What We Did On Our Holidays and Unhalfbricking) until splitting in 1969 during the recording of the third LP. It had become obvious to him that the group's new-found folk/rock direction would involve him far less than its previous contemporary 'underground work'.

The next two years would yield three critically-acclaimed releases for his new band, Matthews Southern Comfort. Due to the fact he felt he wasn't yet ready for a solo career along with his desire to pursue his love of American country music, MSC provided the perfect vehicle for Matthews' musical growth. Some thirty years later, MSC's music continues to be held in high regard. The band went on to chart a #1 single with their version of Joni Mitchell's 'Woodstock'. At the pinnacle of the band's rise to stardom, Matthews found this overwhelming success to be both fulfilling and restricting. He quit the band to pursue a solo career.

The 1970's, from beginning to end, were extremely productive for Matthews – releasing 10 more albums as both solo and member of the band Plainsong. 1970's If You Saw Thro My Eyes would reunite him with his ex-Fairport mates, Richard Thompson and Sandy Denny. Matthews toured the US for the first time in support of this record, the band featuring Thompson, guitarist Andy Roberts and bassist Bob Ronga. Five records followed in the middle of the decade, three with Elektra (including one with Plainsong) and two with Columbia. 1978 brought us Stealin' Home thought by many as Matthews' finest effort of all time. Stealin' Home also yielded the Top 10 US hit 'Shake It'.

Musically, the early eighties proved discouraging for Matthews, and he gave up making music, choosing rather, to take a position as an A&R rep for Island Records and Windham Hill. About a year later, while appearing at the annual Fairport Convention reunion, Matthews began to emerge from the rut that had caused his departure from music. Jumping back in he came up with Walking A Changing Line, a collection of Jules Shear compositions.

Having relocated to Austin, 1990 kicked off the next chapter in Matthews' career. Gold Castle released Pure & Crooked, which included the wonderful cover of Peter Gabriel's 'Mercy Street'. Group efforts followed. Soon came several releases from Plainsong (w/Clive Gregson and Julian Dawson) and one from the country-rock flavoured outfit, Hamilton Pool. In 1994, Matthews signed with Austin label, Watermelon, releasing The Dark Ride followed by God Looked Down. While with Watermelon, he also produced Eric Taylor's debut album.

During the past few years, Iain has appeared on several high-profile releases; What's That I Hear – The Songs of Phil Ochs, (performing 'Flower Lady'), and Nanci Griffith's Other Voices, Too (performing a duet w/Nanci on 'Wall Of Death' and providing guitar/backing vocals on 'Who Knows Where The Time Goes'). He also toured the UK with Nanci in support of her album during the latter half of 1998. Also in 1998 saw the release of Excerpts From Swine Lake on Demon Records, finding Matthews once again, at the top of his game – vocally and musically. Which brings us pretty much up to date with Iain's latest album A Tiniest Wham on which he rediscovers his folk/rock roots with 12 new self penned songs. A UK tour is planned for later in the year.

For media enquiries please contact Mark Anstey at Unique Gravity
phone 01246-567712 fax 01246-567713
email: uniqgrav@globalnet.co.uk
Unique Gravity, P.O. Box 114, Chesterfield, Derbyshire S40 3YU, England

PLAINSONG

Iain Matthews & Andy Roberts

One of contemporary music's all-time great performers, **Iain Matthews'** sublime voice & songwriting are legendary. Co-founder of **Fairport Convention** with Richard Thompson, Ashley Hutchings & Simon Nicol, **Plainsong** with Andy Roberts, **Matthews Southern Comfort** and the #1 hit version of Joni Mitchell's *Woodstock*. Multi-instrumentalist partner **Andy Roberts** helped form terminally mad **The Liverpool Scene** and featured with **Pink Floyd, Cat Stevens, Monty Python, The Bonzos, GRIMMS, Roy Harper, Billy Connolly, The Albion Band, Rolf Harris, Hank Wangford**. On tour with a new recording and a sumptuous feast of acoustic power, lip-smacking harmony & gut-driven numbers. *'An obscene number of great songs!'*

Photograph: Ernst Bozwinkel · Postcard: JADED

April 2001

20	**BANBURY The Mill**	0129
21	**BURTON-ON-TRENT The Brewhouse** www.brewhouse.co.uk	0129
22	**LONDON Ronnie Scott's**	(CC) 020 7
23	**CHESTER Alexandra's Jazz Theatre** www.alexandersjazz.com	0124
25	**BIRMINGHAM mac** www.mac-birmingham.org.uk	0121
26	**WORCESTER Huntingdon Hall** www.huntingdonhall.com	0190
27	**MORECAMBE The Platform**	0152
28	**BURY The Met** www.metarts.demon.co.uk	0161
29	**BEVERLEY Picture Playhouse**	0148
30	**LEEDS New Roscoe Room** www.liveinleeds.com	(CC) 0113

May 2001

1	**BRISTOL QEH** www.qehtheatre-bristol.co.uk	(CC) 0117
2	**TRURO The Hall for Cornwall** with Norma Waterson & Martin Carthy www.hallforcornwall.demon.co.uk	0187
3	**BARNET The Bull Arts Centre** www.thebull.org.uk	020 8
4	**ABERDEEN Lemon Tree** www.lemontree.org	0122
	PERTH Bein Inn Acoustic Sessions www.beininn.com	0157
	GLASGOW The Tron www.tron.co.uk	0141

IAIN MATTHEWS

"Possessed of one of the most gorgeous voices in popular music .... He is a musical treasure" (Austin Chronicle)

"What Richard Thompson is to folk-rock guitar, Iain Matthews is to folk-rock voice"

Appearing at: The Albert Hole
the Albert Inn, West Street, Bedminster, Bristol
Wednesday 12 November
£5/£4.50 ~ 8.30 pm ~ reservations tel. 0117 966 1968

with Ad Vanderveen
A Tiniest Wham

UK TOUR, 8-22 OCT'00

'basically your diamond gig of the month'
***What's On** Birmingham*

'Fairport Convention goes to Nashville' R[...]
Bath Chronicle

One of contemporary music's finest singers, Iain Matthews[...] guitar playing are legendary. Co-founder of **Fairport Conv[...]** Richard Thompson, Ashley Hutchings & Simon Nicol, **Plai[...]** Roberts, **Matthews Southern Comfort** of course and the [...] Joni Mitchell's Woodstock. A solo career that's spanned 3 [...] decades and tours last year with **Nanci Griffith's** *Other Vo[...]* **Plainsong's** *New Place Now*. Long-time resident in Texas[...] Scunthorpe visits Britain with his new album *A Tiniest Wha[...]* more tingling acoustic power, semi-clad emotion & lip-sma[...] than is legally permitted.

http://leden.tref.nl/~tenho003/matthews/inde[...]

S RELEASE

AINSONG

Matthews+Andy Roberts

rt Convention goes to Nashville' **Bath Chronicle**
f the finest British folk/rock bands ever' **Dirty Linen** USA

One of contemporary music's all-time great performers, **Iain Matthews'** sublime voice & are legendary. Co-founder of **Fairport Convention** with Richard Thompson, Ashley Hutchings & l, **Plainsong** with Andy Roberts, **Matthews Southern Comfort** and the #1 hit version of Joni Woodstock. Multi-instrumentalist partner **Andy Roberts** helped form terminally mad **The Liverpool** featured with **Pink Floyd, Cat Stevens, Monty Python, The Bonzos, GRIMMS, Roy Harper, Billy The Albion Band, Rolf Harris, Hank Wangford**. Iain & Andy tour with new cd **From A To B** and on- e a sumptuous feast of acoustic power, lip-smacking harmony & gut-driven numbers. *'An obscene great songs!'* Let it roll! www.iainmatthews.com and http://freespace.virgin.net/dream.tree

ril'01

BANBURY The Mill	01295 279002
BURTON-ON-TRENT The Brewhouse www.brewhouse.co.uk	01283 516030
LONDON Ronnie Scott's	020 7771 2000 (CC)
CHESTER Alexandra's Jazz Theatre www.alexandersjazz.com	01244 340005
BIRMINGHAM mac www.mac-birmingham.org.uk	0121 440 3836
WORCESTER Huntingdon Hall www.huntingdonhall.com	01905 611427
MORECAMBE The Platform	01524 582803
BURY The Met www.metarts.demon.co.uk	0161 761 2216
BEVERLEY Picture Playhouse	01482 867430
LEEDS New Roscoe Room www.liveinleeds.com	0113 245 5570 (CC)

ay'01

BRISTOL QEH www.qehtheatre-bristol.co.uk	0117 987 7877
TRURO The Hall for Cornwall www.hallforcornwall.co.uk with Norma Waterson & Martin Carthy	01872 262466
BARNET The Bull Arts Centre www.thebull.org.uk	020 8449 0048
ABERDEEN Lemon Tree www.lemontree.org	01244 642230
PERTH Bein Inn Acoustic Sessions www.beininn.com	01577 830216
GLASGOW The Tron www.tron.co.uk	0141 552 4267

AINSONG

Guest: Ad Vanderveen

'Fairport Convention goes to Nashville' Bath Chronicle

by singer songwriter & Fairport co-founder Iain Matthews and mentalist Andy Roberts (Liverpool Scene, Pink Floyd, Hank , **Plainsong** reclaims Julian Dawson (also Del Amitri, Lucinda he Roches) and Matthews Southern Comfort 'Woodstock' Griffiths (Hank Marvin, Al Stewart…). Four great voices and to bust with guitars, slide, banjo, dulcimer, harmonicas, bass. New album produced by Andy Metcalfe of Squeeze & lus singer songwriter and guitarist Ad Vanderveen *'a dead ssic period Neil Young'* Record Collector

003

GHAM - mac	0121 440 3838
HILL - Arts Centre	01440 714140
ESTER - Theatre Royal	01962 840440
H - New Wolsey Theatre	01473 295900

03

N - Shire Hall	01840 214220
F BAY - The Point	029 20 230130
VENNY - Borough Theatre	01873 850805
LD - Guildhall	01543 262223
N'S - Citadel	01744 735436
AMPTON - Royal Theatre	01604 624811
R - Telford's Warehouse	01244 390090
NHAM - Town Hall	01242 227979
N - Borderline	020 7395 0777
- Phoenix	01392 667 080
AMBE - The Platform	01524 582803
STLE-UPON-TYNE - Opera House	0191 232 0899
RGH - Queen's Hall	0131 668 2019

photo by Karl Maria Hofer - design by JADED

theiainadventure

IAIN MATTHEWS + AD VANDERVEEN

One of contemporary music's finest singer songwriters, Iain Matthews' sublime voice & tender tough guitar are legendary. Co-founder of Fairport Convention with Richard Thompson, Ashley Hutchings & Simon Nicol, Plainsong with Andy Roberts and Matthews Southern Comfort. The #1 hit version of Joni Mitchell's Woodstock. A solo career that's spanned 3 incredible decades and tours last ye Elliott Murphy… www.iainmatthe Vanderveen (gtr & harmonica) whose The O'Neils, recordings with Flaco made him a lot of friends. www.adv

April 2002

4 CARDIGAN Theatr Mwldan www.mw
5 BANBURY The Mill Arts Centre
6 DERBY Guildhall Theatre www.guild
7 GLASGOW Tron Theatre www.tron.c
8 PERTH The Bein Inn www.beininn.c
9 LINCOLN The Black Horse, Nettlehan
10 YORK Pocklington Civic Arts Centre w

IAIN MATTHEWS & AD VANDERVEEN
THE IAIN AD*VENTURE* 2002

The stylish Norwegian church in Cardiff Bay sees the equally stylish Iain Matthews and Ad Vanderveen visiting on 23rd April during their twenty-date UK tour.

Iain Matthews has been justly described as one of contemporary music's finest singer songwriters, with a sublime voice and a tender tough guitar. He has a rich musical history being a founder member of Fairport Convention, before forming Matthews Southern Comfort, taking his version of "Woodstock" to number one, a song still regularly heard on radio today. Teaming up with Andy Roberts to form Plainsong, they released one album, "In Search Of Amelia Earhart", before Iain moved to America and resumed his solo career. He now has over 50 albums as a solo artist and group member to his credit. Iain based himself in Amsterdam 18 months ago, where he has made several flourishing musical partnerships, in particular with Ad Vanderveen, also working with Eliza Gilkyson, Elliott Murphy, and alongside Andy Roberts in a rejuvinated Plainsong, and solo Iain keeps himself busy both in the studio and live.

***'That voice, one of the best in popular music'* Oklahoma Gazette** *Mike Easterling*

Guitarist, singer and songwriter **Ad Vanderveen**, led the county rock group Personnel in the early 1990's, who enjoyed great success throughout Europe with two albums, "Personnel Only" and "Continuing stories". The latter hailed as one of the most significant records to come out of Holland. In 1993 he started his solo career, which has so far produced six albums. As a counterpoint to this intimate singer songwriter material he also formed "The O'Neills", a bunch of old friends with a passion for the songs of Neil Young, where he gets to really rock and roll.

'A dead ringer for classic period Neil Young' Record Collector

As a duo they have released a live album, **"The Iain Adventure"** and played regularly throughout Holland and further a field, including a UK tour in 2000, when they received a warm welcome, and left audiences very happy indeed.

" Basically your diamond gig of the month' What's On Birmingham *Mike Davies"*

This is their first visit to Cardiff where the acoustics of this very attractive, wood lined church will suit the duo perfectly.

Ian Burgess Apr 2002

The tour coincides with the Perfect Pitch release of
More Than A Song, the album recorded as a trio with Eliza Gilkyson,
and re-releases of
Iain Matthews' **A Tiniest Wham;** and Plainsong's **In Search of Amelia Earhart.**

Press photos of Iain & Ad www.uktouring.org.uk click on Iain Matthews, click on Gallery

'quite simply and without any hyp
Melody Maker

'one of the finest British folk/rock b
Dirty Linen (USA)

www.uktouring.org.uk/plainsong

PLAINSONG

heiainadventure

N MATTHEWS

priest of British folk' City Life Dave Tuxford

AD VANDERVEEN

'a dead ringer for classic period Neil Young' Record Collecto

help us out for the night.

As of 5pm our phone is ringing off the hook. The world is in great turmoil because of the airplanes that flew into the Twin Towers with disastrous consequences. Everyone wants to know if the concert that night is going to take place. Mobile phones aren't yet in fashion so we can't get in touch with the musicians.

When Iain arrives, he has not heard the news. When Jan asks him if he is still going to play, he answers drily, 'Of course, it's my job…'.

That night Iain kept noticing the young woman helping us behind the bar. I'm not gonna tell you everything here, but a romance blossomed between Iain and Marly. They married and had a beautiful young daughter named Luca. Sounds a little bit like a fairytale, doesn't it?

E-WERK

2001/2002, ERLANGEN, GERMANY

JÖRG SZAMEITAT

It must have been in 2001 or 2002. I was a student of Sociology in Erlangen and living near a cool kind of basement club called E-Werk. One night, I was surprised to see Iain Matthews there onstage with some other guy (who I later found out was the great Elliott Murphy, a legend in his own right). They were promoting their album *La Terre Commune*, the only one they did together, as far as I know, and which I bought probably that night.

I did not know the album then, but I recognised the name Iain Matthews from his song 'Horse Left In The Rain' (from 1998's *Excerpts From Swine Lake*). The ballad had been on a CD sampler with the then-current issue of *Rolling Stone Germany* (or maybe a few issues before that) and I just loved the song. It had been love at first listen.

After I heard it, I tried to play it on the guitar, but couldn't figure out one specific chord. This was before YouTube, so there were no video tutorials to look up. My ears and fingers were all I had, and they just hit their limits. So that night at the E-Werk, as I watched Iain and Elliott sing and play their last songs, a simple yet frightening thought popped into my head: 'Why not just ask him? He's here, I'm here... it's never going to be as easy as this, right?' (How could I possibly have foreseen YouTube?) The very source was just a few metres away!

It was love at first listen for Jörg Szameitat (Antje Wiech)

After the concert was over, I plucked up all the courage I had, went down to the stage, introduced myself, and flat-out asked Iain about 'Horse Left In The Rain'. And he picked up a wonderful-sounding acoustic guitar and ran down the song from his memory to get to the crucial chord. Sad thing is, I don't remember it. He definitely showed it to me, but I was, I guess, what you call starstruck. I stood there, probably looking pretty stupid, and heard him talk and play this beautiful song... and didn't pay attention to the damn chord at all.

I thanked him very much and went home very happy. I also came back a few minutes later because I wanted to give Iain a CD of my band and see if he could do anything for us, but he kindly refused. Can't blame a guy for trying, though, eh? Boy, we could have gone places if Iain had just taken our CD to his record company or whoever.

But who am I kidding? We never had a song like 'Horse Left In The Rain' under our belt. Maybe I should try to play it again one of these days and take another shot at that chord. Or simply look it up. Though YouTube will never be as cool as the actual songwriter showing it to me. Thanks, Iain!

PUB GIG

2004, NETTLEHAM, LINCOLNSHIRE, UK

STEVE JACKSON

I was a fresh-faced youth when I first became aware of Ian (as he was then known) via his Matthews Southern Comfort 'Woodstock' hit single. On *Top Of The Pops*, he mostly sang with his eyes closed. I liked his melodic voice and that he had a pedal steel player in his band, which was not a usual add-on in those days. I went out the next day and bought the single. (I still have it.) It's probably what I'd refer to as his pop star period. I didn't really know anything about his early Fairport days until later on.

Next stop was browsing in a record shop where I purchased a copy of *Some Days You Eat The Bear* when it was first released in 1974 and after the album sleeve caught my eye. I investigated further and soon discovered he had a good ear when it came to choosing material. That record has stood the test of time and is still one of his best. Working backwards, I then discovered Plainsong.

My first encounter with Iain live was when he was booked by the landlord to play an intimate pub gig on my doorstep in my village, Nettleham in Lincolnshire, in 2004. He was accompanied by Dutch guitarist Ad Vanderveen. By chance I bumped into Iain the day before as he wandered around the village centre trying to find the overnight accommodation he'd booked. I pointed him in the right direction.

Steve Jackson was a fresh-faced youth when he discovered Iain

I'd actually done a telephone interview with him for the local paper a week or so prior to this, where I discovered his admiration for Miles

Davis and jazz music.

I've seen him in concert a couple of times since (also in Lincolnshire) along with the re-imagined version of Matthews Southern Comfort. He's very down-to-earth, easy to talk to and a normal, likeable guy. What's more he's produced some of my favourite music over a long career, and continues to do so.

BEIN INN

SOMETIME IN 2004, GLENFARG, UK

DAVID MUNDELL

Iain has played for Mundell Music on many occasions. I owned The Famous Bein Inn, which was located in the middle of a wooded glen in central Scotland. One time the legendary Terry Reid played a gig there and, post-gig, there were around four of us in the bar. We were in normal conversation when Terry heard the music playing in the background and looked at me and said, 'Who is singing this? This is my song.' It was 'The Frame'. I informed Terry that the singer was Iain Matthews. He said he had never heard Iain's version before. He loved it. I let him know that Iain had played for me a few times over the years and that I had Iain's phone number. I called Iain there and then and he had a long conversation on the phone with Terry.

IN THE WOODS FESTIVAL

22 NOVEMBER 2005, AMERSFOORT, THE NETHERLANDS

BART HENDRIKS, PROMOTER

Being a music lover all my life I knew and liked the music of Iain very much, from his days as Matthews Southern Comfort, as Plainsong and his solo stuff. I have seen him play many times over the years.

In August 2000, a one-time event organised with friends grew

Bart Hendriks guided Iain to a gas station

into a real phenomenon, an informal low-key stage for real music, where visitors came to listen to music and respect the artist. This was a boyhood dream of mine.

The first time Iain played at *In The Woods* was November 2005. Iain played that night with the likes of Lorrie Singer, Bradley Kopp, Karen Abrahams and Richard Bowden. I had to tell myself I wasn't dreaming as I had this legend on my little stage.

The next time was even more intense. It was 6 December 2006, a cold and grey day. After the soundcheck and dinner, there was still time before the show was to begin. Iain brought up the fact that, living in the south, he had a long drive home after the gig. He said he was running out of gas, and it made it so much easier not to stop at a gas station after the show on his way home.

I offered to guide him to the nearest gas station. During the drive we became two human beings rather than a musician and a fan. For the first time we had a real talk. In his opening up he allowed me to open up. Since then, his music has grown on me even more. The magic of really meeting someone does not break the spell of beauty in the art and the music.

Iain has played many times at *In The Woods* over the years, in different combinations such as Matthews Southern Comfort, with Ad Van der Veen, Eric Andersen, Egbert Derix, Andy Roberts and Mark Griffiths and others. It's always a joy. Keep on doing what you do!

LA POMME D'EVE

6 FEBRUARY 2007, PARIS, FRANCE

HERVÉ OUDET

I must admit that until 2001, when he recorded *La Terre Commune* with Elliott Murphy – who I had been a fan of since 1977 – Iain Matthews had escaped my radar. We met for the first time when the pair played an intimate set at Espace Kiron in Paris and I was hooked by his voice and guitar playing. When I started my *Acoustic in pAris* series in 2004, it became obvious that Iain would be on the list of artists I wanted to present to the small but dedicated audience of La Pomme d'Eve, a 13th century vaulted cellar located close the Pantheon.

Iain performed there for the first time in February of 2007 with two young

Hervé Oudet is a fan

American songwriters, Danny Schmidt and Kreg Visselman. Although I was not familiar with Iain's repertoire, his voice and supple right hand stroked me and to this day, I would rank these two nights in my top three of the *Acoustic in pAris* adventure. Plus, Elliott sat in for a couple of songs, including on Dylan's 'Blind Willie McTell'.

But I am obviously not the only one to hold these two nights as unforgettable, as British label Cherry Red decided to include three songs from the first night in their *Thro' My Eyes* five-disc boxset. And apparently Iain liked it too, as he said he wanted to return. And he did, in December of the same year, this time with long-time partner Andy Roberts in the Plainsong Lite configuration. Six months later, when time came to call it a night on the *Acoustic in pAris* series, Iain immediately agreed to take the train to Paris and join folk legend Eric Andersen and Dutch guitar extraordinaire Ad Vanderveen with their respective wives Inge Andersen and Kersten De Ligny for the last shows.

While both concerts were memorable, the last encore of the second night left a special mark in my memory as Iain and Eric invited me to sing on Eric's 'Close The Door Lightly', an appropriate choice!

In the autumn of 2024, a quick discussion on Facebook sparked the idea of a show in Paris. I had recently discovered a club across the street from where I live called Café du Village, and had organised two shows there in a new iteration of the *Acoustic in pAris* series. This time, I got to know Iain better on a personal basis, as well as his dear wife Marly. When I greeted them at the Gare du Nord station, I could see his smile on his face and I knew I had a new friend. On 19 January 2025, the 120 patrons who attended the show absolutely loved Iain's solo acoustic performance, during which he played many songs off his most recent album, *How Much Is Enough*, and some classics from his repertoire: 'Seven Bridges Road', 'Woodstock', 'From Galway To Graceland' and 'Mercy Street'.

And guess what? We're planning on a Plainsong Lite show in 2026, again with Andy Roberts. I can't wait!

PASTORALE AU PARVIS FESTIVAL
14 JULY 2007, NISSE, THE NETHERLANDS

ELLY KELLNER

I was one of the artists invited to play at the Pastorale Au Parvis festival in the town of Nisse. As I sang a couple of my songs, I noticed a man standing right in front of the stage, listening intently. In his arms he held a sweet, little girl and afterwards we spoke briefly. He turned out to be Iain Matthews, with his daughter, and I had just missed his performance at the festival. We exchanged contact details and when I got home it started to dawn on me who this Iain was. He was the singer I had heard so many times on my favourite version of the song 'Woodstock'. I had never quite registered that it was his band Matthews Southern Comfort that had recorded that version. Now I felt a bit silly.

About a year later, Iain invited me to play at two special evenings of Iain Matthews Common Grounds Series. That was such an uplifting experience for me to have an audience that really listened. It really built up my confidence. After that, I started my own band, even though Iain said I didn't need one. Later, in 2011, I received Iain's call asking if I would like to join

Elly Kellner saw a man in the audience who turned out to be Iain

his band, Matthews Southern Comfort, on tour, together with BJ Baartmans and Bart de Win.

It was such a great honour to go on the road with these musicians. In the two years that followed we sang many beautiful harmonies, performed and hung out together. The tour brought us to Italy, the United Kingdom and of course The Netherlands. It was such an adventure and even though touring was at times stressful I learned so much along the way.

Being on the road together, we all spent a lot of time in each other's presence. After a while Iain felt almost like a father figure to me. I appreciated how balanced, direct and calm he was. He still is someone I love listening to; his voice so warm and soothing. Every single time I shared the stage with Iain I was aware of how unique the experience was. It was something I could have only dreamt of as a little girl. I still feel very happy about all the wonderful songs we sang together and thankful for all the moments shared.

SPIRIT OF 66

15 JULY 2007, VERVIERS, BELGIUM

CHRIS KLEEVEN

Iain and I went to see David Surkamp's band, Pavlov's Dog, at the well-known venue Spirit of 66. David and Iain had formed the short-lived band Hi-Fi during the early eighties in Seattle. Pavlov's Dog were a kind of seventies prog rock band with David singing in a peculiar high-pitched voice with a very fast vibrato almost all the time. (Their most well-known song 'Julia' is on YouTube.)

We went early to Verviers so we would be able to go for a cup of coffee in the city before the show. To our surprise, the concert started at 7.30pm so we were only just in time. The show was very well attended and was sold out.

Mid-show, David suddenly shouted out, 'Iain, are you here? And if you are, please come to the stage!' Iain looked at me and said, 'Don't you dare say a word.' He obviously did not want to go on stage and we stayed at the back of the venue. He later explained to David that he had no idea which song he could have sung with them.

After the show, we met David and the two of them spent 45 minutes having their pictures taken by members of the audience and signing copies of albums by both Pavlov's Dog and Iain. I had no idea they were that well-known and popular in that French-speaking part of Belgium.

WHELAN'S

9 FEBRUARY 2010, DUBLIN, IRELAND

FRITS WIELENS

It all started with the purchase of the Dutch release of 'The Best Of Island' (*You Can All Join In*), a budget-priced sampler. One of the tracks was 'Meet On The Ledge' by Fairport Convention. When, in January 1971, Fairport embarked on a short Dutch tour, I was lucky to see them in Enschede. I was unaware that, by then, their line up and repertoire had changed from the track on the Island sampler. It was the four-piece *Angel Delight* line up and I quickly acquired Fairport's back catalogue, including *What We Did On Our Holidays*. It was on this album that I first heard of Iain. After Iain's departure from Fairport, he recorded his debut solo album, *Matthews Southern Comfort*, which had a few Fairporters backing him. I've been following Iain's career ever since.

Frits Wielens discovered Iain via Fairport Convention on a sampler album

After leaving Southern Comfort, Iain and Andy Roberts

formed Plainsong and their outstanding LP, *In Search Of Amelia Earheart*, has been an all-time favourite of mine ever since it was released. I managed to catch them in 1972, during a Dutch tour, in Winterswijk on a Sunday afternoon.

Iain hasn't been a frequent visitor to Ireland, where I have lived since 1978, but I did see him twice in Whelan's, in Dublin, once with the reformed Plainsong and once solo. It was that latter appearance, while I was waiting at the bar for my pint of Guinness to settle, that Iain appeared beside me and ordered a drink and a packet of crisps. Noticing his disappointment when no crisps were available and knowing that a shop was just beside the venue, I offered to get him a packet, which he was happy to accept. It was a lovely gig with a nice version of 'Brown Eyed Girl'.

That was 15 years ago. Time for another Dublin visit, Iain – and I'll bring the crips!

OSCAR'S GARDEN PARTY

7 AUGUST 2011, DORDRECHT, THE NETHERLANDS

KJETIL GJØEN

I'm from Norway and have been a fan of Iain Matthews for more than 50 years. It started with the album *If You Saw Thro' My Eyes*, a record bought by chance on sale in 1973. I was 16 years old and thought the guy on the cover looked cool. This record has been in regular rotation for almost 52 years. I eventually realised that Iain had a stellar team of musicians on this production, such as Richard Thompson, Sandy Denny, Tim Renwick, Keith Tippet and Andy Roberts.

I later bought all the music from Iain and his various music projects, including a lot of records by Fairport Convention and others who were inspired by this groundbreaking group.

In 2011, my wife Else and I were looking for a holiday destination for the summer. We thought of The Netherlands, where we had been several times. I checked out possible concerts and specifically searched for Iain Matthews concerts, and found one where he was playing with Egbert Derix at something called Oscar's Garden Party. I managed to get two tickets to the concert.

It took time to drive from Ålesund in Norway to Oscar's Garden Party in The Netherlands. We checked into a hotel in Rotterdam, where we had friends nearby. On the day of the show we had a good breakfast and relaxed for a few hours, believing that the concert would start that evening. By chance we discovered that the concert started in the middle of the day and so we drove around at breakneck speed to reach the concert. We Googled to try and find information about the

Kjetil undertook a mammoth trek to 'gatecrash' a private party

concert venue, but without success. There was no information at all about possible concert venues with the name Oscar's Garden Party.

We took the chance to drive towards an address I had received by email. But there was traffic chaos out of Rotterdam, with detours and points where the GPS didn't work. We ended up in a huge traffic jam outside a football stadium and i had to turn and drive against the flow of traffic. Time was passing...

Else checked the address of the party again and thought it best to set the GPS to the address of a hospital next door. I was getting stressed and my face must have changed colour several times while Else gave well-meaning advice about driving direction and traffic patterns. Things became quite tense as I imagined our journey from Norway to The Netherlands was going to end with us missing the concert, the main purpose of our trip.

Eventually we found the hospital that was supposedly right next to Oscar's Garden Party. Else pointed the way, but I was not in the mood to follow good advice. I came up with a cascade of words in which I expressed my clear disgust that she would admit me to 'a fucking hospital'. I certainly did not need any acute psychiatric treatment. But Else saw a group of people who looked like they were going to a concert, asked them and – yes – they were going to see Iain Matthews. But they said it was a private garden party!

We made it to the concert. Oscar and his wife were perfect hosts and welcomed us warmly. Because we had come all the way from Norway, we were immediately introduced to Iain. He also welcomed us kindly but I was completely starstruck after hearing his music all these years and couldn't say anything remotely sensible. Else kept her cool and asked if he really was Iain Matthews? He said no, he was just a good copy!

This was one of our best concert experiences ever. Iain has an exceptionally beautiful voice, with an enormous collection of good songs in stock. The interaction with Egbert Derix on keyboards was impressive. It was a different musical setting than what I was used to, but that's Iain in a nutshell. He, like many other of our best musicians, is constantly searching for something new and better. And that is precisely what makes him a unique and exciting artist. We have seen Iain several times since then and have never been disappointed.

UNION CHAPEL

16 SEPTEMBER 2012, ISLINGTON, LONDON, UK

COLIN ADAMS

I first encountered Iain Matthews in 1972, when on one Sunday evening as a young engineering student I was getting things prepared for the start of my college week at Harrow College of Technology and Art and was listening to the BBC Radio 1 *On Air* sessions. In that one moment I was hooked into the wonderful sound of folk songs with some great vocal harmonies and the silky and mesmerising voice of Iain Matthews. I didn't know it at the time, but listening to this band called Plainsong set me on the path of a musical journey with Iain for the next 50 years that was to become a significant part of my life.

In those days there was no internet and the only social media was through interaction with friends, newspapers and music magazines such as the *NME*, so at some point I made my way to the local record shop searching out any albums recorded by Iain. In the shop I came across *In Search Of Amelia Earhart* by Plainsong which became one of the most played albums on my record player.

A few years later, I came across Iain's album called *Journeys From Gospel Oak* in cassette form. This was an ideal format as I could play this in the car on my journeys to and from college and at the weekends on my cassette player at home. Along with *Amelia Earhart*, it is still one of my favourite albums as well as so many of Iain's musical catalogue. Iain truly has a great ability to write so many amazing songs with wonderful melodies, and he tops each one with some amazing lyrics.

Being a dedicated fan over such a long period, I have been

CELEBRATING 45 YEARS OF PLAINSONG

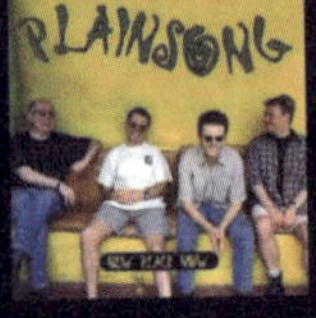

THANK YOU
IAIN MATTHEWS ANDY ROBERTS
MARK GRIFFITHS
JULIAN DAWSON CLIVE GREGSON
DAVE RICHARDS BOB RONGA
ROGER SWALLOW

Plainsong Lite
Iain Matthews & Andy Rober
UK tour October 2025
Special guest Julian Dawson

October
Saturday 11th. Village Hall Brimfield Herefordshire

Sunday 12th. Katie Fitzgeralds Stourbridge

Wednesday 15th. Huntingdon Hall Worcester

Thursday 16th. The Globe Theatre. Hay On Wye

Friday 17th. St Peter's Church Huddersfield

Saturday 18th. Elford Village Hall Tamworth

Sunday 19th. The Cat Club Pontefract

Wednesday 22nd. Cabanas Live Barry

Thursday 23rd. Kitchen Garden Kings Heath. Birmingham

Friday 24th. Cruck Barn Appletreewick. Skipton.

Saturday 25th. Ropewalk Barton Upon Humber

Sunday 26th. Arkenstal Centre Ely

Wednesday 29th. Woolton Village Club. Liverpool

Thursday 30th. Twyford Church Twyford

Friday 31st. The Sound Lounge Sutton. London.

Nove
Saturda
Mary's
Brig

Sunda
Whitstabl
Music
Whits

The *Loft*
at
Limerick Golf Club
(room above Sandtrap SportsPub)

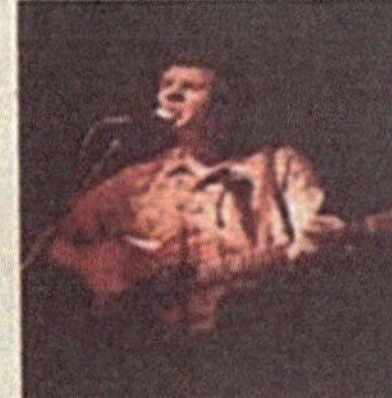

IAIN
MATTHEWS
First United States Performance in 5-years!

Thursday, September 30, 2004
7:00 pm
Tickets: $10.00/person
765 N. Lewis Road
Limerick, PA 19468
610-495-6945 or 610-495-5567
Cash Food and Cash Bar available
Call for Reservations

FOUNDING MEMBER OF FAIRPORT CONVENTION

AND MATTHEW SOUTHERN COMFORT

Iain Matthews
W/JIM FOGART

THE Sandtrap BAR & GRILLE
AT THE LIMERICK GOLF CLUB
765 N. Lewis Rd., Limerick, PA 19468

FREE ADMISSION
SERVING FOOD

1 MILE NORTH LIMERICK/LINF EXIT OF 422

FRIDAY SEPTEMBER 1
5:45 - 8:00
Happy Hour On our outside patio OR INSIDE IF IT RAINS
(610) 495-5567

FAREWELL TOUR 2012
PLAINSONG
MATTHEWS • ANDY ROBERTS • JULIAN DAWSON • MARK GRIFFITHS
WEDNESDAY 12 SEPTEMBER
BIRMINGHAM • TOWN HALL
THURSDAY 13 SEPTEMBER
HEAD • THE SAGE GATESHEAD
FRIDAY 14 SEPTEMBER
SOUTH PETHERTON • DAVID HALL
SATURDAY 15 SEPTEMBER
RYE • RYE ARTS FESTIVAL
NDAY 16 SEPTEMBER • LONDON UNION CHAPEL
NIGHTJAR PROMOTIONS
CELEBRATING 45 YEARS OF MUSIC TOGETHER AND THE MUSIC OF RICHARD FARINA...
PLAINSONG
IAIN MATTHEWS
ANDY ROBERTS
FEATURING SPECIAL GUESTS KEVIN ELLIOTT, JOHN COPPESS, AND JEFF ARRIGO
SUNDAY, SEPTEMBER 25, 2016~5p
INDEPENDENT MEDIA CENTER
202 S. BROADWAY
URBANA, IL
$20
Iain Matthews w/ Jim Fogarty
Havertown, PA - House Concert
Sunday, April 14th, 2019 @ 7:30 PM
1019 Allston Rd, Havertown, PA 19083
Suggested donation: $20 per person (BYOB)
RSVP: Jesse Hubley, jessehubley@gmail.com, 610-223-7957
prepay via PayPal for reserved seating
See a living legend up close in an intimate setting!
Later that same year
Matthews Southern Comfort
IAIN MATTHEWS
'T FADE AWAY THE ROCKBURGH YEARS, 1978-1984
Ian Matthews
Plainsong
FOLLOWING AMELIA
THE 1972 RECORDINGS & MORE

lucky enough to attend many of his concerts and to see and talk to Iain after each performance is the icing on the cake. Perhaps the most memorable gig was in September 2012 when Iain played the magical Union Chapel, Islington, billed as Plainsong's 'farewell tour' and with Andy Roberts, Julian Dawson and Mark Griffiths in the line-up.

I remember it being a memorable concert not only for the musical content and acoustics but also for the fact we were lucky enough to meet Iain's daughter Darcy and have our photograph taken with her, Iain and the rest of the band.

ASSEMBLY ROOMS

23 OCTOBER 2013, DERBY, UK

RICHARD ELY

I saw Iain Matthews in concert twice, both times in 2013. The first time was at Derby Assembly Rooms – or what was standing in for it, as I believe the venue was gutted by fire around that time. This was the reconstituted version of Matthews Southern Comfort, with Iain fronting an all-Dutch band, part of which played a support set.

The concert included re-arranged versions of some Matthews Southern Comfort repertoire, including (of course) 'Woodstock', for which the band was augmented by the original Matthews Southern Comfort bass player. That was an added plus to a very pleasant evening.

About a month later, I saw Iain again, this time playing a support slot to Al Stewart in Halifax (West Yorkshire, not Nova Scotia!). I think this event ended with everyone, including Iain, on stage playing the encores.

I've also read Iain's memoir, which was a real story of struggling against the odds to establish himself in one of the most competitive industries on earth. I'm impressed that Iain has been able to achieve so much, without having rich parents to bail him out or 'old money' to fall back on. I'm particularly appreciative of his work with an early version of Fairport Convention. I know his involvement with that band didn't end well, but the style they explored on *What We Did On Our Holidays* was very rewarding and I sometimes wish they'd continued in that vein. 'Book Song' is one of my favourite Fairport songs and Iain's duet with Sandy Denny on 'I'll Keep It With Mine' is one for the ages.

SCHOOL HALL

MARCH 2013, FEATHERSTONE, UK

EGBERT DERIX

I first met Iain Matthews in The Netherlands in 2003 where he saw me play with the Searing Quartet and asked me to join his jubilee tour of his album, *If You Saw Thro' My Eyes*. We did the tour and starting writing together. We made three albums: *Joy Mining* with the Searing Quartet and *In the Now* and *Afterwords* as Iain Matthews & Egbert Derix. *In The Now* was released by Universal on the Verve label. Between 2003 and 2016 we played in The Netherlands, Belgium, Germany, Denmark, the UK and the US. We played the Cropedy Festival as a duo and co-wrote the songs for Iain's solo album *The Art Of Obscurity*. Iain made a guest appearance on my solo album, *Paintings In Minor Lila*, alongside Supertramp's sax player John Helliwell and Marillion singers Fish and Steve Hogarth.

Egbert Derix feels blessed to have worked with Iain (Jan de Bruyn)

In March 2013, Iain and I played a couple of concerts in England. We did this often, but the reason for this small tour was to play at a benefit concert to raise money for the purchase of instruments for students from a primary school. The benefit concert had already taken place for a number of years under the name

'Billie's Violin'. Billie was the daughter of an English journalist and writer with many beautiful books to his name. In one of his books, he described his passion for music, but as a reader you are suddenly surprised by a very intense story about the death of his daughter Billie. In the book he described how he, nine-year-old Billie and her twin brother went out for a day of canoeing on the River Wye. What should have been a beautiful family day turned into a tragedy. The canoe turned over in the wild water and the father tried to get both his children out of the fast-flowing river but only managed to bring his son to the side while his son screamed 'save Billie first!' He went in search of his daughter but in vain. Billie's lifeless body was only found a few days after, a long way further into the river.

Billie loved music and played the violin. Her parents had named her after the jazz singer Billie Holiday. In memory of their daughter, they decided to turn part of their grief into action, to mean something to others. This resulted in the initiative of the annual benefit concert 'Billie's Violin'.

In the evening after the concert, I sat with Billie's father at the kitchen table in their house. Billie's twin brother played the piano and asked if I had some suggestions for him to improvise on the Miles Davis tune 'All Blues'. The father talked about Billie and what a happy and musical child she was. He talked about how nice the day of canoeing had begun. He described in detail the drama that took place afterwards and the consequences for the family; the lawsuits about who was responsible for the tragic accident. Should the owner of the canoes have warned them better? Or should Billie's father have been more careful? Whatever the answer to those questions, they wouldn't bring back Billie, and the grief and loss would not be less.

I looked at some of Billie's photographs hanging on the wall, a happy nine-year-old girl. I thought of my own daughter, almost nine and also in love with music, singing and playing the piano. Tears started to run down my face. Billie's father smiled kindly. 'I know,' he said softly, 'thank you.'

The next day Iain and I were due to leave by car to Scotland for another concert. Iain stayed with friends a bit further away, and

I was going to spend the night with Billie's parents. Their house was a true museum of music recordings, with a large collection of Bakelite records, including the first recording made by the Italian opera star Caruso and many, many LPs. Their music collection testified to a very broad musical taste, from Bach to Arvo Pärt, from The Beatles to Little Feat and Madness, and from Monk to Keith Jarrett. A collection close to my heart.

Billie's father and I talked late into the night. A bottle of some typical brew from Yorkshire came onto the table. I do not know exactly what it was, but it definitely was alcoholic. Our conversation went from deeply philosophical to so incredibly funny that my stomach hurt from laughter, to meaningfully pleasant silence, and back again. So beautiful can really sharing and really listening be. The bottle was as good as empty when we decided that it was time to go to sleep.

Billie's father brought me to the room where I was allowed to spend the night. It was Billie's room. 'Everything is exactly as on the day we left to go canoeing,' he said. A bit later I pushed my way through the stuffed animals to sleep comfortably in her slightly-too-small bed. I looked around me. Billie's violin case lay on the desk and everything seemed indeed that she could step into her room any time. Again, I thought of my own children, Billie's parents and her twin brother. And, again, tears ran down my face. I climbed out of bed and said a prayer of thanks, as I do every night, but this time I knelt. The big teddy bear on the bed seemed to stare at me. He missed Billie too. I wished beautiful things for Billie's parents and brother, and I thanked for the blessings in my own life. And I thanked Billie for letting me sleep among her stuffed animals.

The next morning, during the 'typical English breakfast', Billie's father and myself could feel that we really emptied the bottle of the Yorkshire brew the night before. We said goodbye, Billie's father embraced me and said, 'Good blessings to you' and Iain and I headed for Scotland. I felt blessed indeed.

A few months later, Billie's father's new book fell through the letterbox. It had the title *Stories From A World Of Music*. I looked through it and saw that there was a foreword. The foreword had the title 'Good Blessings'. I decided to read it and at the end I was surprised by the following paragraph:

At teatime I looked through a window out to the sea. Egbert Derix, the Dutch pianist, was standing at the side of me. We just looked. He pointed out and said: 'Where's that over there?'

I followed his finger and said, 'Well, Denmark, eventually.' He moved his finger to the right. 'Holland,' I said.

'I'll be sailing over there in a few days' time,' he said.

'Yep, you and a lot of blessings.'

Playing, writing, recording and travelling with Iain Matthews are a few of those blessings.

CENTRE CULTUREL DE DISON

11 OCTOBER 2013, DISON, BELGIUM

MARK VOS

While almost half of Belgium was glued to their televisions for football, I was looking forward to the attractive music line-up at Dison, featuring the premiere of the concert series 'Who Knows Where The Time Goes?' by Iain Matthews and Linde Nijland. This was an evening dedicated to the music of British singer Sandy Denny, who had died 35 years before.

After hearing in the car that the Red Devils would be showcasing their footballing skills in Brazil next year, the evening was almost guaranteed to be a success. But the best was yet to come, because music is still a little closer to my heart than football.

The first person we bumped into in the small cultural centre was Iain Matthews, and barely fifteen minutes later we saw him back on stage. A huge football fan himself, he immediately started talking about our national team's fantastic performance, but the audience was clearly much more interested in his music.

And it turned out to be a fantastic musical evening. Iain and Linde were even better than I could have hoped for. We knew, of course, that Matthews is a major player in folk music from his previous concerts, both solo and in duos with Elliott Murphy and Ad Vanderveen, among others.

About ten years before, I had been fortunate to attend a Matthews concert in Horst – his hometown in The Netherlands – where he played his debut album live from start to finish. The recordings were later released on CD and it was a magical concert. Fortunately, Iain Matthews is still very productive and still performs frequently in the Low Countries.

The revelation of the evening, however, was the previously unknown folk singer Linde Nijland and her musicians. Linde sings Sandy Denny better than anyone else; in fact, she sings almost as well as the legendary singer herself. She has already released several CDs and performs quite frequently, in various formations, but mainly in The Netherlands. Incidentally, they had come all the way from the north of Holland for this concert, more than a five-hour drive, she told me. Her CD *Linde Nijland Sings Sandy Danny* is definitely worth listening to.

I loved almost every song Matthews and Nijland sang but the following stood out: 'A Sailor's Life', 'Genesis Hall', 'If You Saw Thro' My Eyes', 'Meet On The Ledge' and, of course, 'Who Knows Where The Time Goes?' This was heartbreakingly beautiful as sung by Linde with Iain as a wonderful second vocalist.

I saw some really great concerts in 2013 – Neil Young, Bruce Springsteen, Hugh Laurie, Johnny Winter, Melanie De Biasio, Emmylou Harris, Eric Andersen – but this might have been the best of them!

DEN HERBERG

5 OCTOBER 2014, BELFELD, THE NETHERLANDS

ROB VAN DER BERG

There I was, a sixteen-year-old lad, crazy about music and with a school assignment to find a place to do a commercial internship. DANG, I can work in a record store! The guy running the

Rob Van Der Berg discovered Iain whilst working in a record shop

shop liked my intro and I was in. Six weeks in heaven. It wasn't a cool indie place, but The Record Store in Roermond, The Netherlands. Hey, it could have been worse. School mates had to spend their time in between shoes or – worse – soap bars...

I was happy, and besides inbounding CDs onto the shelves, sorting out stuff and selling discs, I was learning about music history from my boss. I was already into many genres but this guy taught me about folk, folk-rock, singer-songwriters and obscure prog material. But he could not stop dwelling on two or three singer-songwriters; Donald Fagen, Van Morrison and Iain Matthews. 'Don't start with his eighties stuff, his early work... that's the real deal, but this is hard to get because it was never released on CD.' (We're talking the early nineties so the vinyl revival had not yet kicked in.)

As my training evolved each week (read: history lessons in where all the good stuff started), I started to explore a secondhand book and vinyl store called Het Ezelsoortje ('The Earmark'). I found Lou Reed, early Floyd, Bowie, T. Rex, Steely Dan and... *If You Saw Thro' My Eyes*. My first Iain album.

Mind. Blown. To. Pieces.

Meanwhile my music store mentor started to order CDs for the shop and for me. I purchased 70 CDs in those six weeks, mostly sixties and seventies material, including Matthews Southern

Comfort, Plainsong and also Iain's later solo material. Another thing I got into were the *2 Meter Sessions* recorded by Jan Douwe Kroeske for Dutch public radio. Every few months or so they released a disc containing mostly acoustic originals or covers... and on volume 4 I found Iain's 'A Cross To Bear'. Again, I was struck by the lyrics, voice and the apparent simplicity to absorb the whole. I never had that with any band or singer-songwriter before.

Fast forward a few years. I was following Iain on Facebook and he announced that *If You Saw Thro' My Eyes* was being rereleased 33 and a third years after its' original release. He was going to be playing shows in smaller venues to mark the anniversary and Ad Vanderveen and Egbert Derix would accompany him on the gigs. He played side A and then side B and he told stories about the songs in between. The album had been on constant replay already for years, and this gig being my first Iain gig was awesome.

Many, many gigs followed. In theatres, bars, clubs and – during Covid – in a hay shed. You name it. If it was within driving distance, I was there. Often with my concert mates, sometimes with my wife. Once with my oldest daughter.

Fast forward to 2014. My eldest daughter, Stella, was around six years old and I thought it would be a great idea to bring her to a gig. This one was in a bar/inn called Den Herberg (or In The Inn) in Belfeld. It was the fiftieth birthday of its owner, Puck Bergs, and Iain was going to be playing together with Egbert Derix. (Iain and Egert and the rest of the magnificent Searing Quartet recorded the timeless *In The Now*.) This was a jazz fest with extremely powerful songs and fantastic for a young girl's first live experience.

So there we were, in the inn; first row, best seats of the house. Together with us were Puck's family, Ian's wife and daughters, the six folks that were always at the bar, about 20 to 30 folkies… and my daughter. 40 minutes into the gig a song ended, the cheering silenced and Stella broke the silence with an enormous sigh. Without hesitation, Iain responded, 'This must be hard for you. It's easier to watch *Frozen* for the fifteenth time, right?' Shortly after that, Iain's wife Marly picked up my youngster to go and make some drawings with her kids... and the show continued.

A few months later, a documentary about the creation *of In The Now* was released. The first screening would be in the 'shed' where the album was recorded. This was a great show with the full Searing Quartet as the band as well as a chance to view the documentary.

After the gig, there was the usual stuff; nice chats, discs for sale, autographs. Luca, Iain and Marly's older daughter, was selling her drawings of Iain and Egbert. She was asking one Euro for the drawing. I gave her two Euros and asked Iain and Egbert to sign it. The drawing has been decorating my first version vinyl of *If You Saw Thro' My Eyes* ever since.

These are just a few of my memories of Iain gigs. I've seen him solo, as a duo, as a trio with Plainsong in a chapel, as part of a quartet and backed by a quartet. All the shows had funk and fire, all the shows were pure. Sometimes the mojo was a bit lost, but the next gig could be extremely focussed, with renewed energy and spirit.

I hope the well will never run dry, Iain. You are a companion on the roads that I travel and your songs and voice always bring light.

Rob purchased drawings from Iain's daughter Luca

HALF MOON

2015, PUTNEY, LONDON, UK

ERIC HORRIDGE

It took me 38 years from the time I first heard Iain sing ('Shake It') until I got to see him live in Putney… a night I will never forget. I lived in South Africa (my folks emigrated there from Manchester in '73) and after first hearing 'Stealin' Home' I searched the world to buy every single record and CD Iain has ever made or been part of. I have bought records and CDs in Melbourne, LA, London, Manchester, Singapore and Tokyo and I ordered the memoir *Thro' My Eyes* prior to publication, reading it voraciously upon receipt. I have every solo album, every album by Matthews Southern Comfort (MSC) and Plainsong, every collaboration with Egbert Derix, the Salmon Smokers, Ad Vanderveen (I love *More Than A Song* with Eliza Gilkyson) and many others.

I listened to Iain on my small record player from '77 to '81 every day during my university studies and exam prep…and he got me through each year, the sound of his voice keeping me calm. When I moved to England for four years, you can imagine my excitement when I got to see him for the first time at the Half Moon in Putney in 2015.

He was performing with Egbert and I sat alone in the front row, having arrived two hours early from Cobham in Surrey. I was first through the doors when they opened and, despite the fact that I was going through a divorce at the time, I sat mesmerised, enjoying the happiest two hours of my life.

Since then, I got to see Iain in Plainsong on the Richard Fariña 'tour' in Whitstable as well as when MSC played a gig in Shipley, Yorkshire in 2017.

Iain has been a part of my life for nearly 45 years now. I had one photo taken with him, taken at that first gig, but lost it when my phone was damaged.

Sadly, having moved back to Australia after leaving the UK due to a cancer diagnosis in 2017, I know I'll never see him live again.

But his voice and his ongoing determination to continue with his music are both an inspiration and a pleasure.

I present a show twice a week on Apollo Bay Radio here in Australia and play Iain's songs quite often, especially on my easy listening Ocean Blue show. I wish I could hear him live just one more time.

UNKNOWN VENUE

2016, PITTMAN, NEW JERSEY

RAIN PERRY

I was working on my documentary *The Shopkeeper* (about changes in the music industry as told through the rise and fall of the Congress House studio in Austin, Texas) and Mark Hallman gave me a list of people I should talk to. Iain Matthews was on the list, as he had passed through the Congress House and been in a band with Mark.

Rain Perry interviewed Iain for a documentary she was making

It turned out that Iain was touring in America that year, and I made a plan to meet up with him at a show in Pittman, NJ. I got there, met him backstage and we did a great interview before the show! Me, him, a small camera and a mic pack. He told wonderful stories about fleeing the chilly Seattle winter for the warmth of Austin, and about Mark and him being unable to tell whose voice was whose when they listened back to recordings of the two of them. He also told a wonderful story about when he was doing A&R and Robert Plant told him 'you're not done singing'. Wonderful stuff – I used a lot of it for the film!

And I've hosted him at my house for concerts a time or two as well!

RED DRAGON LISTENING ROOM
15 APRIL 2016, BATON ROUGE, LOUISIANA

BOB RAY

Imagine my excitement when I learned that Iain would make a concert appearance in Baton Rouge, Louisiana at the Red Dragon Listening Room. It was only 350 miles down the Natchez Trace Parkway from my home near Tupelo, Mississippi. I secured the tickets to the show and we were off to New Orleans for a couple of days and then on to Baton Rouge for the concert. I was thrilled when, after taking my seat, Iain was moving through the venue greeting the attendees. As he approached, I stood and extended my hand, telling him we were traveling some 700 miles for his concert appearance. I'll never forget him looking at me and saying, 'I sure hope you won't be disappointed.' I was astonished by his genuine humility.

His character is evident in his writing, but this was my own little bit of validation for the years of dedicated following of his career from London, to LA, Seattle and Austin, from Matthews Southern Comfort, though his solo work and Plainsong. It was an extremely memorable night. His performance was outstanding and an evening I'll treasure forever.

I was *not* disappointed.

URBANA-CHAMPAIGN INDEPENDENT MEDIA CENTER
25 SEPTEMBER 2016, URBANA, ILLINOIS

TOD DURNIL

My introduction to Iain's music came from being a child of the seventies. I fell in love with Iain's amazing recordings and branched out from there. I owe Iain for my connection to Richard Thompson, Sandy Denny, Andy Roberts, Julian Dawson, Clive Gregson, Elliott Murphy, Egbert Derix, Ad

Vanderveen and dozens of others. Through Iain I discovered great songwriters like Jules Shear, Jimmy Webb, Jesse Winchester, Terence Boylan, John Martyn, Terry Reid, Tom Waits, Gene Clark, Paul Siebel, Richard Fariña and so many more.

Iain's connections easily fill a good 50 per cent of my very large record collection, and I often joke that you can exchange Kevin Bacon's name and play the music version of *The Six Degrees Of Iain Matthews*, connecting Iain to literally anyone in music. For example: connect Iain Matthews to late singer Olivia Newton-John. Iain recorded Marc Jordan's 'Survival' on *Siamese Friends;* Jordan and his wife, Amy Sky, were close friends and collaborators with Olivia Newton-John, and Jordan even played her husband in the movie *Score: A Hockey Musical.*

Shortly after Iain made his comeback with *Walking A Changing Line* and reinvented himself as an Austin-based singer/songwriter, I connected with Iain's management to propose a box-set. I submitted an extensive selection of songs up to his most recent albums, the three masterworks *Pure & Crooked*, *Skeleton Keys* and *The Dark Ride*. Unfortunately, the set never happened as Iain had recently changed management.

I did get to see Iain in concert several times during this period, in Bloomington, Illinois (with Hamilton Pool collaborator Michael Fracaso) and twice at FitzGerald's in Berwyn/Chicago (once featuring my friend Steve Dawson as the opening act). But my favourite connection was when Iain and Andy Roberts were touring the Midwest in 2016 to promote their Plainsong tribute to Richard Fariña, *Reinventing Richard*. I contacted Iain to see if he had any dates in Champaign, Illinois and he said he did not, but had time available to hit there! I set up a show at the IMC in Urbana and was so happy to have hosted two music legends in my hometown.

Thank you, Iain, for 60 years of fantastic music and memories!

Todd Durnil promoted a show in Urbana, Illinois

'CARTWHEEL AVENUE'

PETE MANCINI

Pete Mancini was flattered to receive an email from Iain (Bart Gallagher)

It was around the time my band Butchers Blind released our first album in 2011. The bass player who ran our band email account said, 'Some guy just wrote us a really nice email, his name is Iain Matthews.' Sounds familiar, I thought. I did a quick online search and realised it was *that* Iain Matthews. I was blown away! How did he get our album? How did he find us? That correspondence was the beginning of a friendship that changed my trajectory as an artist and songwriter. Iain's encouragement and support gave me the confidence I needed to keep moving forward, even as the band suffered some setbacks and challenges.

Discovering his vast discography and his influence on Americana music inspired me to make my first solo album, *Foothill Freeway*. I wanted to make an album like *Valley Hi*. I don't know how close I got to that goal, but the highlight for me was when Iain did a guest vocal on a rendition of his song 'Cartwheel Avenue'. I look at that recording as a snapshot of a great time of doing shows and hanging with Iain, something I'll never forget. I am glad we crossed paths.

RECORD STORE

SUMMER 2017, SOUTH JERSEY

ETHAN KURZWEIL

When I was a teenager all my dad ever seemed to listen to was Iain Matthews' music. In the summer of 2017, he told me and my brother we were going on a road trip. We drove like two hours and checked into a hotel in South Jersey. Then we went to this little record store to see Iain perform live. We got to meet him and listen to him sing. My dad asked him a special request, to play 'A Spanish Guitar' by Gene Clark, and he added that song during the set. It was a great thrill for my father. Iain seems like a really nice guy, and my brother and I enjoyed the music.

Ethan was taken on a road trip to see Iain

CROPREDY FESTIVAL

12 AUGUST 2017, CROPREDY, UK

MICK DONOVAN

Iain Matthews, to my mind, completed a stunning job in the two years he was with the nascent and fast-developing Fairport Convention. Having the task of singing harmony alongside my favourite singer of all time (Sandy Denny) after Judy Dyble might have seemed a role destined to put him in the shade. Even the chap himself played down the part he played in the band taking off when he said in an interview with author Richie Unterberger, 'I was at that point simply a pawn in the Fairport game. I was the male vocal energy on the right side of the stage. Ultimately, I can't think of any long-lasting effect that my presence in the band had.'

Fairport might have been inspired by the dual vocal set-up of San Francisco's Jefferson Airplane with Marty Balin and the incomparable Grace Slick to introduce our subject to their fold. But I felt Iain underplayed his role while chatting to Unterberger. He certainly complemented Sandy's vocal with his gentle but distinctive tone of voice. And he helped the band record a few landmark moments in their recording career, not least Richard Thompson's 'Meet On The Ledge' on *What We Did On Our Holidays*, setting them off on the path to folk-rock immortality, if that's not overblowing things.

I instantly appreciated his impact on their live performance when I saw him with what many view as the classic Fairport line-up of Sandy Denny (vocal), Richard Thompson (guitar), Simon Nicol (guitar), Ashley Hutchings (bass) and Martin Lamble (drums) early in 1969. It was at the Country Club, a small establishment just round the back from Belsize Park Station on the Northern Line on the London Underground. The date was 2nd February 1969. Of course, it was Sandy Denny who took most of my breath away, but Iain stole a little as well.

His time with the band was all too short. After the *What We Did On Our Holidays* album which set Fairport on the path to becoming a trail-blazer for British folk rock and recording 'Percy's Song' for their follow-up, *Unhalfbricking*, he and the band parted company.

Yet not too long afterwards, I pottered down to the Roundhouse in Chalk Farm, north London – a regular haunt for me and my mates – and there was Iain on stage with his own band, Matthews Southern Comfort.

It must have been one of their earliest gigs, the combo formed to promote his solo album of the same name. I remember Iain's lovely tones on a cover of 'Woodstock', the Joni Mitchell song I saw her perform at the seminal 1970 Isle of Wight Festival. That became a hit single. A number 1. And I was struck by Iain's country-tinged folk-rock collective. I bought the album, which was packed with fine Iain-penned songs, and its' follow up, *Second Spring*, on the back of it.

Mick Donovan first saw Iain in 1969

It would be 47 years before I saw Iain on stage again, with him relocating abroad after a spell with Plainsong, following MSC. It was at Fairport's 50th anniversary at the Cropredy Festival. He performed with a revived Plainsong, alongside Andy Roberts and Mark Griffiths. His voice was as good as ever. The playing was wonderful, the songs more than decent.

After their superb performance, I met the band at the signings tent and got them to sign their latest album, *Reinventing Richard*, a tribute to Richard Farina. Iain was wearing a blue and red-checked shirt. His full head of hair was flecked with grey, but with a matching five o'clock shadow stubble. I was struck at how youthful he still looked.

To the embarrassment of my partner, I asked him to pose for a picture with me to capture the moment. He was friendly and accommodating. Later that day, I saw him perform with Fairport in celebration of their half-century milestone, alongside the band's first female singer, the now-late and lovely Judy Dyble (knitting while performing), plus other former members Ashley Hutchings and Richard Thompson, with the then Fairport line-up which included founder Simon Nicol, the now late Gerry Conway, bassist Dave Pegg, Ric Sanders (violin) and multi-instrumentalist and vocalist Chris Leslie.

I saw Iain in the tent again at Cropredy the following year, promoting his memoir *Thro' My Eyes*, kindly signing it for my partner and I. From his Lincolnshire upbringing to working in Carnaby Street to becoming a survivor in the fickle world of music. Still touring, doing a recent one in the UK promoted by my colleague Terry Baker.

Now that book had – and will always have – a special resonance for me and my wife. It was the one I read while we were in Rome celebrating our fortieth wedding anniversary not long before the 2018 renewal of the family festival we always return to.

Thank you, Iain Matthews, for the words, music and tent talk.

THE EVENING MUSE

14 SEPTEMBER 2017, CHARLOTTE, NORTH CAROLINA

WES KNAPE

I first got to know Iain – or, at the time, Ian Matthews – in 1970 with the release of Matthews Southern Comfort's *Later That Same Year.* Full disclosure requires that I clarify that the meeting was strictly through the music when a friend of mine turned me on to it. The quality of the work was exceptional, and the music was instantly accessible. That led me back to his time with Fairport Convention and I have followed all the creative twists and turns since.

I became head of the UNC-Wilmington Concert Committee in 1971 and we had a great run presenting upcoming acts such as Yes, Tranquility, Cheap Trick, Steely Dan, Renaissance and more, always with the emphasis on making sure the opening act was as artistically talented as the headliner. I tried unsuccessfully for years to book two artistically important acts, Horslips and Ian Matthews, but could never work at the logistics. (The American South after the rise of the Allman Brothers became less accepting of as wide a variety of international acts.)

Fast forward to 2017 and word came to the coast that Iain would be playing in Charlotte, North Carolina at a club called

Wes has 'known' Iain since 1970

The Evening Muse. It would be a 400-mile odyssey and though the time had long passed when my friends and I would drive hundreds of miles to see a performer, this was simply not to be missed. Visions of multitudes from all over North Carolina descending on this small club made me anxious to secure my ticket and I called the club immediately. After 37 years and untold albums and CDs, I would finally get to see 'the voice'.

Arriving at the club early, I was informed that Iain was doing a sound check and doors would open later. I had been in the professional music business for nearly ten years and realised how important a sound check is. On the other hand, I had waited 37 years and sitting in the back unnoticed was a chance that could not be passed up. As security walked away, I started through the door, when my wife grabbed my arm and told me that I knew better than to sneak into a sound check. I had stopped many a person from doing the same thing at my own shows. I could have died. She was right, of course.

When the doors opened, there wasn't a crush. Perhaps the venue owner did not have the money to really promote the show properly. It was a small crowd. Iain was standing around, so I took the opportunity to introduce myself and express my appreciation of his work over the years. He was reserved but gracious.

The show was great. Much of his career has been noted for his ability to champion either material by performers on the rise or those wrongly overlooked. I appreciated that he dwelt on material by Richard Fariña and Jules Shear. The material covered quite a lot of his storied career. 'Darkness, Darkness' was a real treat. He talked to the audience and told stories. It was a truly great evening of song.

After the show he took the time to interact with the audience for pictures and autographs. He graciously signed the album covers that I had brought and it was neat to be able to purchase the Richard Fariña tribute album that I was unaware of.

So what is Iain Matthews really like? A voice as exceptional as Iain's – a man in the same league as, say, Art Garfunkel – has the power to invoke empathy and it is easy for the listener to assume that he has an insight and understands the inner nature of what is in realty a perfect stranger. The fact that this 'stranger' probably regularly meets people that assume a closer connection than can possibly exist, and throw in the difference in the predominant cultures in which we are raised and the number of years this minstrel has toiled on the road, and it is easy to understand why he might not immediately need another new best friend.

What you can expect is a truly exceptional performance by an obviously gifted vocalist with the songwriting chops that equals or surpasses most anyone else. If you are lucky, he will not only masterfully interpret other's material but also showcase his own, such as 'Thro' My Eyes', 'Rains Of '62', 'Timing', 'Christoforo' Eyes' and so many, many more.

Will Iain Matthews ever venture to the American South again? There is always hope and if he does, even though my travelling long distances for concerts are from the distant past, I would gladly repeat the odyssey.

Hope to see you on the road, my enigmatic musical friend.

CAT CLUB

OCTOBER 2018, PONTEFRACT, UK

DAVID POLLARD

I have seen Iain many times in concert, but my favourite has to be the gig I saw at the Cat Club in Pontefract, a small and very intimate venue. I was sat right at the front for Matthews Southern Comfort and could have leaned forward and tuned Iain's guitar for him, though I don't think he'd have thanked me! A superb venue to hear an excellent band and Iain's beautiful voice.

David Pollard was so close to Iain he could have tuned his guitar

UNKNOWN VENUE

OCTOBER 2019

PETER MILLS

I'm not by nature an 'act hassler', but in October 2019 when I finally got to see Iain Matthews play live in the neighbourhood, and there he was at the merch table in the interval, well, what could be nicer? He was touring with the collaborator on his memoir and later author of the Plainsong biography, Ian Clayton.

Peter Mills & Pat Thomas, a mutual acquaintance of him & Iain

As it happened, I had a couple of stories to tell – firstly, he'd been very helpful to me in recalling via email his memories of working with Michael Nesmith while making *Valley Hi* at Nesmith's Countryside studios for a book I was writing about The Monkees, so I wanted to thank him for that. Secondly it turned out that we had an acquaintance in common, a Californian fellow called Pat Thomas – a true music fan, reissue label boss and indisputably one of the good guys. Iain surprised me by saying that Pat was also periodically his percussionist for stretches of touring in the States. That I'd like to see.

We also discussed our mutual admiration for Van Morrison and I told him that I had heard his version of 'Brown Eyed Girl' as a kid long before I heard Morrison's original. It's a luscious, super-driven pop cover I still thrill to. He told me a funny story about Van that's included in his memoir *Thro' My Eyes* – no spoilers, you can buy the book, it's a great read – which, if I needed it (I didn't), was an added incentive to buy the book right there and then. Which I did.

I've seen him since doing a Plainsong set with Andy Roberts at a great bespoke venue in Pontefract; both evenings were little marvels, with his voice and musical gift undimmed by time it seems. It was a pleasure to meet him and, while I'm still not an act hassler, I'm glad I said hello.

HALF MOON

12 AUGUST 2021, PUTNEY, LONDON, UK

SANDIE RITTER

In the 1970s, I was a fan of Matthews Southern Comfort and Plainsong. I loved playing their albums at home, but never found the opportunity to see them perform live. Decades later I went to their final appearance in London's fabulous Union Chapel, but did not speak to Iain.

More recently I saw Iain perform at the Half Moon in Putney twice – the first time when his autobiography had just been released and the second time when he and Andy Roberts performed their tribute to American folk singer-songwriter Richard Fariña, whose music I was not familiar with, but thoroughly enjoyed.

At the gig to mark the release of Iain's autobiography, I purchased his book and waited for him to sign it. I have no clue how our conversation moved to my love of rural coastal northern California, where I own a second home, but Iain was keen to talk about Northern California as he had visited friends who lived in a town called Fort Bragg – I knew I'd visited that town (about 55 miles from my holiday home), but in the moment when he asked where my home was in relation to it, I confused it with Fort Ross, a coastal town south of my home.

He spoke of how he worked in the music industry in Los Angeles and would have preferred to live in Northern California, but needed to make a living. Suddenly I realised I was talking to a man who did not always live the troubadour's lifestyle, but at times needed a nine-to-five job within Los Angeles' music scene. I went home and read his entire autobiography in just a few days. Iain's songwriting clearly overlaps with his honest and poetic style of autobiographical writing.

Fast forward to 2024 and I had sold my Northern California home and purchased another one further north, about eight miles south of Fort Bragg, the town Iain had mentioned to me. That summer I visited the local bookstore in Fort Bragg, and while there saw a magazine about Amelia Earheart. I was so excited because I knew I'd be seeing Iain performing live in April 2025 at the Costa Festival in Ibiza, and so I purchased two copies: one for me and one for Iain.

I attended the Costa Festival in Ibiza for the first time in 2024 and at the end they asked for us to suggest artists we'd like to perform there. I submitted Iain's name and to my surprise a few hours later I discovered that Iain was already booked to appear there in 2025! I am a firm believer in synchronicity. Sometimes the world feels really small and cozy!

Thank you for your music, Iain, for more than 50 years. It continues to bring me hours of enjoyment.

TOWN HALL LIVE

11 FEBRUARY 2022, KIRTON-IN-LINDSEY, UK

BRIAN CHUDLEY

I live in Kirton-in-Lindsey, a small town in North Lincolnshire where Iain worked at Jack Tighes as a teenager before moving down to London. I have followed Iain's career since his days with Matthews Southern Comfort and their hit single 'Woodstock'. It is incredible that this is the only song of Iain's that I have heard played on national radio and sad that the British public do not know what a great singer and songwriter Iain is. One reason may be that Iain spent many years in America as a young man and then many more in Holland.

Brian is a fan of Iain and has promoted shows of his

I believe that I have all of Iain's album releases, either on vinyl throughout the seventies and on CD since. My collection started with Matthews Southern Comfort and continued with his solo albums and his various bands and collaborations since. Those include Plainsong, Hamilton Pool (with Mark Hallman and Michael Fracasso), Julian Dawson, Andy Roberts, The Iain Adventure (with Ad Vanderveen), No Grey Faith, More Than A Song (with Eliza Gilkyson and Ad Vanderveen), Eliott Murphy, The Searing Quartet, The Trio Amen (with Mike Roelofs and Bart Oostindie), Egbert Derix, The Salmon Smokers, The Matthews Baartmans Conspiracy and the new Matthews Southern Comfort. That is some list.

Throughout the years Iain's vocals have always been pitch perfect, and still are. He couldn't have named the solo albums released on his 'Perfect Pitch' label any better.

I have been fortunate enough to promote several concerts involving Iain. The first, featuring The Iain Adventure, was at the turn of the century at the Angel Ballroom in Brigg, North Lincolnshire. It was my first ever attempt at promoting concerts. In 2012 I started promoting Town Hall Live events in Kirton and have had the pleasure of hosting Iain on two occasions, once with the new Matthews Southern Comfort in 2018 and once with The Matthews Baartmans Conspiracy in 2022.

In 2024 it is great to see the release of Iain's latest album, *How Much Is Enough Volume One*. The fact that it is entitled *Volume One* gives hope that more volumes will follow. Knowing Iain I bet there will be!

MUSICA DEL RIO

MAY 2022, ATASCADERO, CALIFORNIA

JOHN SCHMITZ

I was driving. I didn't catch all the lyrics, but I heard this amazing voice on the car radio: 'She's been with me now for a long, long time and I feel fine.' The DJ mentioned Matthews. You mean the guy who sang 'Woodstock'? Since I couldn't research it – there was no internet then – the song was filed away in one of my dusty cranial filing cabinets.

A year or two later I heard, again on the car radio, 'I was standing on the sidewalk; had a noise in my head…' from Iain's *Tigers Will Survive* LP. The music was forceful yet refined. Again, the vocals – man!

John Schmitz, pictured with Oreo, has been a fan since 'Something In The Way She Moves'

I was sitting in my living room, listening to the *Second Spring* LP from Matthews' Southern Comfort, which I had just bought. The opening chords to 'Something In The Way She Moves' floated across the room. I perked up. This sounded familiar. I got goosebumps! As soon as the vocals began, I cried out. Yes! I dragged out my acoustic guitar and began to figure out the chords. I've been a fan ever since.

Iain's *Valley Hi* and Plainsong's *In Search Of Amelia Earhart* LPs remained on my turntable as I figured out more chords to the wonderful tunes. Iain's music helped me with my playing and singing, encouraging me to play more, play better. These were exciting times!

I saw Iain at The Back Door, a coffee house at San Diego State University, when he was promoting his *Hit And Run* release in 1977. He had a talented band behind him; his saxophone player (Steven Hooks?) played two saxes simultaneously. I'd never seen that done before.

Fast forward to May 2022 and a house concert at Musica Del Rio in Atascadero, California. Iain and Steve Postell were appearing. It had been over 40 years since I had seen Iain and there was no doubt in my mind. I had to go!

Iain was such a pleasant man. We had a nice conversation, talked about some of his hard-to-find CDs, watched him sign his book, entitled *It's About Time* that another gentleman had brought. Iain said there were 50 copies printed; he had two. So, with his two copies and this one, that would mean there were 47 copies still out there. Six months later, I found and bought a copy. (That means there are still 46 copies out there, if you're keeping count.)

In March 2025, I saw Iain at Rain Perry's house concert in Ojai, California. He walked out on 'stage' holding a cup of tea, a little detail I will always remember. He opened with 'Meaning Of Life', a song he first performed with the band, More Than A Song. Sitting there, I reflected on just how much this man has accomplished in the music world since the early 1960s. He's lost track of the number of releases he's made; he's produced records and added harmony vocals on innumerable releases. That's not to mention his influence on my life and playing. I try not to be awed by this, I mean, he is only human, like the rest of us. But I think it's important to remember those people who join us on our path for a little while and be thankful for their kindness, encouragement and positive vibes.

Now, if you'll excuse me, I think I'll break out the guitar and play for a bit.

WORLEYS AT THE SWAN

10 AUGUST 2022, STOURPORT- ON-SEVERN, UK

PHILIP DELAFIELD

Being a big fan of Fairport Convention, when I first got to read about the band, I discovered that one of the original members had left early on and set up Matthew Southern Comfort, who recorded the coolest single, 'Woodstock'. On 10 August 2022 I dragged my wife Karen over to Stourport- on-Severn where Iain was playing at Worleys at the Swan pub, just before Cropredy. It was a great evening listening to Iain and got even better when his friend Robert Plant joined us.

I've found Iain so pleased to talk to people and after the concert I messaged him about coming to the Stables in Milton Keynes near where I live. He responded and eventually I saw that he was booked in for a concert with Plumhall in June 2024. I took a gang of family and friends to see him and he kindly mentioned me during the performance. We had a chat during the interval and he signed my copy of the 'Woodstock' single, which now hangs proudly on my wall.

Not only do Karen and I love listening to his music, he sings his words so clearly, something a sound engineer commented on just recently when I mentioned seeing Iain.

HOUSE CONCERT

DECEMBER 2022, KINGSTON-UPON-HILL, UK

MARY CRYAN

The pandemic was an awful time for musicians and music lovers alike. By the end of summer 2022 many folk clubs in England were still not reopened, festivals had been cancelled, and lots of our musician friends were getting very worried that live music could never be the same. Mike and I wondered were dismayed by the situation and wondered if there was any small way in which we could help. We had a chat with the great duo Plumhall and decided to try running a house concert with them as guests. It would be very small numbers, as people were still nervous about being out in a crowd, and supper would be provided to ensure good value. So in October 2022 the HU5 sessions were born.

This first concert was an immense success, and we decided we would organise more on an occasional basis. Imagine my surprise when the following week I was contacted by a friend, Gerry McNeice, who said he would like to put me in touch with Iain Matthews who would like to play for us. My initial response was that that this was a joke, a wind up! *The* Iain Matthews could not possibly want to play to twenty people in a house in Hull? Gerry reassured me that this was not a joke and, after a conversation with Iain, we set a date for the gig.

Iain came, along with musician BJ Baartmans, in early

Mary thought it was a wind up when she heard Iain was interested in her hosting a house concert

December 2022 to play to a small group of fans in my sitting room. The standard of music would have been at home in the Royal Albert Hall. I had to keep pinching myself that this was real, that a man I had last seen play live with Matthews Southern Comfort in 1970, was singing 'Woodstock' in my front room. This was a very memorable evening and one I thought would never be repeated.

About nine months later, Iain contacted me as he was planning a small tour with Andy Roberts to promote a new book, *In Search Of Plainsong*, the story of the band by Yorkshire author Ian Clayton. We set up another house concert with Iain and Andy and with Ian the author along to promote the book. Another amazing evening followed, with Plainsong's music to the fore. Iain and Andy were our house guests, and we learnt a lot about their lives in music and their love of football as we talked into the night.

Two incredible nights of music never to be forgotten.

THE GREYS
12 DECEMBER 2022, BRIGHTON, UK

TOBY GOODYER

We have seen Iain many times in the field at Cropredy and stopped to chat. Always a pleasure. Seeing him at smaller venues near home in Brighton is a really special experience and allows me to listen to wonderful music and attempt to capture some magic and memories in my drawing. Always a bit too dark to draw but it's part of the experience. His version of 'Woodstock' accompanied by the marvellous Plumhall was truly magical.

SHINJUKU MARZ
24 FEBRUARY 2023, TOKYO, JAPAN

PETER GALLWAY

Peter Gallway didn't think he'd make it to Japan because of Covid

In January of 2023 I came down with Covid after nearly three years of masking, hand washing, social distancing and periods of full-on quarantine. Two days later, my wife Annie showed symptoms. In four weeks, I was scheduled to fly to Japan to co-headline a series of concerts with Iain Matthews. Until nearly the last moment, including near-divine intervention to secure my work visa after my papers were lost in transit from the consulate in Boston, I wasn't certain I would be able to make the trip, but less than a week before departure I confirmed with our promoters I would be coming as planned.

I had never met Iain but had heard his name for years and was aware several of my musician friends in Austin and

Los Angeles had worked with him. On the plane to Haneda Airport in Tokyo, my excitement grew. The various tours and production trips to Japan were always rich experiences and this would prove no exception.

Izumi collected me after clearing customs and we bused to Shinjuku Station and took a short taxi ride to a small hotel in the neighbouring Kabuki-cho, the district known for Yakuza-controlled nightclubs, escorts and love hotels. Being from Greenwich Village, I felt at home.

I met Iain, his wife Marly and guitarist BJ Baartmans the following day, and the journey began through our series of promotions and concerts in Tokyo and Osaka. Iain, Marly and BJ were gracious and kind, and we each practised our ways of being on the road; managing jetlag, securing nurturing food, enjoying snippets of time off, seeing to the tasks at hand and getting to know one another.

And there was the music. Music connects musicians and audiences in similar and different ways. For musicians it is a language; it is like lifers without parole, it is unspoken, it is a look in the eye, it is with eyes closed.

I have had and continue to have a prolific career, and as I came to know Iain during this short time together, I was astonished at his level of productivity; the sheer number of albums he has released. The sense of connection was nearly instantaneous. I too had numerous recent albums in different musical configurations. I too was completing a memoir. And as we shared stories it came to light that we had many friends, collaborators, and acquaintances in common. It is said there are six degrees of separation. In my experience, more often than not there are none.

What struck me deeply was Iain's effortless yet intentional singing. His vocal ability was moving and surprising. When I complimented him, he said it was a gift, something I understand. Since meeting and sharing those concert stages in Japan in 2023, Iain has been generous and thoughtful, as I suspect he has always been, and he has become a friend.

GLENN WILLIAMS

I first saw Iain at the De Montfort Hall in Leicester in September 1978 – he was supporting Renaissance. I hadn't even heard of him to be honest and I don't recall much about that show but I do remember admiring how he played the guitar. There was a strength and clarity in his strumming I had never heard before.

Some (gulp!) forty-five years later, I was asked to interview him to promote some shows he was doing in Tokyo with Peter Gallway. I wrote the questions, sent them off to him and he sent back the answers. My final question was about a well-known aviation mystery: 'What do you think happened to Amelia Earheart?'

The answer came back, 'She crashed and died.' Great answer and I actually felt a bit daft for asking it. Never mind. He signed off the answers with a 'Look forward to meeting you' message.

Friday 24 February 2023 was a bloody cold day in Tokyo but the venue, Shinjuku Marz, was sold out. Peter went on first and played a set so enchanting, he had the audience hanging on every note. There was a half an hour toilet/beer break and then Ian took the stage with BJ Baartmans, ie. The Matthews Baartmans Conspiracy. He opened with 'The Frame' and there was that instantly recognisable strum again. Solid and percussive, it gave BJ a lot of room to lead, enhance and fill-in whilst never overshadowing the key elements of the songs; Iain's singing was glorious.

Post show, both Peter and Iain were available to meet. Approaching Iain, he looked at me and said, 'Well I know who you are!' I threw one back at him. 'I know who you are as well!' He broke into a broad grin, held out his hand and we shook. He thanked me for coming and for the interview. We chatted about this, that and the other, the conversation ebbing and flowing naturally as if we were just picking up from a chat the day before. Fans were waiting for autographs so after a few minutes, we shook hands again and I moved on. Observing from a distance, I watched him meet and greet every fan like they were his only fan. He was genuinely pleased to be there, to meet people and spend as much time as they wanted with him. I caught his eye as I was leaving and he waved me a cheery goodbye.

Set List
The Frame
God Looked Down
The Corner Of Sad And Lonely
Reno Nevada
Working In The New Mine
Fourteen Months
Blood Red Roses
I've Gone Missing
Like A Radio
Is This It
Me And Mr Hohner
Woodstock

Encore
Right As Rain

AVENEL PERFORMING ARTS CENTER
7 MAY 2023, WOODBRIDGE, NEW JERSEY

ANDY PINESS

I had the pleasure of seeing Iain in performance at the Avenel Performing Arts Center. James Maddock was the opener. I am an avid audiophile who (still) buys and collects CDs. To date I have 25 of Iain's, including the brand new *How Much Is Enough*. I so enjoyed his performance, and his accompanist was a wonderful addition and counterpoint to Iain's playing and singing. Many years prior, my first introduction to hearing Iain live was with Hamilton Pool at the now-defunct Fez Under Time Café in New York City, sometime in the mid to late nineties.

I so admire Iain's prolific output of recordings and the various musical incarnations he has aligned himself with. I love 'La

Terre Commune' with Elliott Murphy. As for his solo work, it's truly difficult to choose, but favourites are 'The Dark Ride' and 'Walking A Changing Line' – what a stroke of genius to have covered the brilliant Jules Shear! My Spotify/Wrapped account listed him as my Top Artist of the Year. And his memoir *Thro' My Eyes* is an epic narrative of your life and long career.

He is a true renaissance man. Sounds like an album title to me!

Andy has 25 of Iain's CDs

PAVILION ARTS CENTRE
13 AUGUST 2023, BUXTON, UK

NEIL HARRIS

My wife Pauline and I went to see Iain on a short tour he was doing. He introduced a song as being stolen (my word, not his) from him and said something about how he heard a somewhat well-known band play a version that became a hit and which sounded very much like his much earlier version. He said he wanted to do a different rendition of it, as a way of reclaiming the song. Pauline knew straight away that it was 'Seven Bridges Road'. I didn't until he started singing it.

Afterwards, when he was speaking to people, I came over and said I was really glad he had reintroduced it as it was such a beautiful song. What I didn't say (but should have done) was that I didn't know The Eagles had done a version. I only know the version on *Valley Hi*, which has always been one of my favourite albums.

HUNTINGDON HALL

15 AUGUST 2023, WORCESTER, UK

IAN GIBBONS, IMG MUSIC

Ian Gibbons was delighted to find himself working with one of his favourite ever folk musicians

I first saw Iain Matthews perform live at Huntingdon Hall in Worcester in August 2023. I had always been a huge admirer of Iain's work and the show did not disappoint. He had the audience in the palm of his hand from the very first note. He delivered the goods as always and received a standing ovation from a packed auditorium. I was lucky enough to get to meet him after the show and I had a long conversation with him about my work as a concert promoter and agent. Little did I realise then that, just under twelve months later, I would be working with Iain putting his 2025 UK tour dates together. It's been a pleasure working with him, particularly because he is one of my favourite folk musicians ever.

GREEN NOTE

16 AUGUST 2023, CAMDEN, LONDON, UK

TOM ARVIDSSON

I had been listening to Iain Matthews for more than 50 years and still I had not heard him play and sing live in concert. When early in 2023 I read that he would be playing at Green Note in Camden, I asked my eldest son Martin if he would like to join me for a trip to London to see Iain play. Martin gave me a quick nod and said that it 'would be nice'. Afraid it might sell out – it only had a 65 capacity – I got tickets fast.

I had been to Green Note twice before, to see Austin singer-songwriter Darden Smith in 2013, who impressed with his funny stories and songs, and Canadian bluegrass group The Eastpointers two years later, which was a nice evening with some workmates.

Tom Arvissson caught up with Iain live after listening to him for 50 years

I reckoned that Green Note would be the perfect place to see Iain. I'd first heard him with Fairport Convention. It might have been 'Percy's Song' from *Unhalfbricking*. Then I bought *Second Spring* and loved it. When *If You Saw Thro' My Eyes* was released in 1971, it just smashed into my life. This LP simply set the standard for what an album should be: a neat production that sounded great on my new hi-fi stereo system with Wharfedale speakers. Melodies that stood out, lyrics that meant something, awesome guitar playing from Tim Renwick, Richard Thompson and Andy Roberts (even on the same track!) and a voice far above the usual.

I thought (and still do) it was one of the best records I've ever heard. It was followed by another great album, *Tigers Will Survive* and the first Plainsong album, but I was a bit disappointed by *Valley Hi* and by the time *Siamese Friends* was released I dropped out.

In 1988 I was listening to *Tio I Topp* (Swedish for 'Ten At The Top'), a radio chart-programme, whilst painting some chairs, and 'Following Every Finger' was introduced. I thought that it *must* be Iain singing and it surely was…

Since then, I believe I have all the albums and there have been many of them! My favourite songs include 'For Better Or Worse', 'Falling Stars', 'To Be White', 'Pebbles In The Road', 'Alone Again Blues', 'Every Crushing Blow', 'Joy Mining', 'Fading Fast', 'A Cross To Bear', 'You'll Know Lightning', 'Ash In The Wind' and the whole 'If You Saw Thro' My Eyes' album. I could go on (and on…).

After 53 years of listening there we finally were: Iain singing and playing right in front of us. At the start there were some problems with the amplifier, but when he began playing it became obvious what a professional artist he really is. His singing is surely stunning and with that voice, how could he go wrong…? His guitar playing is really fine nowadays. He told stories and made us enjoy ourselves. I believe he was enjoying himself too.

On some songs, Iain was joined by Joe Harvey-Whyte on steel guitar, but it sounded more like a lap steel. Joe is a young guy who had recently bought a guitar from Iain and he was there to collect it. After never playing together before, they did very well indeed.

TIVOLI THEATRE

17 AUGUST 2023, WIMBORNE, UK

DAVID JOHNSON

My first date with my now wife was in April 1991 to see Al Stewart, with Iain Matthews supporting. We knew him mainly from Fairport and were not prepared for such a stunning set, so much so that we booked to see him again a few months later at Reading. Fast forward to post Covid, in 2023, and somehow we found out about a small gig in a Brighton pub with Andy

Roberts. And then we saw him again in Wimborne. On both occasions I could only say 'thank you'.

TERRY BAKER

Terry Baker (pictured with wife Freda) shares a love of Manchester United with Iain

I came across a mention of Iain's potential UK tour dates in 2022 on his Facebook page and reached out. Having booked theatre shows for sports personalities, and being a fan of Iain's music from years ago, I was keen to arrange some dates for him. I even used a phrase from one of his albums from the seventies – 'some days you eat the bear, some days the bear eats you' – without realising its origin until recently!

I organized around eight shows for him and while I only had the chance to meet him once, at the Tivoli Theatre in Wimborne, it was a memorable performance. The audience may have been smaller than deserved, but everyone thoroughly enjoyed it. I particularly loved his renditions of Jackson Browne's 'These Days' and 'Seven Bridges Road'. It was his version of 'These Days' that introduced me to Jackson Browne's music many years ago.

We also connected over our shared love for Manchester United, and I was able to get Iain signed memorabilia from some of the athletes I work with, including Wayne Rooney and Eric Cantona. I'm also friendly with an agent for Sir Geoff Hurst. Iain and Geoff are the only people I know who look so good for their age – at least 15 years younger! It's inspiring that Iain's still touring and creating new music.

Keep up the great work, and let's hope we both live to see Manchester United back at the top of the Premier League.

FOLKLORE ROOMS

13 JUNE 2024, BRIGHTON, UK

NICK HALL

I remember the first time I met Iain Matthews (but he probably won't remember this) was backstage at Cropredy some years ago. He and his lovely family members were staying with my friends John and Bev and I was introduced to Iain and Andy Roberts (who won't remember this either!) in the cool camper van that John and Bev had hired.

I recall I was nervous to meet such a famous ex-Fairport member but Iain immediately put me at ease and was kind and friendly, with his characteristic, very welcoming smile. He was courteous enough to be interested in what I was doing musically as well, which was lovely. We passed a very friendly couple of hours in good company with nice wine.

It was great to later see Iain and Andy perform brilliantly with Mark Griffiths on the Cropredy main stage with their superb Richard Fariña show.

At a later Cropredy, Michelle (my wife and half of Plumhall) also loved Iain's set with BJ Baartmans on guitar. Just the two of them managed to captivate the crowd and it was a masterclass in

Nick Hall first met Iain backstage at Cropredy

performing and connecting with a huge audience.

Fast forward to 2023 and John and Bev kindly invited Michelle and me round to their house to have a meal with them, Iain and Marly. It was lovely to meet Marly properly and great to reconnect with Iain. We all got on like a house on fire – so much so that Iain very kindly invited us to his show in Ilkley the next night.

Iain's show was brilliant – a superb set of his own great songs interspersed with inspired covers (his version of 'Mercy Street' sent shivers down my spine). After the show we said hi to Marly, bought Iain's autobiography and said a fond farewell to them both – not knowing when we'd see them again…

Fast forward to 2024 and, having come off the back of the Fairport tour, Michelle and I were itching to tour again and were so excited to be playing some great venues opening for Iain. The first show, at the atmospheric Folklore Rooms, was such great fun, especially as Andy was guesting with Iain. We had worked up an encore of 'Woodstock' and 'Killing The Blues' where Michelle and I would join Iain on guitar and backing vocals. It was such an honour to share the stage with Iain and I think we made a very good racket! Throughout the tour it was great to watch Iain perform at close quarters and get to know more of his songs. Having read his autobiography, I really felt we were getting to know him well.

He is a very generous person to tour with and his audiences were all lovely people, interested in music and kind enough to give us a good listen too. After Brighton, we played the Sound Lounge in London (one of the favourite nights I've ever had in a venue – thank you Iain for introducing us all these fab places!), a sold-out Milton Keynes Stables and then headed north for shows at John and Bev's house (for Iain's birthday), Appletreewick Cruck Barn and Chapel Allerton Seven Arts.

At every stop on the tour, Iain mesmerised the audiences with his lovely songs, ageless voice and warm stage presence.

It was great to tour with Marly, John and Bev too and it was a happy touring family.

When the tour ended - much too quickly - conversations were had and plans put in place… watch this space! I hope we'll be working with Iain again in the very near future and I for one can't wait. We've already had a successful go at writing a song together (I have to pinch myself writing that) and we're looking forward to more collaboration.

It's been a joy to meet and get to know Iain and here's to whatever comes next. As Iain likes to say: 'Onwards!'

SOUND LOUNGE

14 JUNE 2024, SUTTON, UK

NEVILLE DALTON

I met Iain for the first and only time when I visited the Sound Lounge in Sutton, south London, to see my friends, Plumhall, who were his support. I was fortunate enough to spend the hours leading up to the gig with my friends and Iain and his charming wife, Marly, who regaled me with stories of previous shows and tours over his lifetime in music.

I watched his sound check and complimented him on a superb cover of Jackson Browne's 'These Days' and another stunning song, the title of which I can't recall. He played neither in his set that night!

Iain with Nick Hall at the Sound Lounge (Neville Dalton)

Neville Dalton saw Iain at Sutton's Sound Lounge

What struck me about him was his modesty and amiability. He has been at the forefront of some of the UK's greatest music in a career that stretches way beyond that of most of his peers. He has worked with Richard Thompson and Sandy Denny but stands as tall as any of them. Yet he chatted as though he had known me for years (as did Marly) and seemed genuinely interested in the songs I liked and why I liked them.

He was trying desperately for last-minute tickets to see Crowded House that month. I looked up their availability on my phone and let him know as he settled down at my table to watch Plumhall. I hope he got the tickets in the end.

HOUSE CONCERT

16 JUNE 2024

JOHN & BEVERLEY WALSH

We've been close friends with Iain for many years and had numerous curries, road trips and nights spent discussing his odd choice in football teams. But he's a top guy, a super unique talent and we're so pleased to have hosted a house concert for him right on his birthday. We hope to do it all again soon.

John Walsh with Iain

SEVEN ARTS THEATRE

23 JUNE 2024, CHAPEL ALLERTON, LEEDS, UK

SHAUN HUNTER

I had just arrived home from a show in Newark, New Jersey when I received a text message from a dear friend and supporter of my work, John Walsh:

Hi Shaun, hope all is good. I've got Iain Matthews (Fairport Convention, Matthews Southern Comfort) and his wife staying with us and he's breathless watching your videos. Absolutely blown away by your music.

I thought, 'Wow, woah… how utterly wonderful to receive such a message from a peer of note.' The substance and great weight of Iain's art in the world of true songwriters always felt apparent and deeply resonated with me. His long-time collaboration friend, Andy Roberts, had just finished a video about his musical exploits with my filmmaker friend, Nick Bloomfield, who has made numerous videos for me over the years. It felt like a joyous little synchronicity.

Iain was playing the Seven Arts Theatre in Chapel Allerton, Leeds. I told John I'd love to be at the show… He replied, 'Please do come, Shaun. I know that Iain would love to meet you. I'll put you and yours on the guest list.'

The show was a warm excursion of an energy akin to that of meeting an old friend… strangely familiar. Great songs and wonderful stories of the events that formulated much of Iain's life were poured forth, from the inescapable heat and hard circumstances and conditions of his time in Texas to the latter years spent in the heart of Europe, primarily The Netherlands, where a belated contentment seemed evident. Iain's voice, awash with gravitas, sounding age defying yet, paradoxically, full of experience and heartfelt reflection, resulting in simmering sonic story segues overlaying his fine and sensitive guitar playing.

He was supported by the dulcet tones of Plumhall, the husband-and-wife team of Nick and Michelle, who played a magical little opening set and then returned to join Iain on a couple of numbers, culminating in a rousing emotive version of Fairport's 'Meet On The Ledge' as an encore.

After the show we hugged in a nourishing wide-eyed fashion, embracing like two young school friends who had been forcibly absent. Iain said in my ear, 'That Captain thing, it's like nothing else, it's art, you've nailed it totally, absolutely completely.'

The conversation continued in jocular exchanges as we morphed into memories of sweets; Iain opened up a bag of Pontefract Cakes (liquorice) that he always loved. What greater honour than sharing one of a man's childhood favourites? We laughed, reflected momentarily on the difference of our journeys and tried to succinctly see where our paths dissected and momentarily might cross.

With that we exchanged physical albums and our curated catalogues, Iain carefully choosing the albums he really wanted me to have, and we had a photo together.

Iain said, 'I'd love to do a version of that great song of yours, 'Drifting'. I hope I can do it justice.' I retorted, 'I'd love nothing more than to hear that, it would be a wonderful thing to behold.' Equally, I'd like to translate one of Iain's songs and hopefully it'll be a welcome surprise when I deliver it to him.

What hit me with Iain in the short time we spent together was his gentle kindness, his ability to truly listen and his humility and grace. If you'd listened to us and didn't know who was who, it wasn't clear that it was Iain who had the seminal success and inhabited the musical spheres of well-worn, well-known names in the history of the music business.

There was a bond and a connection that evening, which remains, to this day, a rather mystical one. As if we saw each other beyond name and form… and what we revealed was that which operates far beyond the confines of music or stories; a cosmic law felt as if it was all enveloping in that potent and magical meet.

Alongside my wife, Lucy and my 18-year-old son, Harry, we shared laughter and frivolity with him and his dear and delightful wife, Marly.

Thank you, Iain.

LISA COMMENTUCCI-LOWDEN

I'm so glad to have the opportunity to express my love for Iain's music! Playing in three bands with my husband (Steve Lowden), we love to search for unique work and Iain's songwriting and his vocals are so inspiring! Besides having a 'velvet' voice, we have enjoyed the many albums, bands and other works he has done. Thank you so much for your lovely contribution to music!

Lisa is a big fan of Iain

HAVERFORD TOWNSHIP MUSIC FESTIVAL

7 SEPTEMBER 2024, HAVERTOWN, PENNSYLVANIA

JESSE HUBLEY

I first saw Iain Matthews perform in 2012 at a coffee shop in the Philadelphia suburbs. Iain was touring with a friend and bandmate of mine, Jim Fogarty, who at that time I had met several months prior. I didn't know much about Iain other than that he was at one time a member of Fairport Convention, and that he toured the Mid-Atlantic region with Fogarty as his sideman every year or two. I came out of that show impressed with what I heard and proceeded to dig into his studio album catalogue. The more I listened, the more I began to enjoy and appreciate songs from solo and collaborative albums from all eras of his music.

After again seeing Iain on his next area tour in 2013 at the Sellersville Theater, I was planning to see him again in 2014, when I saw a Facebook post from Fogarty mentioning that a local venue had accidentally double-booked Iain and another band on the same night and as a result he was asking if anyone knew of another venue where they might be able to slot in on that date. Mostly as a joke, I added a comment to his post that read, 'How about you play here at my house?' Later, Fogarty asked me if I was joking or not, and I said I mostly was, but if Iain really wanted to give that a go, I would be up for hosting a house concert, even though I had never done that before.

Iain and Jim Fogarty at Haverford Music Festival (Patti Hubley)

The three of us all decided to do it, and the first ever Iain Matthews house concert in Havertown, Pennsylvania turned out to be a success. It was a surreal event for me, having a living legend perform in my living room. About half the crowd were family and friends that I already knew, but the rest were new or only slightly familiar faces, which in several cases became long-term friendships. And another long-term friendship that grew out of that was with Iain, who I not only remain in touch with to this day, but for whom I have since hosted four more house concerts on Iain's subsequent mid-Atlantic tours, in 2017, 2019, 2021 and 2023.

During his 2023 tour, I even had a chance to tag along with Ian and Fogarty to a Philadelphia Phillies game (over the years, Iain had picked up some of Fogarty's Philadelphia sports fandom, and additionally the Phillies were playing the Seattle Mariners, with Seattle being a place that Iain lived for a stretch early in his US residency). It was 'dollar dog night' at the stadium that night, which intrigued Iain (normally a vegetarian) enough to try a ballpark hot dog. And by his own admission, he enjoyed it.

My experiences with Iain came full circle on his most recent mid-Atlantic tour in September of 2024 when Iain performed with Fogarty and a percussionist as a headlining act of the Haverford Music Festival, an annual event run by a non-profit organisation of which I am a volunteer member. During Iain's set, a light rain gave way to a clearing sky, and a bright rainbow appeared overhead that landed directly in the backdrop of the stage behind Iain.

The most amusing anecdote from the five Iain / Jim house concerts I hosted was during the 2021 show when the two biggest Iain fans I know, Jeff and Delight Roberts (who attended all five of my house concerts, plus the 2024 festival), sat outside on my patio behind Iain and Jim and listened through the windows because they were being extra cautious about Covid. (They were taking care of Delight's 99-year-old mother at the time.) At one point during the show between songs, I told Iain that his two biggest fans came despite having to sit outside, and as he thought I was joking, we got him to turn around and look out the window, and sure enough there were Jeff and Delight waving back at him.

One last story I would be remiss not to share is that the 2019 house concert came during a difficult time in my life when I was fighting depression for about six months. During the leadup time to Iain's arrival that year, I read his recently released autobiography *Thro' My Eyes* which included many poignant introspective tales of life on the road, often living and travelling alone. This resonated with me greatly. And I became immersed in the 1999 Plainsong album *New Place Now*, which helped me get through that difficult time.

I hope that my friend from across the ocean can continue to make it back to Philadelphia in the coming years. Until then,

I continue to be a fan of Iain's music, and hold on to my vinyl copy of the Matthews Southern Comfort self-titled album, which Ian signed at the first house concert in 2014 with the personalised note:

'Jesse – This album is old.'

PATTI HUBLEY

It was 2014 and my husband and I were waiting with anticipation looking forward to meeting and hearing Iain Matthews live for the first time. We are from the United States and we first heard of Matthews Southern Comfort with their hit of Joni Mitchell's 'Woodstock' at the ages of 18 and 19 in 1971. We didn't specifically know who the 'Matthews' was in the group's name at that time.

Fast forward to 2014 and our son, who is and has been a drummer in local bands over the years, asked my husband and I if we knew of the group Matthews Southern Comfort. We said that we did and he told us that Iain Matthews, the band's founder, was going to do a concert at his house along with an accomplished local guitar player, Jim Fogarty.

We were very impressed with Iain's mellow, harmonious voice especially for someone who has been singing for decades. Afterwards, he stayed and conversed with anyone that was attending the concert that wanted to meet him. He was cordial, very interesting and we enjoyed listening to his smooth British accent. Since we met him in 2014, he has returned several times to tour the US East Coast which usually included our son's home and we have attended each time. That has allowed us to get to know him personally to a small degree and we continue to follow him on the internet and listen to his music.

We also really enjoyed his performance (once again accompanied by Jim Fogarty) at the 2024 Haverford Music Festival outside of Philadelphia. The weather that day included on and off light rain. As Iain and Jim walked on to the stage they were almost magically accompanied by an amazing rainbow! Now it's 2025 and we look forward to Iain hopefully returning again for another East Coast visit.

HOUSE CONCERT
14 SEPTEMBER 2024, USA

TOM FLECK

I have been very lucky to have seen over 500 artists in my life. Being able to see Iain live and at a house concert was truly a once-in-a-lifetime event. After attending so many shows in my life, it's really great to have a venue where not only do you hear your favourite songs but also the artist's thoughts about those songs. Iain put on a great show with support from Tommy Geddes and Jim Fogarty. It was as if the band and attendees were long-time friends with us. He played so many of his songs which brought me back to when I heard the song for the first time.

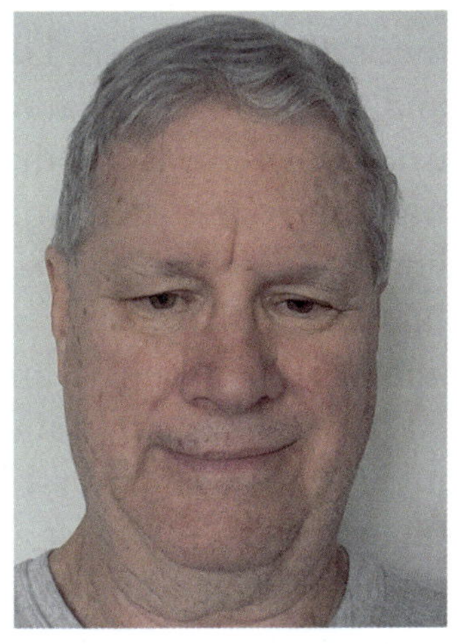

Tom feels like he's a friend of Iain's via his music

My invitation had come a couple of months before the show. I recently downsized my record collection from just under 3,000 albums to 25 or so, and *Stealin' Home* is one of those I kept. I was listening to it when the email came through announcing the show.

'Let There Be Blues' is one of my favourite songs by any artist. 'Man In The Station' is another favourite, but the whole album is great. Talking to Iain and the band after the show was great. As in his music, a picture of the artist comes through and that picture was painted vividly by his interactions with me and everyone at the show. It was a one-off experience and I'm so glad I went and met Iain, a great writer and performer, After the show he made me feel like I was one of his friends, although we were already friends through his music.

HOUSE CONCERT

20 SEPTEMBER 2024, STROUDSBURG, PENNSYLVANIA

TOM HAMPTON

In the mid-nineties, I was floundering in the throes of a musical identity crisis. I'd been playing underneath dart boards and televisions in restaurants and corner bars for some time, wondering how it was that people eventually managed to transition out of that world and into the next. I don't remember how I got the gig, but I was offered an opportunity to open for Iain and Jim Fogarty at a show in a town between Philadelphia and Reading, Pennsylvania.

I had no idea who Iain was prior to that show, but his set that night was a revelation. I brought home five CDs from his merch table (spending at least as much as I was paid for the opening slot) and while I loved *Pure And Crooked*, the *Complete Notebook Series* discs stayed in rotation for the space of a couple years after that. I grew to prefer his version of 'Mercy Street' to the Peter Gabriel original.

Years went by. Our paths crossed again a dozen years ago when an artist whose record I'd helped produce opened a show for him in NJ, and then in the summer of 2024 I split a bill with him at a house concert just outside Philadelphia. It struck me, listening to him that night, that he hasn't lost a step in the nearly 30 years since I first encountered him and his music.

He's a true original – never afraid to colour outside the lines when the mood strikes – but his musical identity is a thread that leaves its mark on everything he's done over the course of a truly remarkable career.

SJOERD VAN BOMMEL, DRUMMER, MUSICIAN

I met Iain later in life as a studio musician. I had heard about his existence through the grapevine but I had a different road to walk with my choice of music, hard-funk, fusion and rock before I came to an appreciation of roots-Americana and folk and country. I knew of Matthews Southern Comfort and their hit 'Woodstock' and I knew that Iain had decided to live in Holland but that was all.

Having great friends in Germany where there was a tradition of inviting musicians from all over the world to play in their venue, my German girlfriend told me that out of all those acts they hired through decades of gigs, her favourite was Iain Matthews. At the time it went in one ear and out the other.

Being a drummer, I'm usually the first musician to lay down the carpet for others to add their instruments to and sing upon, mostly when I'm already gone, so when I got a CD in my postbox of a recording with different singers singing songs from one singer-songwriter, my ear got stuck to one song called 'Private Ways'.

The way the guest singer filled in that song was amazing, with a gripping strong vocal. Not that the others weren't also great, but he stood out and, sure enough, it was my German friend's favourite. I sent her that song and she was over the moon.

Since then, I have met Iain Matthews during various recordings. I have played on at least three albums as his drummer and now we work together in the studio, so the interaction is one-on-one. He is a delight to work with because he is plain and simple, an amazing songsmith. His lyrics are strong and down to earth about the greater scheme of things. He is clear in his opinions about the way the world is turning, but his songs on a domestic level are always honest observations of his day-to-day life and how he interacts with his little family and the ones he loves.

The Netherlands has an amazingly good scene of singer-songwriters in the traditions of folk, roots and Americana with a hint of country, but Iain stands out with his use of words and how he employs his vocal cords. The average singer has to accept the diminishing of his vocals with age, but not so for Iain Matthews. Even when singing on his demos, he is consistent in delivering an amazing quality. It's like he's never aloof about his art, which makes it a breeze to work with him.

That said, before I played with him I heard that he wasn't the easiest cookie to work with. But to my surprise he was a nice bloke with interest in all kinds of things beside making music. He is an avid reader, which I am too, so we exchange book titles and find we have a lot in common.

We made two albums together in 2024 and in an age where the average rock star is repeating his greatest hits, this guy is still on the barricades finding ways to come up with songs that are still of this time. His urgency is genuine. He is a young man inside and out, and we still can't draw any conclusions about the future. This man isn't done yet!

HOW MUCH IS ENOUGH (VOLUME ONE)
RELEASED 25 OCTOBER 2024

SUSAN PARK

When I left my parents' home in '71 and moved down to teach art at Fennville High School, I was a new teacher and flat broke except for babysitting money from the summer months. LPs cost $11 to $14 then, so I didn't own many records. I had whatever Beatle LPs were out then plus three more… *Sweet Baby James* by James Taylor, *The Thorn In Mrs Rose's Side* by Biff Rose and *If You Saw Thro' My Eyes.* When Iain performed in Spring Lake, Michigan, I had him sign it.

I bought a used car in November 2024. It had no CD player, which made me crazy, so I bought a portable one that hardly reached to the USB port. I had just purchased Iain's new CD, *How Much Is Enough (Volume One)*, and I couldn't bear to change it. My favourite songs off it? 'It's Complicated', 'The New Dark Ages', 'Ripples In The Stream', 'Good Intentions' and the title track, but I really love them all. I was driving with his new CD playing when 'To Baby' came on… I was totally knocked out. I had to pull into a parking lot and stop the car until I pulled myself together.

Iain has asked how much is enough and my reply is *please* don't stop! I've had his songs playing in my car since the second week in December… and I'm *still* not ready to change the CD for something new!

JOOST HARTOG

My connection with Iain's music comes from the early solo years. I loved most of his work in these years and listened to the albums often in my attic room, lying on the floor with my eyes closed. I remember all of them, but maybe the most the moments I drifted away on 'Biloxi', with his smooth voice and the brilliant lapsteel of David Lindley, whose sound I already knew from my other distant friend, Jackson Browne.

Joost Hartog would listen to Iain's music with his eyes closed

Much later, Iain's version of 'Woodstock' inspired me to write a song, which in name ('Southern Comfort') referred to his band and in its lyrics asked listeners to keep the message in mind. (I'm afraid the recording, in BJ's studio Wild Verband, drew a bit too little attention.)

EDUARDO TORRES

It was 2020 when I discovered Matthew Southern Comfort's music through the song 'Woodstock'. I liked the band's – and the vocalist's – style. I'm a huge fan of folk, country and rock but in my country, only Pink Floyd and Led Zeppelin were heard in the seventies. Unfortunately, we can't get Iain's music in El Salvador. But I am very happy to know that we have YouTube. There it teaches us that for a long time we ignored the existence of many facts that we did not know. Well, I highly praise the music, the songs, the unmatched style of the group and Matthews' slow and melodic voice, like most of the songs where he uses that great voice.

NIKOS KIRITSIS

I first learned about Iain 25 years ago, while I was student in Crete, Greece. His music was introduced to me by a hippie at a flower power place called Janis Farm. Listening first to Fairport Convention and, later on, Matthews Southern Comfort and Iain's early solo recordings really changed my way of thinking about life. I have heard many stories about Iain's visit to Janis Farm, and although I have never really met Iain, one day I believe we will reunite with Iain at Janis Farm and celebrate the music that we love so much.

JAN WIM SCHOENMAKERS

In the early seventies I was a member of a youth choir and one of my friends played the music of Matthews Southern Comfort to us. We liked it and for quite a long time we sang together songs like 'Mare, Take Me Home', 'D'arcy Farrow', 'Even As' and – our big favourite – 'Blood Red Roses'.

Jan Wim bought a guitar off Iain

Later I kept following Iain as a solo artist. His album *If You Saw Thro' My Eyes* is still an all-time favourite of mine. (Besides being a fan, I am a singer-songwriter myself and Iain is a big inspiration to me.)

Over the past years BJ Baartmans worked a lot with Iain. They recorded a bunch of songs in BJ 's studio, played together on stages and BJ is a member of Matthews Southern Comfort. I know BJ because he played all kind of instruments on several of my songs I recorded and released.

In 2015 Iain sold a few of his guitars through BJ Baartmans.

I was immediately interested and bought one of them. BJ asked me to pick up the guitar from his house. I did that and when I walked into the living room, to my great surprise, I saw not only the guitar I had purchased but also Iain Matthews himself. BJ hadn't let me know that Iain would be there too. I was thrilled and, at first, I didn't know what to say. After a while we had a nice conversation about his music, and why and how I became fan, especially of his solo work.

He told me some things about the guitar, who built it and what he mainly used it for; practising in hotel rooms and writing songs. I also told him about the youth choir from long ago and how we sang his songs for fun. I paid for the guitar and he signed the body. I said I would take good care of the guitar and he replied, 'Oh you can break it now!' Very funny!

I've met Iain again a few times in the past years in BJ Baartmans' studio and during concerts with Matthews Southern Comfort, and every time BJ explains to him, 'That's the guy who bought one of your guitars.'

Some years ago, MSC played in my hometown and a few of my old friends of the youth choir came too and sang along of course and we had a little chat with Iain.

He is a very nice guy and a fantastic musician. Secretly I hope to work together as songwriters one day. Then a dream of mine would come true.

JULIAN DAWSON

My first ever trip to the USA began in New York with a visit to a music industry shindig called the 'New Music Seminar'. I was wearing a badge saying 'Artist' with Warner Chappell, my publisher. The event was held in a giant steel and glass palace somewhere in Manhattan and on the very first day I was riding up an escalator and spotted the unmistakable figure of Iain Matthews. (As a fan who had worn out his copy of Matthews' Southern Comfort's *Second Spring*, I knew what he looked like.)

My recollection is that Iain's badge said 'A & R, Windham Hill', which surprised me. I trusted myself to talk to him, but didn't manage much more than, 'I'm a big fan'. He was obviously busy, probably with meetings to attend, so that was the end of our scintillating conversation. Who'd have thought that from that chance encounter, we would share 20 years of Plainsong and (with occasional blips) a lifetime of friendship. Harmony singing is still the most fun you can have without taking your clothes off!

Keep on sailing…

ÅKE BANKSELL

I think I first heard Mr Matthews when Matthews Southern Comfort's 'Second Spring' was played on the radio here in Sweden. The record was later sold in our staff shop at Philips, where I worked in the factory. As a part-time musician, I was fascinated by all the nice sounds they created and I liked the vocals at the same time. Ian's voice was of course a big foundation. I was convinced that he was a great musical leader in the band.

Åke Banksell first heard Iain via MSC

When they had a big hit with 'Woodstock' I thought that the band would appear again on the charts so I wouldn't have to keep an eye on them. When *If You Saw Thro' My Eyes* came out, it expanded my musical horizons. I often played guitar in my free time with Ove at the military base and I taught him many of the songs on Matthews' record. We learned by listening to the record a lot anyway. It's about timing and such. I did military service and forgot about both Matthews and other favourites and started listening more to Poco, The Eagles and Jackson Browne but eventually Ian's voice came back to my head because it is so special. *Later That Same Year* is another great record.

In the late eighties, a colleague in a band I played with told me that he knew everything about Iain Matthews and of course he had all the LPs. I can only say that Ian has one of the finest voices in the music industry and that he was fired from Fairport Convention seems crazy but it was probably because they were too young and inexperienced to understand what a really good singer he is.

CHRISTOPHER SHUTTY

When I think of Iain and his music, I am greeted by this artist who says to me, 'I want to inspire people, I want to tell a story that both entertains yet causes reflection. I want you to look at me and say because of you I didn't give up.' As a physician, his career to me was inspirational, especially during my training years. Listening to his music during rough patches was something that reinforced hope and provided inspiration.

The first time I heard Iain was back in 1999 in college. The song was a Jimmy Webb song, 'Met Her On A Plane'. I began to think of the meaning of the song and its meaning for me. Subsequently, I searched out more of his songs and was hooked.

Iain has a melodic voice that can sing anything and make it sound good. Along with his own writing, Iain really knows how to pick songs to sing. Musically, he always knows how to choose an arrangement for that time and place. Over the years, he has

Christopher Shutty first heard Iain in 1999

continued to evolve a variety of songs to make them fit the era. Some of my favourites include 'Tigers Will Survive', 'Pebbles In The Road', 'Right As Rain', 'How Much Is Enough' and 'The Letter (1944)'. I continue to follow his career and never miss the chance to see him when he is on tour.

So I will conclude simply by saying thank you, Iain. Thank you for the music, the memories and the inspiration.

JON CROUSE

My memories of Iain date back to as long as I can remember. Growing up, there was always music playing, consuming every corner of my atmosphere. My father's favourite artists spilled out of every stereo and speaker system imaginable. One of those artists was Iain Matthews.

Over my growing years I have been absorbing his musical output from his time with Fairport Convention, Matthews Southern Comfort, Plainsong and his extensive solo work. The variety and scope of his discography meant there was hardly any musical landscape untouched by his talents as a singer and songwriter. Its influence on me once I decided to pick up a guitar and sing myself has been insurmountable. Whether it was learning how to harmonise from his records or taking a song you didn't write and interpreting it to fit your singularity.

My father ran a nightclub and invited Iain to sing, and over the years I've gotten to know Iain outside of the vast records I grew up on. I've gotten to know the kind soul, laid back and funny as hell person that he truly is!

Several years ago, I had the honour of opening for Iain for the first time. To my surprise I was asked to do so several more times afterwards. Since then, he has become a mentor of sorts to me. He would give great advice, constructive criticism when needed and was very supportive and nurturing of my skills as a singer and songwriting.

I grew up listening to Iain Matthews as just a regular fan, but am now lucky to have the privilege to listen to Iain not only as fan, but as a friend as well.

'WOODSTOCK'

HELEN STADLER

When I was a teenager, we had a stereo with a record player at home and a portable cassette player at the side for daily use. One of the cassette tapes was called *Flower Power* and it was my favourite. It contained a collection of different songs from the sixties and seventies including a beautiful song that I knew as 'Stardust'.

Years later, during my student days, one of my best friends worked in the croissant shop in Horst. Marly usually worked there alone on Saturdays, but if there was a fair or another party in the village it was too busy for one person and so I would come and help out for the day. We always played nice music there, and because there was no CD player, I'd take my *Flower Power* cassette tape with me. They were wonderful days, working together with nice music in the background.

Years later, the same friend called me. After a concert in Cambrinus in Belgium, Marly had got into conversation with an English singer and they couldn't stop talking. I was happy for her because she had been through a tough time with a divorce. He was a bit older she said, and maybe I knew him? He had had a worldwide hit, in the year my friend and I were both born, with the song 'Woodstock'. It didn't immediately mean anything to me, but when I started looking, I was almost speechless. It was the song I knew as 'Stardust'! I had always thought the song was sung by a woman, but it was the voice of the young Iain… How special.

The singer of one of my favourite songs is now married to one of my best friends. The CD about his meeting with her melts my heart again and again.

BART DE WIN

One day I was playing keyboard parts on Matthews Southern Comfort tracks that still had so-called 'scratch vocals', just to let me know where the song was going, and with Iain Matthews in the room apologising for whatever he thought was worth apologising for. Meanwhile I was thinking, 'What could've been done better on that vocal track?' I'm just saying, Iain is not a sloppy guy when it comes to singing. I admire that kind of conviction. And apparently it comes easy. It just has to sound good. Period. And it always does.

Iain and I met around 2010 when he needed a keyboard player with a voice for Matthews Southern Comfort. BJ Baartmans and I already played together. I am still grateful he and Egbert Derix endorsed me. So here I was playing with an icon. Elly Kellner (and later Eric Devries) made it all complete.

In the meantime, I had my friendship with Texan songwriter and producer Walt Wilkins. Every year me and my wife, Arianne Knegt, go to Texas to meet him and Bill Small and the rest of a huge circle of fans and fellow musicians. In November they come

Bart De Win has played keyboards with Iain

to The Netherlands to stay with us. We play as much as we can during the two or three weeks they are present, so every now and again I wouldn't be available for Iain.

'How do you know Walt?' Iain asked me. 'We know each other. I lived in Austin for years.'

'Are you in a band with Iain? I've been a fan since I was a kid!' said Walt.

It turns out they met a bit in the past but lost contact when Iain left Austin. And now I was some kind of spider in the web of musical liaisons.

In 2008 I met Walt for the first time in the monastery of Roepaen where he played with Sam Baker. Arianne saw him and Sam earlier that year and she promised me a blast. The only two seats were right in front of Walt. First row. I loved everything about it. Sam asked for requests. Arianne jumped up and asked (without being aware) for a Walt Wilkins song, since she remembered the title from the previous concert. Everybody laughed, especially Sam Baker, and they played the song. When I told Iain about this, he replied, 'Aha, so Arianne was the one in the first row jumping up. I was standing in the back!'

Synchronicity. I love it.

ATJA OUT

One of my darkest years was the year of my divorce. Although it was my decision, it was a hard thing to do, because it included my two sons. My former husband's effect on our marriage and our lives was devastating, so I left with our two boys, then aged five and seven. With no job and no desire for alimony from my husband (which would give him power over me), I was lucky enough to quickly get an apartment for us.

So far, so good. But then the finances, problem. I ended up on assistance. Not very nice nor funny…

But I had an old record player and my records, including a lot of Fairport Convention albums, a band I had discovered in my teens and have followed ever since. From those albums I discovered Iain and his voice and the bands he formed. Even the name 'Southern Comfort'. Comfort was what I was looking for and what I got. Man, his music pulled me through!

I cried, sang and danced to Iain's lovely songs and still admire his sound and voice. When I found out he had chosen Holland and a Dutch girl to play a lead role in his life I was (crazy but true) proud. Our country! A Dutch girl!

Thank you, Iain, for the wonderful music such as 'Tigers Will Survive' and 'If You Saw Thro' My Eyes'. And thank whoever rules the world for your magnificent voice.

BILL HIGGINS

Bill is never disappointed by Iain

I've been following Iain's career for years, from Fairport Convention to the present. Every performance is always different and exciting due in large part to his vast catalogue. He is a master 'wordsmith' in the same league as Bob Dylan and Richard Fariña. He has an emotional impact throughout his lyrics and arrangements. He's a great artist in every sense of the word. As a composer, musician, singer and performer, he never disappoints.

BRADLEY KOPP

Over the course of the nineties, I had the pleasure of joining Iain on multiple tours in the US, Japan and Europe. We travelled tens of thousands of miles together. When working in Europe, we would fly into Berlin's Tegal airport, rent a car and head towards our first venue. Typically, we would tour for three weeks. When touring, if you're not playing and making money, you are spending money so we worked as many dates in those three weeks as possible. We'd drive to a gig, do the sound check, check in to our hotel, grab a meal, do the show, go to the hotel, chill out, get some sleep, rinse and repeat daily. We jokingly started writing a song which in its entirely went 'we eat, we sleep, we drive, we play…'.

Bradley Kopp remembers getting lost in Berlin

As you can imagine, touring like that can be a grind. We would share the driving chores and sometimes there were some long hauls. At the end of one tour, we were headed back to Berlin for the last show. It was a long travel day. Those German cities have loops around them that we called 'ring roads'. They are basically concentric circles of roads around the city not unlike the interstate loops around big cities in the US like Loop 610 around Houston (for those of you who know). It was before the days of GPS.

Iain was taking his turn at the wheel. We were approaching the outskirts of Berlin and searching for the right 'ring road' to take us to the road into Berlin where our hotel was. We were tired. We'd been hard at it for three weeks. We were having a hard time figuring out which ring road to take. Then Iain said, 'I'm just going to take this one.' After a bit, we randomly turned onto a north bound street heading into Berlin. It had gotten dark and it was difficult to see the street signs and we weren't sure we'd taken the right road.

We were driving and driving and straining to see the signs. Every mile or so the name of the street we were on would change. We were both getting a little tired and anxious. I was looking at the signs, saying, 'No, that's not it! I don't know where the hell we are!' We drove further and Iain said, 'What does that one say?' I said, 'That's not it either.' Then Iain said, 'I'm just going to pull over and fight.' I said, 'I'm not fighting, I'm just trying to figure out where we are!' He said, 'Well, I'm not either!'

We looked up at the street sign and found we were on the right road. We laughed and started back driving. Pretty soon we saw Tegal Airport on our right and a few blocks past we found our hotel. We looked for parking and there was none. People had parked on the sidewalk. We decided to check into the hotel, return the rental car at the nearby airport and walk back. Just another day in the life of a touring musician.

We've known each other for almost 40 years. Who'd have thought that a British ex-pat and a kid from a hick town in the panhandle of Texas would end up being the best of friends? We've logged countless miles, worked on many records together including four solo records, which I had the honour of producing for him.

Thank you, Iain, for believing in my talent. But most of all, thank you for being my friend. Love you, bud!

DAVID FARRELL

I have been a fan of Iain for a lot of years, in the early years without fully realising it, initially from hearing 'Woodstock' by Matthews Southern Comfort. In 1973 I bought my mother a sampler LP from Elektra Records (because I loved the cover!). She didn't like it, so *The One That Got Away* became mine... I loved all the tracks and later bought the 'second' sampler album, *New Magic In A Dusty World*. Both featured Plainsong, but *The One That Got Away* featured 'Goodnight Loving Trail' and someone called Ian Matthews with 'These Days'. Both entered my favourites track list.

Roll on 20 plus years and I was listening to a lot of the Bob Harris overnight shows and especially loving the interviews. One night in the early hours I was listening to Bob talking to 'someone interesting' and it dawned on me that it was Iain Matthews. All the pieces then started to fall into place.

Roll on a few more years. I was now married and I took my wife along to see Plainsong in Banbury. Mid-show I was chuffed to be able to call out from the front row a suggestion for 'Goodnight Loving Trail'.

After the show, as the band and a few people had gathered in the stage area, I was able to say a personal thank you to Iain and explain how long I had been a fan. I added the account of hearing the overnight radio interview that had made all the pieces drop into place and a few glances were exchanged around the band. I made my excuses and left.

As I walked back to my wife, she said, 'Did you just speak to Bob Harris as well?' Doh!

I have been able to see several more UK shows. I now always make sure to know all those on stage…

ANDY MILLS

My wife, Julia Mills, was a major fan of Iain from his early solo days. Even at 14 and being obsessed with Slade she had the album sleeve for *If You Saw Thro' My Eyes* on her wall. When we dated, she introduced me to his musical genius and I was hooked. Other LPs were purchased and then life got in the way – university, marriage, career and two sons were the priority.

One day early in 1990, we were looking in a local paper and saw a concert in Cheltenham featuring Iain Matthews. We decided to organise baby sitters and invite friends. On a snowy evening, Julia rediscovered Iain and became hooked on his music and shows. Over the next few years, we travelled all over England to Iain's solo shows (many on the same tour) and those with the reformed Plainsong. At each show we would chat with Iain and sometimes help him sell merchandise. He

Andy with his late wife Julia, who was a big fan of Iain

was always gracious and willing to talk to his fans. We bought all his CDs and played his music frequently. The most memorable show was at the Half Moon in Putney, which I thought was a solo show but actually had Andy and Mark playing as well. We chatted to the other fans and also to Iain.

I told him that it was Julia's birthday and to our surprise he asked her to pick the final song of the evening. She chose 'And Me' from *Later That Same Year*. The trio surrounded our table and performed it beautifully – perfect harmonies and Andy's guitar. This was one of the highlights of her life – she talked about that evening often. Sadly, Julia died suddenly in 2021 – a fan of Iain until the end.

RAY WEAVER

I'm a musician, working primarily in the acoustic singer-songwriter /Americana realm – whatever they're calling it these days.

Throughout my musical journey, I've been deeply influenced by Iain Matthews. His exceptional songwriting and brilliant covers made his albums a constant source of inspiration, especially when I set out on my own musical path in the seventies.

The *Matthews Southern Comfort* version of 'Woodstock' was the first I ever heard, and his rendition of 'Ol '55' introduced me to the world of Tom Waits – a rabbit hole I still explore to this day. Through Iain, I also discovered Terence Boylan and other artists I might have otherwise overlooked.

Ray has discovered the music of Tom Waits thanks to Iain

I've long been the enthusiastic (and probably annoying) friend telling everyone that Iain's version of 'Seven Bridges Road' was the one The Eagles borrowed and made famous. His sparse, respectful arrangements gave songs space to breathe, allowing his voice and playing to shine. Those qualities made his tracks staples of the mix tapes I'd play in my old Chevy station wagon.

Beyond his covers, Iain's original songs stand tall among the greats. I'd put tracks like 'If You Saw Thro' My Eyes' or 'Home' up against any classic from the singer-songwriter canon.

Though I've yet to meet Iain in person, I follow him on Facebook to stay updated on his tours and music. A while back, he posted about selling some guitars, one of which was a travel guitar I'd been eyeing. He offered it at a more-than-fair price, and the fanboy in me couldn't resist the idea of playing a guitar once owned by one of my musical heroes.

I bought it, and Iain kindly packed it up and shipped it to me in Denmark. It arrived in perfect condition, and I've loved it ever since. Every time I take it out at a session, I can't help but share its history – though I wish Iain had remembered to sign it!

BERT PIJPERS, MUST HAVE MUSIC/CRS

Iain and I did not start in the best way. Around 2010, our mutual friend and musical contact BJ Baartmans introduced me to Iain. I run a small record company specialising in roots music, and BJ thought we would be a great fit. I guess musically we were, but although I try not to make any false promises and in fact usually try to wreck an artist's expectations of lots of sales and (in this case regained) unlimited glory, our work did not really bring what Iain might have expected from the Dutch reincarnation of Matthews Southern Comfort.

And as so very often: the grass looked far greener elsewhere, so Iain decided to take back control of *Kind Of New* and hand the rights over to English partners.

Now, I don't even know if their grass actually was greener than ours. But I am happy to say that some 15 years later I have had the honour and the pleasure to work with Iain on the release of Matthews Southern Comfort's Woodstock and some other releases including his latest master piece, *How Much Is Enough.*

I hope there will be many more.

MARK SWANSON

I first found Iain Matthews through his music back when I was 17. I became a fan right away. I was delighted to see him play in concert in 1973 on one of his early American tours. I kept listening through the years and then along came Facebook, where I found Iain active there. It then became clear that we had a mutual interest in the acoustic guitar and since I am luthier, we had a lot to talk about! So the guitar has brought us together as friends and since becoming close with Iain I have restored three vintage guitars for him and built one completely. That makes me very happy but along with that good fortune, I have been able to play with Iain and travel across the Midwest, joining him as a backing musician on a couple of small tours. After being a fan for so many years, finding him to be such a genuine, kind person has been fantastic!

Mark has restored guitars for Iain

DARCY JONES

Many years ago, I dated a rather famous rock star. One evening we were chatting about music and I happened to mention my father, Iain Matthews, and the bands that he'd been in. Said rock star was good friends at the time with Sean Lennon who happened to be in possession of his father's record collection. And guess who featured in that very record collection belonging to John Lennon? You guessed it – Iain Matthews.

GREG BOONE

I had been a fan of Iain's music since I was a kid in high school and had even met him at shows on a couple of occasions. But I came to be close friends in the early nineties when Iain came to Columbus, Ohio during a Midwest tour. His manager at the time, Charlie Hunter, had asked if I knew anyone he might stay with while he was there and, of course, my wife Kim and I volunteered.

I must admit that I was a bit concerned early in his visit. Despite his lively demeanour on stage, he was pretty shy and quiet when he was at our home. It was in our way to his soundcheck that the ice finally broke. I believe it was Iain who made an off-the-cuff comment about being a Gemini, to which I responded that I was too. When he asked exactly when I was born, we were both surprised to find that that we shared the same birthday.

After that it was like we'd been friends forever. Before he left Ohio, we'd made plans for me to come to Texas, where he lived

Greg Boone, pictured with Iain on Christmas Eve 2021 in Ohio, ended up writing Iain's fan newsletter

at the time, to watch him record the next Plainsong album and by the time I left Texas, I was writing his fan newsletter and running his fan club out of my home, a task my wife and I happily did for several years before the internet came along and ended such things as newsletters.

We've remained close friends and now consider Iain and Marly and their girls our 'Dutch family'.

The Matthews & Boone families celebrating Christmas in Ohio in 2021

DUNCAN SMITH

I have fervently followed the career of Iain Matthews since 1970 and his hit with 'Woodstock' when he fronted Matthews Southern Comfort. I own all his albums plus releases by his various offshoots, in particular Plainsong.

I have been hosting my own community radio show here in Perth, Western Australia since 2001. It's called Top Shelf Music on 89.7 FM.

Some time ago I wrote to Iain to respectfully ask him if he would voice a promo for my show. You can imagine my delight and thrill when he acceded to my request and I have been playing the promo weekly ever since. To have a radio sting by a true hero and icon is overwhelmingly amazing, and something I could only have dreamt of as a 14-year-old way back in 1970.

JOHNNY CARLSEN

I have followed Iain's music since 1967 and met him a few times. In 2015, I was staying at the Banbury House Hotel with friends, where we'd stay in Cropredy days, but went early to bed. Suddenly, my friends came to my room, woke me up and said someone was waiting for me in the bar. I got up, washed my face, put on clean clothes and went to the bar, where I met Iain and Egbert Derix. We had a fantastic time together. The next evening, they played the Fairport song 'Sloth' at the festival and dedicated it to we 'Crazy Norwegians'. Some years later, outside the same hotel, my friends and I were having a beer together when I began singing an Iain Matthews song. Someone touched my back and said, 'Not bad, Johnny.' It was Iain.

MADELIEF KLEEVEN

My mom and Iain met at a concert in Horst. They have been married for 21 years now. The first time I met Iain was when I was one and a half years old. He and my mom told me this story and I love hearing about it. Iain came over for dinner when I met him and he kept trying to make me laugh but all it did was make me cry.

Iain has been in my life for over 23 years and I can't imagine my life without him. I'm very proud to call him my extra papa.

JOHN SELLARDS

In high school in the eighties, I worked part-time at a local radio station, a small AM oldies channel. My boss, Jim Owston, quickly realised that our music tastes were similar – The Byrds, Airplane, Tim Hardin – and began nudging me toward exploring the catalogue of his favourite artist, Iain Matthews. I borrowed his Vertigo LPs and his Columbia records, which were all out of print in the US. Within a couple of years, I started actively searching for Matthews' work and discovered *Skeleton Keys* when it was new. It became the number 1 album on my personal chart for about a year. Listening now, it still sounds fresh and clean, and the songs remain some of Iain's best.

Around this time, I found copies of his Elektra albums and listened to them obsessively. Eventually, I bought import CDs of some of his Rockburgh albums. His entire catalogue wasn't easily available in the US 30 years ago, but the hunt was always rewarding.

Later on, I heard that Iain was looking for a designer for an upcoming project. I wrote to him introducing myself, and in very short order, I was designing covers for his and Andy's Richard Fariña tribute album. It was a real joy to get to know them both and to meet them briefly at the historic Club Passim in Cambridge when they were promoting the release.

I've since been part of quite a few of Iain's projects, including several of his current albums – his new one is incredible and sits alongside my beloved *Skeleton Keys* as a favourite. I've also worked on box sets covering his demos, Vertigo and Rockburgh years, and the expansive and enduring legacy of *In Search of Amelia Earhart* LP, which was expanded into a six-CD box set.

While his voice is justifiably celebrated all over the planet, it's really his songwriting that connects with me in a big way. I have loved hearing his growth over the years as his ability to express his ideas has developed. Listening to one of his songs is like having a conversation with him – it speaks to the level of communication he has achieved. If you don't know Iain and want to feel like you've spoken to him, just listen to *Shakespeare's Typewriter*. He's speaking to you, me, and all of us, as himself.

I consider both Iain and Andy to be friends and am honoured to be a small part of their ongoing body of work.

BJ BAARTMANS

Reflecting on the 22 years that I've known Iain Matthews – or rather, known in person touring, recording and writing with him – the first thing that comes to mind is that these last couple of 'post pandemic' years have been very productive. Only in the last two of them we finished three completely different albums. In a way they sum up quite a bit of the entire body of Matthews' work I've been involved with as a player, co-writer and producer.

There's Matthews Southern Comfort's *The Woodstock Album* with lovingly rearranged cover versions of songs that were performed at the legendary festival. There's Iain's latest (last? he thinks and says so) solo album, *How Much Is Enough*, and a new version of 1973's *Valley Hi*, with remarkable remakes of the classic songs from that album, performed with my current band Wild Verband.

We had a blast making those albums, experiencing a very creative workflow in a peaceful, easygoing mindset and without losing the musical and lyrical edge. It's not always been like that. But we go back a long time now and I think we know each other very well, sharing a deep connection in music and in life.

I first met Iain at a show with my early 2000s band, BJ's Pawnshop, at the Cambrinus Café in Horst. He was invited to come and see us by owner Jan Duijf, who knew that Iain was looking for professional regional musicians for possible collaborations since he'd just moved into the area, finding a good home with his later wife Marly.

BJ's Pawnshop were doing a double date tour with New York singer Eugene Ruffalo, (brother of actor Mark) opening the evening with a set of my original songs before backing him up. But that first part was what really drew Iain to me, he told me after introducing himself. I was puzzled. I sort of knew who he was from reading articles in rock magazines at my older cousins' house, but having being born in 1965, I had spent the years in which Fairport Convention or Matthews Southern Comfort were defining folk rock in shorts, playing soccer on the streets or singing playback to Slade, The Sweet and Mud in my boy's room.

Before we knew it, I had a legend in the Studio, Leon's Farm, where I worked at the time, singing magnificent harmonies to my gravelly leads, in exchange for which I produced a demo of a cool new song he was working on, 'My Favourite Son'.

He was nice to hang out with, and interested and complimentary, although I must say that when I apologised for my rough, shaky way of singing he said, 'I will make you sound good,' with a subtle yet superior smile. It made me feel slightly intimidated. But he was right. He knows how to do that.

From there on we formed a very fruitful bond. Being driven by a mutual passion, finding common ground but also realising that both of us are strong individuals. We love connecting with musicians, or people involved in music in a different way, but still we're just as much soloists. Stubborn, protective, insecure at times. Struggling with the business side and the responsibilities that come with leading a band, carrying a name. Iain and I had to overcome a few serious bumps in the road, like when he pulled the plug on the first new version of MSC in 2005, just after we recorded a heartfelt, wonderful album, *Kind Of New* (eventually released in 2010) and were looking at a very promising tour booked to follow the launch of it. That did hurt.

We wouldn't always agree on decisions regarding professional issues or even personal choices and had to get over a serious clash here and there. But we always did. The friendship does it. The amazing feeling the music can give us does it. The stories we share. The discoveries we make. During those 22 years we recorded more than ten albums either as a duo or with a band, did hundreds of shows all over Europe and even Japan. It can still feel like we're just at the beginning of something beautiful. I'm a fortunate man getting the opportunity to share a big part of my life in sound with such a great singer, writer, guitar-loving and soccer-loving companion.

KRZYSZTOF OPALSKI

When I was still in primary school I heard the song 'Woodstock' on Polish radio. I had no idea who the artist was or who composed it. In 1976 I bought the Island sampler, *Bumpers*, which included the Fairport Convention track 'Walk Awhile'. I liked it very much and started to look for their records. It was not easy in Poland at that time, because there were no Western-pressed records in shops. Such records were only bought at records fairs or during foreign trips.

Becoming a big fan of Fairport Convention, I also decided to collect the solo records of the musicians who passed through the band. While in Oslo in Norway in the summer of 1987, I bought a bunch of records. Besides Fairport Convention LPs and a Sandy Denny box set, these included a compilation album entitled *Best Of Matthews Southern Comfort.* I was surprised to find a version of 'Woodstock' on it and remembered it from my school days. I already knew Joni Mitchell's original version and the rock interpretation by Crosby, Stills Nash and Young, but Iain Matthews' version is my favourite. It best reflects the beauty of the melody of this composition. I really like the vocal harmonies and the atmospheric intro along with the background and solos played on pedal steel guitar.

Over the years I have managed to collect almost the entire discography of Iain Matthews, both solo and with his bands – Matthews Southern Comfort, Plainsong and Hi-Fi. One of my favourite albums of his is *If You Saw Thro' My Eyes*. The versions of Richard Fariña's 'Reno, Nevada' and 'Morgan The Pirate' are amazing with their masterful interpretation and interesting arrangements. These compositions are enhanced by the wonderful guitar solos of his former Fairport colleague, Richard Thompson.

The album's closing (and title) track is also amazing, being a beautiful duet with the unforgettable Sandy Denny. In 2000, during my visit to the Cropredy Festival, I had the opportunity to see Iain live for the first and only time when he performed as part of the reunited Plainsong along with Andy Roberts and Mark Griffiths. It was one of the best performances at this edition of the festival, along with the concerts of Robert Plant, Fairport Convention and Stackridge. Thanks to Fairport's Dave Pegg, who invited me and my wife to this festival, I had the opportunity to take photos in the front of the stage and had backstage access, allowing me to talk to Iain after the concert and have my photo taken with him. I also reviewed his appearance at Cropredy in the Polish folk magazine *Gatki z Chatki*.

MARLY KLEEVEN-MATTHEWS, IAIN'S WIFE

Having been married to Iain for as long as I have now (23 years), I've come to understand what it's like to be 'on the road'. Especially as a solo artist.

Just like most people I guess, I always felt that it must be quite easy. People love seeing you and you are in a different place every night. Until I went on an English tour with him, a couple of years ago… Of course it was great. It was great to see Iain perform. It was great to see the reaction of the crowd, it was great talking to fans after the shows…and it was the best feeling being there with him, to share these experiences.

But what I never realised is that that's just the tip of the iceberg of daily life on the road.

You wake up in the morning in a hotel room. You have to be out, usually around 10am or 11am. You get in the car, you set your Google maps to the next destination and then you drive… and as everyone knows, it always takes longer than what Google maps promises…

Then you arrive at the next hotel, check in and go to the venue. You unload all the gear for the concert, there is a soundcheck and then you're on your own. Find a place for something to eat, back to the venue to do the show…

Perform, sell CDs, pack everything back in the car, go to the hotel to sleep…

And next morning, you do it all again…

So on one of these nights, we were waiting in a gloomy basement dressing room and I looked at Iain and asked him, 'How on earth do you do this when you're alone and - more importantly – *why*?' (I would be immensely depressed if I had to do that.)

He looked at me with a smile and said, 'It's not easy, I get lonely and depressed sometimes. But it's only small part of it. The playing for people and sharing my music is what I love doing most, so everything else is just a small sacrifice for doing what I love doing.'

It was such a truthful and emotional answer, I was taken aback by it. Imagine doing this for over 50 years. Iain turned 79 in June. And still he cannot stop working. He says he wants to, but in our house we've stopped believing him.

YVONNE ELENBAAS

A man in my attic.
Lonesome and heartbroken.
No home or country to call his own.
Simple clothes, CDs, books and a guitar.
A notebook for thoughts and reflections.
No desire to eat; jam on toast, eggs and homemade fries.
Curtains closed, a dark brown wall as testament to his mood.
Hardly room for the sun to shed some light.
An occasional visit to my living room for talks and tea.
Then slowly times are changing.
Long walks in the city, making new friends and opening up to the world.
Reconnecting with the love of his life; his voice in music.
New projects emerge, news songs are written and his sweet voice is shared.
Slowly a new man rises up, embracing the hard lessons learned.
Brave and gently taking on the world again.
And then his angel arrives, out of the blue as if she was waiting.
Walls are broken down and hopes and dreams are shared.
His heart starts to sing again and a new future is on the horizon.
As their love grows it's time to move on, away from his solitary life in the attic.
With some clothes, CDs, books and his guitar away on a new adventure.
With grace and humility and a new found voice.
No longer lonely and his heart mended.
The sweetest soul who despite his troubles taught me to move forward.
Not to ask but to give, unconditionally.
My housemate, my dear friend, a gentle man.
The man in my attic.

ACKNOWLEDGEMENTS

Richard Houghton would like to thank everyone who contributed material for this book but particularly Ian Burgess for access to his archive. He would also like to thank Bruce Graham (Night Owl) for the design and layout, and Iain Matthews for wanting to do the book. Richard would also like to thank his lovely wife Kate, who keeps the ship afloat.

SPECIAL THANKS

Iain Matthews would like to thank the following for their support for this book: Alan Skingsley, Alistair Hawtin, Andrew Mills, Andy Morton, Arne Rasmussen, Arthur Ticknor, Barry Eaton, Beverley Perrin, Bob Rose, Bob Young, Brian Chudley, Bryan Bance, Chris Bennett, Christian Globisch, Christopher Shutty, Christopher Todd Durnil, Colin Adams, Craig Green, D M Butcher, David Clarke, David Morgan, David Mundell, David Pollard, David Summers, Debra Watkins, Dennis Fisher, Dermot Ferguson, Dolf Beckers, Duncan Smith, Eric Horridge, Frits Wielens, Greg Borgartz, Gregory Boone, Ian Jones, Ian Treasaden, James Unwin, Jean-Luc Temporel, Jennifer Wilson, Jim Marks, Jim Owston, John Elder, John Herbert, John Lester, John Schmitz, John Sellards, John Slaytor, John Wilson, Johnny Fewings, Julia Mills, Julian Christou, Kim Simpson, Kingsley Abbott, Kjetil Gjoen, Lacey Gordon, Lisa Lowden, Marc Vos, Mark Hart, Maureen Everett, Mauro Regis, Michael Pearce, Michael Yeomans, Mike Donovan, Neil Harris, Neville Dalton, Nicola Hurt, Nigel Bamford, Norman Reid, Pat Thomas, Paul Harper, Paul Sampson, Peter Holmstedt, Peter Turner, Philip Delafield, Richard Hammond, Richard Lewis, Rick Jones, Robert Bodger, Robert Osman, Robert Phipps, Robert Thornton, Roger Mercer, Ron Hooijenga, Ron Kurzweil, Ron Yaxley, Roy Trimble, Stephen Blundell, Stephen Royston, Steve Mckinney, Thomas Fleck, Tim Payne, Tom Arvidsson, Ulf Dalheim, Wes Knape, William J Martin Jr.

ABOUT THE AUTHOR

Richard Houghton lives in Manchester, UK. He is the author of more than 20 books on music and managing director of Spenwood Books, who specialise in 'people's histories' of acts. More details can be found at spenwoodbooks.com

AFTERWORD

Thank you so much to everyone who contributed to this book. It brought back lots of pleasant (mostly) memories and is very much appreciated. I hope to see you all on the road.

IAIN MATTHEWS